Imagination, Cognition & Language Acquisition

A UNIFIED APPROACH TO THEORY AND PRACTICE

Clyde Coreil, Ph.D., Editor-in-Chief

Ninah Beliavsky, Ph.D., Associate Editor
St. John's University, New York

Robert Lake, Ed.D, Assistant Editor
University of South Georgia

Claudia Ferradas Moi, Argentina, Assistant Editor
International Teacher

Monika Yadav, Editorial Assistant
New Jersey City University

Published by
New Jersey City University
Jersey City, New Jersey 07305

NEW JERSEY
CITY
UNIVERSITY

Book design by Ronald Bogusz, Director of Publications and Special Programs,
    New Jersey City University.

Illustrations are by Dennis Dittrich, Assistant Professor of Art, New Jersey City University.

This anthology replaces Volume VIII of *The Journal of the Imagination in Language Learning and Teaching*. Volume IX of that *Journal* will appear in 2008.

Additional copies may be ordered through the distributor:

Bastos Educational Books
P.O. Box 770-433
Woodside, New York 11377
Voice mail: 800-662-0301
Fax: 718-997-6445

ISBN: 978-1-883514-11-2

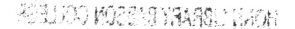

Imagination, Cognition & Language Acquisition

A UNIFIED APPROACH TO THEORY AND PRACTICE

Contents

Dedication

For

Lev Semenovitch Vygotsky

A Spirit that Endures

Words of Tribute

Gita L'Vovna Vygotskaya, Daughter of L.S. Vygotsky
and
Dr. Elena Evge'evna Kravtsova, Granddaughter of L.S. Vygotsky
Russian State University for Humanities, Moscow

Our father and grandfather, Lev Semenovich Vygotsky (1896-1934), was one of the most famous and influential psychologists of the twentieth century. He lived a very short life, passing away before he reached thirty-eight. Although he spent only the last ten years in pursuit of his scientific dreams, Vygotsky remains one of the most quoted and respected of psychologists.

Lev Vygotsky is founder of the cultural-historical theory of human psychological development—a new approach. Non-traditional rather than scientific, this approach allows psychologists to develop a fresh and dynamic way to study human development.

We are referring to one of Vygotsky's main theoretical achievements: expansion of the boundaries of the science of psychology, thereby introducing psychological principles into the humanities, art, education, and other aspects of the cultural developments of a human being. Perhaps this is why scholars from different academic fields actively study the works of L. S. Vygotsky, respect his achievements, and use his notions and theories in their own research.

Another of Vygotsky's original ideas is his concept of the "Zone of Proximal Development." Vygotsky theorized that human development was dependent on social interaction. With the help of this interaction, the individual is transformed into an intelligent and intellectual human being, beyond what he or she would otherwise have been.

L.S. Vygotsky was a man many decades ahead of his time. He has chartered the course for the new generation of scientists who rely on his work as a beacon of the future of psychology.

This dedication was translated from the original Russian by Dr. Ninah Beliavsky of St. John's University in New York City. The publication at New Jersey City University deeply appreciates the efforts Dr. Beliavsky took, not only in rendering a meaningful translation but in her persistent and successful efforts in communication with L.S. Vigotsky's family.

The Muscular Eye, Swift Mentation, and the Dark Side of the Imagination

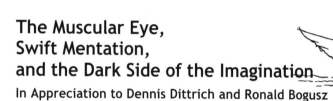

In Appreciation to Dennis Dittrich and Ronald Bogusz

There is an inverse relationship between the simplicity of the illustrations in this book and the somewhat complex nature of the text. That is to say, the delightful Rube Goldberg-type drawings tell one simple story that involves a chain of events that ultimately result in an answer being chosen on a multiple-choice test by a monkey. These irreverent episodes serve as part of the background for the rather complicated but unified theme of this volume: i.e., the nature of one of the most precious gifts of the human mind—the imagination. Readers are advised to look at the composite fold-out at the back of the book. Possibly, the different parts of that simple drawing— many of which are printed with the individual articles—will bring to mind the complexity of the role played by the imagination in both children and adults.

Unfortunately, there are two sides to the imagination: one bright, one treacherous. When you have a developed a bomb that can find its way down a stairway from 30,000 feet—that is the dark side of the imagination. To destroy thousands of lives and two magnificent, gleaming towers of metal and light—that is also the dark side of the imagination. Another opponent of the bright side is "Teaching through Testing" which seems to be undercutting many programs of elementary and secondary education in the USA. In short, "Teaching through Testing" is concerned with showing students how to take a test instead of showing them some of the wonders of life itself.

It has been demonstrated time and again that it is virtually impossible to separate young children from the imagination. If ever anything seemed inherently part of the human mind, it is the imagination. Yet at some age, children seem to become vulneralble to efforts to stifle the bright side. Unfortunately, the dark side of the imagination seems able to slither away more effectively.

How are we to pursue the preservation of brightness? By writing about it as brilliantly as Dr. Kieran Egan is doing in Canada. And by doing such simple things as publicly thanking Mr. Dennis Dittrich, the illustrator of this volume, and Mr. Ronald Bogusz, the designer. In their bubbling cauldron, they have mixed paper, ink, design and enough good will to allow us to put Rube Goldbergesque drawings in a book that attempts to call on the wisdom of science, philosophy, music, literature, math—and even mystic resonances in exploring and sharing the angelic imagination.

In Gratitude

I welcome this chance to express deep appreciation to my wife, Vivan Tsao, who was always there, quietly painting, waiting.

Clyde Coreil

Imagination, Cognition & Language Acquisition:

A Unified Approach to Theory and Practice

The Alchemist's Swan

Clyde Coreil

The Statement

What is "the imagination"? Such a question implies that there is a single answer. Of course there are countless aspects, some more relevant to ontology, others to areas such as physics, philosophy, mathematics, theology, brain science and mysticism. But if we step back to acquire a greater perspective, does the word "imagination" denote essentially one distinct concept or does it simply designate a vague level of intensity and creativity of approach and nothing more specific? This latter is generally the meaning attributed to the imagination.

A more compelling if difficult case, however, can be made for the imagination as a single, quantifiable and fixed mode of mental operation. If this is so, we can ask that this concept of the imagination be characterized. Such a characterization should generally be as applicable at the lowest level of some game-like activity as well as at the lofty abstract realms of advanced physics. In the metaphor of the Alchemist's Swan, I will present such a characterization through the use of metaphor. Before I do that, however, I will attempt to delineate in the most concrete of terms the meaning of the word "imagination."

The Essence of the Imagination

1st. The genesis of all acts of the imagination refers to at least a duality of concepts.
2nd. An activity representing or constituting a problem must be present.
3rd. The sealed concepts are opened and several of the contents of each are removed.
4th. These contents are rearranged or recombined in such a way that a third concept comes into being.
5th. This recombination is carried out with the original problem in mind.
6th. The third concept which is new is applied to the existing problem.
7th. This exercise is always carried out in the presence of at least relatively high concentration.
8th. If the problem is solved, the imaginer will experience some degree of emotional satisfaction.
9th. This process is recursive: that is, if two new concepts are formed as a result of two separate acts of imagination, then these new concepts can be treated as any other two concepts.
10th. Activated as parts of a single operation, this operation is the essence of the imagination.

Of course, there are virtually infinite variations that arise in every exercise of this mental operation. However, all of the above characteristics will be present in every act of imagination. This hypothetical analysis is useful in terms of understanding what we mean when we say that a particular solution to a problem is imaginative, or that a person himself or herself is imaginative—that is that his or her thought processes often employ this approach.

However, a far more valuable purpose of the above ten steps will emerge if we find that the imagination is effective in the teaching-learning exchange. The ten steps can serve as a checklist against which new lessons and books of lessons are evaluated at any level. Such a checklist can lead away from the "automated teaching" that is found more and more in the schools, and back to a strong concern for students as human beings who are fully capable of responding to the thematic and intellectual concerns of authentic literature.

The Metaphor

As the drape coving the large statue at its exhibition is ready to be lifted by a rope and a pulley, everyone is filled with apprehension. There is a long pause, then up the cover climbs very slowly. Finally revealed in their entirety are two highly polished golden ovals, each five feet in length. They are both standing on end. There is a murmur here and there, but generally everyone is waiting, sitting on the edge of their seats. Then the magic begins. The ceiling of the Secret Transformational Laboratory (SLS) is high, and the air is amazingly fresh despite its thick aroma of magic, potent herbs and boiling flasks. Enter "The Alchemist" in gorgeous, deep purple robes and a long and floppy cloth hat that Oscar Wilde would have behaved himself for. The surface of the fabric ambiguously played with the image of a night sky in the aboriginal Rockies. The Divine Creator had outdone himself on that one. The stars filled the deep black with distant, beautiful chords of heavenly subtlety.

"Each oval represents a concept," the aging alchemist said, and produced an object covered in a deep red cloth. There seemed to be movement under the cloth, but no one could be sure. He put the object next to one of the ovals, and the object and the oval seemed to interact. At times the motion was incredibly fast; at other time, everything seemed perfectly still. Finally, The Alchemist lifted the red cloth and there was a round opening in the oval. He reached inside and took out two sparkling gems. The audience caught its breath. Then, before they could say anything, he put the cloth and the object next to the other oval. The action was the same. He removed three gems and placed them beside the other two on the table before him. The Alchemist waved his wand over the concepts and the opening were instantly closed. His old and wrinkled hands took up the gems and molded and spun them into a beautiful swan which looked at the audience demurely and then paddled away effortlessly.

"I have given you," The Alchemist said and paused to make certain that the attention of everyone in the room was focused on him as though he were the hard-burning fire that could answer their most precious question. "I have given you the metaphor of the imagination. It is the single secret I hold most dear in my heart. Study it and tell your children and close friends that, next to love, tolerance and true humility, it is the most precious and meaningful of lessons they will ever encounter. It will guide them to the most distant stars and through the blackness of the deepest ocean. The only thing that can ever stop its magical transformations is the loss of confidence. The imagination is the key to all of creation: all it asks is that you never let its glow be hidden. If you do, you will doubt that it was ever anything but the idle fantasy of a lazy child. He turned and the room had become a bower, and he was walking very near the edge of the water where the seemingly translucent bird was floating gracefully. He reached into his pocket and took out an assortment of nuts and grain that the swan began to eat ravenously.

Then a rough man in the back of the room said, "Hey! Is that all? The guy who sold me the ticket said that a divine secret would be revealed in here. So I gives him a dollar and comes inside and all I hear is this yakking about a big goose." Immediately, he saw that the magnificent swan turned into a goose, honking angrily like one of those old-fashioned brass horns that are attached to black rubber bulbs. For the man who had spoken out, The Alchemist turned into a small and ugly creature whose face was full of displeasure and even hate. He was a walking bomb, waiting for the smallest reason to explode into the foul stink of a dozen really rotten eggs. Across the room, there were small poppings as the swan and The Alchemist became the honker around whose neck was a noose and a thick cord held by the nasty guy who suddenly stopped. The goose squawked and wanted to get away, but every time he did, the cord became tighter.

The owner of the goose with dirty feathers yanked his bird and came back to the center of the room. He looked at each man, woman and child in the crowded enclosure which had begun to smell of tobacco, unflushed toilets, overflowing garbage cans and everything else that made one choke and threaten to vomit. ""Hah!" the man said and squeezed the head of the goose which had become an old and cracked rubber duck. "Hear that?" He squeezed again and the duck responded with a wheezing, whistling sound. "That stinking old bum had almost bamboozled you again. 'The Glorious Imagination,'" he said rolling his protruding eyes skyward and mocking. "What a crock. And you'd a'sworn that he was giving you a secret he got from his own private angel." The man then leaned into the crowd and whispered and everyone told everyone else to "Shut up!"

The old man waited until the hall was as quiet as a mouse. "He's looney, he is. Crazy as the day is long. Don't you go believing all that malarkey about the imagination. That'll get you into big trouble. Things is what you see, not some fairy tale about an old woman who lived in a shoe, or some little boy who blew a flute and some sort of genie whooshed out." He stopped and looked into each eye. Then all at once he shouted, and the little children started to cry: "If you think you got it bad in your stinking lives now, you just go along and believe all that nonsense. The only thing he ever cracked with his 'magic wand' was a peanut and maybe the head of an old lady whose purse had caught his eye."

A Modest Credo

So there you have it. And in metaphor in the form of an old-fashioned tale to boot! Why didn't I just come right out and say that the loss of confidence in the imagination is among the most treacherous obstacles in the path to a fuller and fuller realization of what the human mind can hold? I do believe that. I also believe that for some dark reason, we keep on calling, not for the magical swan but for the cracked and wheezing rubber duck which represents propriety and prestige. The swan, on the other hand, represents the existential magic of becoming what we and the things around us are not. A cosmos of possibilities is ours for the asking. In each of our minds, there are countless shining ovals and the red cloth of the imagination is always a wish away. But again and again, we turn from the swan and the magnificent possibilities and go with the rubber duck of propriety and prestige. So that, if we want the swan, we must remain vigilant lest we lose faith and thereby let ourselves be fooled into tragic belief that the imagination is nothing but a "big goose." I believe that metaphor is the home of the imagination. And that the human capacity to perceive the truth of things as they are is severely limited. And that the imagination is the one divine gift that can light our night.

Revisiting Vygotsky & Gardner– Realizing Human Potential

Ninah Beliavsky

Four components have long been the goal of our educational systems. The idea of teaching and learning that will allow the educators (1) to teach ahead of development, (2) to teach for understanding, (3) to motivate and promote students' creativity and imagination, and (4) to encourage their personal, social and academic growth. This paper suggests that by joining the visionary forces of two great educators, Lev Vygotsky and Howard Gardner, we can achieve this lofty goal. By maximizing Vygotsky's concept of the Zone of Proximal Development and utilizing Gardner's Theory of Multiple Intelligences educators can develop a universal approach of furthering children's abilities as we nurture their individual intelligences.

Journey to the Self

My journey from Moscow to Jerusalem to Paris to New York has made me who I am today. I cannot separate or isolate my love for the arts, music, opera, literature and languages from my people's history, my heritage, my culture, my society, and the environment where I was brought up. My own views on education stem from the rich traditions and heritage of my own people, on the one hand, and an abundant wealth of all human accomplishments throughout the history of the world, on the other. The two individuals who have had a tremendous influence on my own theories and my own philosophy of education are the Russian psychologist, intellectual, and social activist Lev Semenovich Vygotsky (1896 -1934), and the leading American developmental psychologist Howard Gardner (b 1944). The philosophies of Vygotsky and Gardner have much in common, even though their lives have been separated by different continents, by different political regimes, by different languages, by different cultures, and almost a century of innovative research in the fields of psychology and education.

I think that Vygotsky's ideas should be viewed through the prism of Gardner's theory of Multiple Intelligences. The combination of these concepts can shed new light on education, on teaching and learning. By doing so, we would enable the students to reach a higher level of cognitive development. This article intends to suggest that Vygotsky's dream of maximizing the Zone of Proximal Development can be realized by utilizing Gardner's approach of nurturing the students' combination of intelligences. This idea of teaching and learning will allow the educators to teach ahead of development, to teach for understanding, to motivate and promote the students creativity and imagination, and to encourage their personal, social and academic growth.

Lev Vygotsky

Seventy years have passed since Vygotsky died on June 11, 1934. He was only 37 years old. "Vygotsky was a product of his time: an intellectual, a Jew, [one] who took as much pleasure in thinking through the intricacies of speech impediments and language acquisition as he did in contemplating Shakespeare's Hamlet or the psychology of Art" (Kerr, 1997, 92). Fundamental to Vygotsky theory was the idea that higher mental functions, such as thinking, logical memory, and human consciousness have their origins in human social life.

Vygotsky believed that culture should be passed down to future generations, in a Socratic, not a dogmatic way. He believed that everyone should be given the tools to live up to their highest potential! For Vygotsky, psychological development could not be separated from human history and human culture. The notion of development as growing out of the interaction of human beings with one another, especially the interaction of adults and children, offers a collectivist vision of human psychological growth, especially different from American ideas of individualism and pre-determined stages of psychological growth (Kerr, 1997). Vygotsky believed that the child has to be exposed to the array of the intellectual and cognitive "tools", developed over the centuries by human beings—tools such as language, mathematics, music and art.

He stressed that systematic instruction in the formal disciplines—Latin, Greek, mathematics, and composition—is beneficial to the development of students' mental facilities in general. Studying the formal disciplines would lead to higher-order thinking and thus enhance "scientific" concepts. In other words, the systematic learning of scientific concepts in one field translates into developmental changes, abstract thinking, and greater logical thinking/and logical flexibility. This notion is being recently welcomed by American psychologists. For example, in one study in the United States, a group of American psychologists demonstrated that specialized training in medicine, law and psychology seems to have an effect on real-life problem solving requiring statistical and logical reasoning (see Kozulin, 1990, 170-172).

In American educational psychology, Vygotsky is famous for his concept of the Zone of Proximal Development (ZPD). Behind this is the notion that a child's cognitive development occurs within a social milieu. The teaching-learning process (instruction) does not occur in isolation. The role of instruction for enhancing cognitive development is a joint activity, a collaborative effort between the child and a more knowledgeable partner-such as an older sibling, a parent, or a teacher. Therefore, the analysis of cognitive functioning requires studying how a child's social interaction with more competent peers of their culture is mastered and internalized. In other words, to understand a child's cognitive development, we need to examine specific patterns of social interaction in which this child participates (Rogoff & Wertsch, 1984). The most detailed description of the concept of ZPD can be found in a lecture "Dinamika umstvennogo razvitia sckol'nika v svjazi s obucheniem" delivered by Vygotsky at the Bubnov Pedagogical Institute on December 23, 1933, a year before he died (see Van Der Veer & Valsiner, 1991). In that lecture, Vygotsky was challenging such researchers as Binet and Meumann who claimed that one can not start teaching children unless they have reached a certain level of development. These researchers tried to establish the "lowest possible thresholds" from which the teaching of various school subjects might be started. As the way to establish these thresholds, a child was asked to perform certain tasks independently, without the aid of the experimenters. The degree to which the child was able to solve the task was measured and calculated, and this "score" became indicative of the development of his intellect—hence, his IQ score. The IQ test was devised by the French psychologist Alfred Binet back in 1900 in Paris as a measure that would predict which kids would succeed and which would fail in primary grades in school. This test became a success, and "like other Parisian fashions, the IQ test soon...made its way the United States..." (Gardner, 1993, 5).

IQ to SAT

Psychologists and educators like Henry Goddard (1919), Lewis Terman (1916), Robert Yerkes (1921) saw the great potential of the IQ test and devised them in such a way that they could be administered to hundreds of students at one time. By the 1930's the tests became very popular. Work on the development of such tests continued through 1950's and they are still being improved to this day (SAT, GRE, LSAT among others). Vygotsky argued that this testing gives only a partial picture of the child's intellectual development. He claimed that in addition to this "lowest threshold" there exists another dimension; call it an "upper boundary". If the same child is asked to perform the same task, but now with the aid of the experimenter, this child can reach a higher performance score—hence an "upper boundary". A different child, for that matter, may not profit as much from the above assistance. In other words, children with the same mental age may perform the same when working independently, but differently when help is offered. Some will benefit more compared to others. This difference between independent performance and aided performance seems to be characteristic of the child.

Zone of Proximal Development

Based on this, Vygotsky proposed his notion of the Zone of Proximal Development. "The zone of proximal development of the child is the distance between his actual development, determined with the help of independently solved tasks, and the level of the potential development of the child, determined with the help of tasks solved by the child under the guidance of adults and in cooperation with his more intelligent partners" (Vygotsky in Van Der Veer & Valsiner, 1991, 337). Vygotsky believed that the measurement of ZPD is a more accurate means to predict the child's future development or potential. The first level can be called the actual development level. This is a level of development of a child's mental functions that has been established as a result of certain completed development cycles; it represents the already matured functions. In other words, it represents the results of yesterday.

When a child's mental age is determined with the help of IQ tests, it almost always points to the actual developmental level (Vygotsky, 1978). Suppose that now we offer leading questions or show that same child how the problem is to be solved, and the child then solves the problem much better. Vygotsky claims that the performance of this child, who is cooperating with a more knowledgeable partner, is characteristic of his future development. Thus, the child's performance reveals the results of tomorrow. This level is the second level of the child's development. This assisted performance represents the child's future development or the child's potential. Therefore, the Zone of Proximal Development defines those functions that have not yet matured but are in the process of maturation. "The actual developmental level characterizes mental development retrospectively, while the Zone of Proximal Development characterizes mental development prospectively" (Vygotsky, 1978, 87 emphasis added).

This child who is able to profit from jointly performed tasks, has a larger Zone of Proximal Development and will do better in school, because what he can do with help today, he will do independently tomorrow. To substantiate this claim, Vygotsky referred to the results of the American researcher Dorothea McCarthy. Her research showed that among children between the ages of three and five, there are two groups of functions. One group of functions was the ones the children already possessed, and the second group of functions they could only perform with aid but could not perform independently.

In other words, there were some tasks they could perform independently and other tasks that they could perform only under the guidance of or in cooperation with an adult. McCarthy demonstrated that the second group of functions is at the actual development level of five-to-seven-year-olds. What these children could do with help at the age of three-to-five years, they could do independently when they reached the age of five-to-seven years. Therefore, Vygotsky claimed that based on the above, educators can judge what will happen with a child between five and seven, if other conditions of development stay the same, of course.

Vygotsky's Zone of Proximal Development empowers psychologists and educators with a tool through which they can understand better the maturation processes that have already been completed and those that are beginning to mature and develop. The state of a child's mental development can only be determined with the two levels—the actual development level and the Zone of Proximal Development. Vygotsky believed that the measurement of Zone of Proximal Development is a more accurate means to predict the child's future IQ development or potential.

A Change Needed

The above concepts supported the idea that the philosophy of education needs to be changed; the interaction between learning and development needs to be revisited. What can educators draw from the diagnostic tests of development? Before educators believed that instruction should not exceed the limits of development. This meant that this type of instruction was directed toward the developmental stages that were already completed. Educators discovered that this philosophy of education was flawed while looking at studies involving children suffering from mental retardation. Earlier studies have established that mentally retarded children are not capable of abstract thinking. Based on this, educators decided to eliminate teachings of abstract thinking, and base all education on the use of concrete methods. It was quickly observed that this teaching system failed, not only because it did not help these children overcome their innate handicaps but also because it reinforced their handicap by suppressing any traces of abstract thought that such children have.

This is also true with normally developing children. When learning is oriented toward development levels that have already been completed, learning fails. This type of instruction is ineffective because it does not aim for a new stage of development but instead lags behind. Vygotsky argued that learning must be in advance of development. His notion of Zone of Proximal Development will enable educators to do just that.

Critical Factor: Interaction with others

According to Vygotsky, an essential feature of learning is that it created the Zone of Proximal Development. In other words, learning awakens a variety of internal developmental processes, and that can take place only when the child is interacting with people in his environment. Once these processes are internalized, they become part of the child's independent development achievement. Therefore, learning is a necessary and universal aspect of the process of developing culturally organized, specifically human, psychological functions (Vygotsky, 1978). From this perspective, "instruction is good only when it proceeds ahead of development, when it awakens and rouses to life those functions which are in the process of maturing or in the zone of proximal development. It is in this way that instruction plays an extremely important role in development" (Vygotsky, 1956, 278, in Rogoff & Wertsch, 1984, 46). For us, it means that instruction has to be challenging.

Conclusion

The concept of ZPD, the relation of teaching to cognitive development, as well as Vygotsky's other ideas attracted the attention of Western psychologists only in the 1970s. Its acceptance although delayed was enthusiastic. (Kozulin, 1990, 170) This was the time when Western psychologists such as Skinner (behaviorism) and Piaget (individually oriented cognitive psychology) were beginning to be called into question as being too simplistic (see Kerr, 1997). In the USA, the concept of culture has finally emerged in the post-Piagetian period. It grew most centrally out of the work of Vygotsky and has been reinforced by such supporters as Jerome Bruner, Michael Cole and Howard Gardner.

Howard Gardner

Human beings are not only biological creatures, they are also cultural creatures. In fact, as Gardner states it "much of the story of human development must be written in the light of cultural influences in general, and of the particular persons, practices, and paraphernalia of one's culture" (Gardner, 1991, 39). In other words, the stages of psychological growth cannot be predetermined, like hair color, because "intelligence, or intelligences, are always an interaction between biological proclivities and the opportunities for learning that exist in a culture" (Gardner, 1993, 221).

If there are opportunities both biological and cultural, intelligences may be realized. But if there are no cultural opportunities intelligence may not be realized. Imagine Beethoven without the musical culture…The student is not alone in school or in the environment. He draws inferences and learns concepts with the help of other people or props in his environment. His intellect cannot be isolated or decontextualized. In Gardner's terminology, intelligence is "distributed" in the environment, as well as in the head, and the "intelligent student" makes use of the intelligence distributed throughout his environment (Gardner, 1991, 136-137). This view of the intellect being "distributed" within the environment challenges the isolated view of the intellect and thus leads to a contextualized view of intelligence. Furthermore, people do not learn in the same way. Studies of cognition suggest that there exist many different ways of acquiring and representing knowledge. These individual differences need to be taken into account in our pedagogy as well as in our assessment. These notions have lead Gardner to his theory of Multiple Intelligences (MI), which is a critique of the notion that there exists but one single human intelligence that can be assessed by standard psychometric instruments.

Different Potentials in the Brain

MI Theory claims that there are multiple ways to understand the world around us. Not one potential but many different potentials inside the brain. Gardner suggests that there are at least seven or eight intelligences. We all have them. This makes us human. However, no two people, not even twins, have the same combinations of these intelligences (see Appendix A). That is important for teachers to know because you can count on every one of your students to have all eight intelligences albeit in different configurations. Because there are many intelligences, there are many ways to understand the world. Ideas should be taught in more than one way. This will enable you to reach more students and teach your students what is it like to think in more than one way. In other words, teach your students flexibility and provide a multiple view to understanding the physical world, the social world, the human world, the artistic world. If you teach only one way, you will reach only one kind of student.

Most teachers teach through the first two intelligences—linguistic and mathematical—because that's the way schools operate and intelligence is assessed. Those students who have other intelligences are left out and lose motivation, self-esteem and are not praised rightfully for their other talents and abilities (other than linguistic and mathematic). Think of famous violinists Yehudi Menuhin, Yasha Heifetz or pianists Vladimir Horowitz or Glenn Gould, or composers—Ludwig Van Beethoven, Peotr Ilyich Tchaikovsky, famous dancers Maya Plisetskaya, Anna Pavlova, Isadora Duncan or Martha Graham, famous painters—Francisco Goya, Henri Matisse, Vasili Kandinsky or Marc Chagall and Ilya Repin. Are they considered intelligent in our society?

What happens to those students who are not strong in the first two intelligences—the linguistic and the mathematical but have other strengths, such as musical or spatial? They feel left out and unmotivated; they lose their self-esteem—school becomes very difficult. Therefore, Gardner suggests that if we want those students, and all the rest to understand, we should take advantage of multiple intelligences. How do teachers take advantage of multiple intelligences? Well, teachers need to approach the explanation of a certain concept in different ways. If you understand something well, you can think about it in more than one way—you can capture it in many forms of intelligence. We can think of a concept linguistically, musically, artistically, and so on.

Gardner suggests to think of a topic as a room with five entry points or five different doors. Students will choose to enter through one that is most convenient, at first, and then they can explore other perspectives, thus developing multiple perspectives on an issue. Awareness of these entry points can help the teacher introduce new material in ways in which it can be easily grasped by a range of students. A skilled teacher is the one who can open a number of "doors" on the same concept—the one who can shine light from different perspectives and motivate students. These entry points roughly correspond to the seven or eight intelligences. An example of this approach follows.

1. **Linguistics**: Students love stories. When teaching about Beethoven, the German composer (1770-1827) you can tell students short anecdotes about his romantic nature, sloppy handwriting and the misnaming of a romantic composition because of his poor hand writing.
2. **Mathematical entry**: People love numbers, for example, an eight-year-old might understand everything in numbers. "How many minutes do I need to practice the piano?" or "If I practice, how much candy can I get?" In contrast to someone more artistic, this approach through numbers may be inappropriate.
3. **Logic**: Most topics that we teach contain logic an eight-year-old, for example will see the logic and follow instructions if he or she sees the benefit. Such situation stresses cause and effects.
4. **Musical and Art**: Some people love art and music. You can explain major concepts through listening to music, watching and discussing films and looking at art. So when you are teaching history—a historical event such as the French Revolu-

tion and Napoleon's rule—don't just ask your students to memorize the dates and facts. Tell them about "Eroica" and listen to the music, Beethoven's 3rd Symphony—his ripping up the dedication page to Napoleon, in rage—when Napoleon crowned himself the Emperor of France in 1804. Show the students paintings by a famous French painter Jacques-Louis David (1748-1825)—"The Consecration of the Emperor Napoleon and the Coronation of Empress Josephine." This painting and many others are in Louvre in Paris. You can show your students clips from art videos and reproductions from art books.

5. **Hands-On**: Some people do not like to listen or to watch—but they like to do things—a hands-on approach is more helpful. This includes working in groups, collaborating with classmates, role playing, debates, and drama. If you are teaching about Helen Keller, the deaf and blind child, you can teach the students to make a few signs from the American Sign Language (ASL). You can also tell students to work in groups and come up with questions for an imaginary meeting and an interview with Helen Keller.

The above are certainly not intended as a guide but as examples of taking advantage of different learning styles. Everything cannot be taught five, six, seven or eight ways. That's not realistic or practical. But everything should be taught in more than one way. If we teach more than way we reach more students and we show them what it is like to really understand something from many angles. We thus provide a very rich representation of a concept.

Through a New Lens

I believe that Gardner's Multiple Intelligences Theory can help students reach their potentials by developing their particular spectrum of intelligence through a multi-faceted approach to understanding. By teaching in more than one way and by approaching the given topic through numerous angles, we do not only reach many more students, and show our students what it is like to really understand something by providing a rich representation of a concept, but most importantly, we motivate the students and thus provide an opportunity for creative growth. Motivation, I believe, is a key element for successful education, which, in turn, promotes imagination and creativity.

I argue that Gardner's MI theory can be used as a tool for bringing to life Vygotsky's concept of the Zone of Proximal Development. Remember that Vygotsky's dream was to restructure the educational experience and to find a way to help children reach their potentials. His ideology rested on the notion that one has to teach ahead of development so as to maximize the child's Zone of Proximal Development. Today we can do it with the approach offered by Gardner. We also need to restructure our educational experience by thinking of teaching in a new light. I believe that by incorporating Gardner's MI theory into our instructional approaches we can maximize cognitive development and thus expand the Zone of Proximal Development.

The idea of teaching and learning that will allow the educators to teach ahead of development, to teach for understanding, to motivate and promote the students' creativity and imagination, and to encourage their personal, social and academic growth—these have long been the goal of our educational system. By joining the visionary forces of two great educators, Lev Vygotsky and Howard Gardner, we now can achieve this noble goal. By maximizing Vygotsky's concept of the Zone of Proximal Development and utilizing Gardner's Theory of Multiple Intelligences, educators can develop a universal approach of furthering children's abilities as we nurture their individual intelligences.

Conclusion

Therefore, our goal for today's education should be to carry Vygotsky's legacy and bring his ideas to life using Gardner's Multiple Intelligences theory. Our goal is to expand the Zone of Proximal Development in order to maximize individual potential. The way to do this is to recognize and understand the student's cognitive profile, his strengths and passions, and then nurture the combination of his intelligences. This will undoubtedly yield motivation which I consider the foundation of imagination and creativity. This kind of learning and teaching will thus lead the student to a higher level of cognitive development and place him on a new level of intellectual possibilities, a new plateau with the richness of the world within his reach.

Beliavsky's Epilogue:
A Tale of Two Cities

I was eight when I last set foot on Russian soil; my mother, my father, my older brother, and I were leaving Moscow forever. My childhood friends, my school, my music teacher—whom I adored—my grandfather, and my aunt shed an ocean of tears for one last time. This was 1971 and we were immigrating to our Jewish homeland, Israel. We closed the final chapter of our lives in Soviet Russia. My father was fired from the Moscow Symphony Orchestra because there was no more room for a Jewish violinist—soon to become an Israeli citizen.

At the Visa Central Office of Immigration my mother was shamed for her lack of loyalty and gratitude to the Soviet State, which had after all, provided her with education and a life to be only envied by the capitalist world. There was an appeal to her conscience and sense of patriotic duty, to at the very least, leave her two children behind, who would be taken care of by mother Russia herself and would not have to endure the embarrassment that she was about to inflict upon them. My mother thanked the authorities profusely, but nevertheless opted not to leave her eight-year-old daughter and fourteen-year-old son in the communist cradle.

My own life as a second grader was no different than that of any child—or so it seemed. Until one day my brother and I were taken to our aunt and uncle. The next thing that I remember were the embraces, the cold sweat on my father's face, the cool and collected demeanor of my beautiful mother, my brother being sent back to those staying behind the iron curtain to get some extra rubles from our grandfather, my aunt's disheveled hair, tearing eyes, and aged face and the four suitcases, one for each member of the family—with some clothes, music records and books. We were at Sheremetievo airport leaving our life behind forever. We knew that if my father would not be arrested for being an activist with the Zionist movement and trying to help the refusniks, this would be a one-way trip. I remember walking through the very last patrol stand, and seeing my father's eyes—there was so much light in them and hope for freedom to come and a gift of a lifetime to give to his children. His body was tense, hands shaking, never looking back at his past, one more step and we would all be free, free to take a breath, free of anti-Semitism, free of oppression and hatred, free of the chains of Soviet Russia that it so skillfully draped around the necks of all the Jewish people. These were the endless moments in my parents' lives. I still see us walking—as if in a slow motion—taking those final steps to freedom.

Cut to 33 Years Later

On November 15, 2003, 33 years later, my face glued to the window of the Finnair aircraft, holding my breath and filled with incredible curiosity and bewilderment at what was awaiting me, I was anticipating the landing at the very same Sheremetievo airport, in Moscow, Russia. I had been invited to participate and present a paper at an international conference on Lev Semenovich Vygotsky, a famous Soviet psychologist, at the Russian State University for the Humanities in Moscow. I knew that this would be an opportunity of a lifetime to meet Gita L'vovna Vygotsky, Lev Semenovich's daughter. My mother was accompanying me, feeling somewhat nervous and responsible for the safety of her now grown daughter, a wife and a mother. My husband and our two little girls, were impatiently awaiting our return on American soil.

First we decided to visit my uncle Boris and my aunt Yelena. Boris is a well-respected professor and dean at the Moscow State University. He is tall and handsome, and looks just like my older brother. Instead of taking the metro that day, we decided to walk all the way to my uncle Boris.

We walked on the central street in the heart of Moscow's downtown, Tverskaya Street, once called Gorky Street. It is a magnificent and wide boulevard lined with grand looking buildings. Before World Word II—the street was rebuilt—some of the original buildings were lifted and moved slightly into the inside, closer to the courtyard, and new buildings were erected in their place. There is even a children's poem written by a famous Russian poet, Samuel Marshak, called "Dom Pereyehal," in which a young boy comes home from a summer camp but cannot find his apartment building. After making sure that he is on the right street, and after endless searching, he realizes that his house has migrated!

We passed by the famous Moscow Art Theater, also called the home of Chekov. There the premier of Chekov's *Sea Gull* was first staged. At the time, Anton Pavlovich Chekov was living in Yalta, Crimea, suffering from tuberculosis. Because he was not able to attend the premier, the whole troupe traveled to Yalta to perform the *Sea Gull* for Chekov himself. Shortly after, Chekov passed away. In his honor and memory the emblem of the sea gull was embroidered on the curtains in the Moscow Art Theater. When I was five, I watched a magical children's play in that same theater called *The Blue Bird* by the German writer Mauris Meterling.

And then we came across a small café that used to be the well-known Philipov's Bakery. Before the 1917 Revolution this bakery was famous for its fresh breads, rolls, and patisserie. Once a well-to-do lady walked in and purchased a roll, sat down, ready to enjoy it but all of a sudden screamed, "There is a cockroach in my roll!" Philipov, the owner, without wincing ever so slightly, held the cockroach in his two fingers, opened his mouth and ate it. Then, with a smile he exclaimed, "Oh madam, it is only one of our freshest and plumpest raisins!" Then we passed the monument of Prince Yuri Dolgorukiy, who founded Moscow in 1147. The noble Prince is proudly mounted on his iron horse. More than 850 years had passed since. It was evening and Moscow November snow was dancing in the streetlights. Its soft shimmer lit the long Tverskaya street which weaved ahead of us. We were hungry and exhausted. Caviar, blintzes, and of course my aunt's red borsht awaited us, as my uncle and aunt ran outside to embrace us. Today, when I think about that evening, it seems that it took place so long ago, in a land so distant…My uncle handed me a short, scientific autobiography by Alexander R. Luria, and began his own story. Boris' family and Luria's family used to spend Russia's long summers in neighboring *dachas* (summer cottages). Boris was a mere child then, not older than three or four years old, yet already extremely gifted in mathematical abilities and abstract thinking. Boris' mother was friendly with the Lurias and used to show off her young prodigy. In a game of cards with Alexander Luria, who was in his 30s, Boris, who was four, would invariably win, to everyone's great surprise and excitement! Boris laughed wholeheartedly, and continued his amusing story—"You see, I used to memorize the cards, so winning was really not difficult in the least!"

The Troika

Alexander Luria (1902-1977) was one of the most prominent Soviet neuropsychologists of the 20th century. He met his future teacher and colleague Lev Semenovich Vygotsky (1896-1934) on January 6, 1924, at the Second All-Russian Psychoneurological Congress in Leningrad. Luria recounts that this initial encounter, and that day changed his life forever. He remembers Vygotsky getting up to deliver his very controversial speech without any printed text or any notes, yet his delivery was crystal clear. This presentation earned Vygotsky an invitation to join the Psychological Institute in Moscow. After Vygotsky's arrival in Moscow, A.R. Luria and A.N. Leont'ev (1904-1979) joined him as students and colleagues. They became known as the *troika*, threesome, of the Vygotskian school. While Vygotsky was only about 30 and his students were about 23 years of age at the time, his students' respect for him was immeasurable. To hear Vygotsky's lectures, his students would crowd outside the packed auditoriums and listen through open windows. Tragically, Vygotsky, as did Chekov, died from tuberculosis on June 2, 1934, when he was only 37 years old. Very few of his writings were published after his death due to the politics of the time. His work was banned in the USSR until Stalin's death in 1953.

Present Bridges

Lev Semenovich Vygotsky was born on November 5, 1896, and this year's International Conference was being held in honor of his 107th birthday. The conference was dedicated to creativity and imagination in education, and it was held at the Vygotsky Foundation, at the Russian State University for the Humanities. It was a great success and I met scholars from all over the world in the fields of linguistics, psycholinguistics, psychology, English as a second language, and education.

Vygotsky's daughter, Gita L. Vygotsky spoke warmly of her father's short but meaningful life, recollecting her own childhood memories. She spoke of many of his colleagues, especially of his dearest and closest one, Alexander Luria. Later that day, Gita and I spoke at length, and Gita Lvovna shared with me incredible and rare photographs from her father's life. I can't describe in mere words how fortunate I was to be able to attend this conference and present my own paper in which I shared my own theories and philosophy of education. I believe that today we have a unique opportunity to exchange our ideas with the rest of the world—and not only promote cross-culturalism, but to promote education across disciplines. I believe that building bridges of erudition between countries is our future.

And the Beat Goes On

"And I want to be part of that noble mission," I said to my uncle, as I hugged him one last time before we left. I held Luria's autobiography close to my heart, a gift I shall treasure along with my endless memories.

Appendix A

Howard Gardner's *Multiple Intelligences*

1) Linguistic—The ability to think in words and use language effectively both orally and in writing. That of a poet or a writer.
  - *Vygotsky
  - *Tolstoy
  - *Shakespeare
2) Mathematical/Logical—The ability to think logically and use numbers. That of a scientist, a law professor, a mathematician, a programmer.
  - *Albert Einstein
  - *Bill Gates
3) Musical—The ability to think musically, recognize rhythm, pitch, and melody. That of a musician.
  - *Verdi
  - *Beethoven
  - *Tchaikovsky
  - *Gould
4) Visual/Spatial—The ability to imagine spaces, form, color, line, shape. That of a pilot, a sculptor, an architect, or a chess player.
  - *Bobby Fisher
  - *Yury Gagarin
5) Bodily–Kinesiological—The ability to "think" with the body. That of a dancer or an athlete.
  - *Isadora Duncan
  - *Maya Plissetskaya
6) Interpersonal—The ability to understand other people; another person's motivations, intentions, and to respond effectively. That of a teacher, the salesperson, the religious leader, the politician.
  - *Anne Sullivan
  - *Mao Tsetung
  - *Gandhi
7) Intrapersonal—The ability to understand yourself. When we have to make decisions about where to live, whom to live with, what work to pursue, what to do if we have to change arrears, spouses, countries, etc.
8) Naturalistic—The ability to make fine discriminations in the world of nature and to recognize and classify plants, minerals and animals in nature.
  - *Charles Darwin

References

Coreil, R. C., ed., 2003. *Multiple Intelligences, Howard Gardner and New Methods of Teaching in College.* New Jersey City University: Jersey City, NJ

Gardner, H., 1983, *Frames of Mind*, Basic Books.

—, 1991, *The Unschooled Mind*, Basic Books.

—, 1993, *Multiple Intelligences*, Basic Books.

—, 2003, "Multiple Intelligences after Twenty Years". Paper presented at the American Educational Research Association (AERA), Chicago, Illinois, April 21, 2003.

Kazulin, A., 1990, *Vygotsky's Psychology: A Biography of Ideas*, Harvard University Press.

Kerr, S. J., 1997 "Why Vygotsky: The Role of Theoretical Psychology in Russian Education Reform." http:/webpages.charter.net/schmozel/vygotsky/kerr.htm

Lipman, M., 1996, *Natasha, Vygotskian Dialogues*, Teachers College: Columbia University Press.

Rieber, R. W., ed., 1987, *The Collected Works of L. S. Vygotsky*, vol 4, The History of the Development of Higher Mental Function.

Robbins, D., 2001 *Vygotsky's Psychology-Philosophy. Cognition and Language*, a series in psycholinguistics, ed. by R. W. Rieber, Klewer Academic/Plenum Publishers.

Rogoff, B., & Wertsch, J., eds., 1984. *"Children's Learning in the 'Zone of Proximal Development', New Directions for Child Development"* vol 23, Jossey-Bass Inc. Publishers.

Veer, Van Der R. & Valsiner, J., (eds.), 1994. *The Vygotsky Reader*, Blackwell.

Veer, Van Der R., & Valsiner, J., 1991. *Understanding Vygotsky*, Blackwell.

Vygotskaya, G. L., 1995. "His Life" Gita's reflections on her father L. S. Vygotsky; published in School Psychology International, vol 16.

Vygotsky, L., 1987. *Thought and Language*, revised and edited by Kazulin, A., The MIT Press.

Vygotsky, L.S., 1978. *Mind in Society*, edited by M. Cole, V. John-Steiner, S. Scribner, E. Souberman, Harvard University Press

Wertsch, J., 1985. *Vygotsky and the Social Formation of Mind*, Harvard University Press.

Introduction

Creativity: The Realizing of the Imagination

Elena Kravtsova
Translated by Olga Rowe and Shawn Rowe

Most often, when one talks about Vygotsky's significance for educational psychology, one means first and foremost the concept of the Zone of Proximal Development which he introduced. Indeed, Vygotsky's idea that the only good teaching is the kind that leads to development became a basis for the elaboration and construction of various systems of developmental teaching both in Russia and abroad. However, no matter how fruitful and revolutionary this idea is, it does not exhaust Vygotsky's role in building psychologically adequate instruction for the different stages of ontogeny.

From the cultural-historical[1] point of view, an important principle of teaching is the inclusion in it of various modes of artistic expression. It is also important to note that Vygotsky's life in science was closely connected with theater, that his first work in psychology was devoted to psychology of art, and that during his entire life he worked around and was close to many famous artists[2]. The incorporation of art in teaching is, as a rule, connected with cultivating creative teaching rather than teaching that is based on reproducing tasks. Therefore, it seems important to determine the psychological content of the concept of creativity in Vygotsky's cultural-historical theory.

Psychology and Creativity

Among Vygotsky's works there is only one devoted directly to the issues of creativity— "Imagination and Creativity During Childhood." The main idea of the author who espoused the cultural-historical theory is that creativity is closely connected with imagination, or, as Vygotsky calls it, "creative imagination". Moreover, he mentions originality as the main criterion of the "creativeness" of an activity and writes, "Everything that surrounds us and that is made by human hands, the whole world of culture unlike the world of nature is all a product of human imagination and creativity that is based on that imagination" (Vygotsky, 1991, 5). Thus, according to Vygotsky, creativity is based on imagination. Vygotsky describes the psychological mechanism of creative imagination as separating out the single elements of an object, modifying these elements, composing the modified elements into new integrated images, systematizing these images, and crystallizing them into their objective embodiment.

External Reality and Internal Imagination

It follows from this thesis that imagination implies two processes going in different directions. One process is connected with making meaning out of objects in the everyday world: in other words, with thinking and rethinking external objects and situations. The other process suggests the construction of one's own new image which captures the surrounding reality in an original way. In other words, it is possible to say that on the one hand imagina-

---

[1] Readers in the US may be accustomed to associate Vygotsky's work with the name "socio-cultural theory" or "socio-cultural approach," as suggested by authors such as J. Wertsch (1985). Here and further in the paper, the author uses the name "cultural-historical theory" (kul'turno-istoricheskaya teoriya) for Vygotsky's approach in accord with the Russian academic tradition. (Translators' remark).
[2] Such as Stanislavsky and Eisenstein, for instance. (Translators' remark).

tion, or, more accurately, its mechanism, suggests working with external reality, and, on the other hand, it suggests creating some internal subject of imagination.

Images Yearning for Embodiment

If we try to define the specific character of creativity in cultural-historical theory based on these positions, we should say that Vygotsky emphasizes the unity of these processes in creative activity. He believes that the "throes of creation" are caused by the images of imagination yearning for embodiment. "This is the genuine basis and prime mover of creativity," Vygotsky writes (Vygotsky, 1991, 34). We believe that this thesis is very important for understanding what Vygotsky meant by the psychological content of the concept of creativity. For him, imagination is a process without an external product. This is easy to prove using Vygotsky's own words about a game which he calls imagination at work (voobrazhenie v dejstvii). In this context, creativity is a process of the realization of the products of imagination in real life.

What has been stated does not mean that cultural-historical theory recognizes a process as creative only if the process is directed from the subject outward. It is possible to assume that the realization of the images of imagination has a double mechanism—in one case a subject imagines something depending on a concrete situation, and in another case the subject is determined by internal rather than external goals and motives.

Both of these cases are easy to trace in the following examples. For instance, a person needs some object for his or her practical activity. If the object is absent, this person can take another object, most likely the one that has some characteristics necessary for completing the activity, and use it as an object-substitution. In this case it is very clear that the subject is directed towards external worlds from the very start, and his/her ability to use an object-substitution is connected with an image of the object that is necessary for the realization of her/his activity. In another case, a person takes on a certain image or role and builds his/her relationships with the surroundings from the perspective of this role. The most prominent example is "play"—when the subject rethinks both different situations and different objects through the "glasses" of the role that the subject is realizing.

Creativity/External Imagination/Internal

Such a double directedness of creativity allows us to emphasize the connection of imagination with various sides of the human psyche[3] and personality. Thus, in the first case imagination is fused with the subject's perception, and in the second case the connection between imagination and personality development can be clearly traced. Traditionally, psychologists distinguish two types of imagination—re-creative and creative. From this point of view, it is easy to see that the outward directionality is connected most prevalently with re-creative imagination, whereas the activity directed toward creating an internal image may be characterized as creative imagination.

The analysis of re-creative and creative imagination allows us to determine their principal difference from each other. The subject of re-creative imagination is directly connected with objective reality, with the characteristics of one or another object which the subject uses or is going to use in his or her activity. Moreover, as is emphasized in psychological literature, the subject may—on the one hand— "guess at" or supplement a non-existing object or its part, and on the other hand, recreate some integrated situation based on the separate elements. It is easy to notice that the main mechanisms of such kind of imagination are directly connected with perception and memory, since the origins of a subject's ability to supplement or guess at an object or situation based on its elements are products of the subject's perception and memory based on real experience.

On the one hand, creative imagination is built on the basis of a subject's real experience as well. On the other hand, in the process of creative imagination a subject uses this experience in significantly different ways than in the process of re-creative imagination. It seems possible to say that the subject of re-creative imagination to a significant measure—is not the human being but the objective reality in which the re-creative imagination occurs. Certainly, it appears that a human being is absolutely free in his or her making sense of objective reality. At the same time, it seems to us that this freedom is restricted to a large degree. For example, in filmmaking, different kinds of music suggests different moods or expectations in viewers. And in the majority of cases it works according to the directors intentions. Having heard some music, the viewer already understands or guesses that a declaration of love, a murder, or a chase is coming next. Thus, in spite of the viewer's external freedom, in this case, s/he remains in the captivity of the intention of the film's director.

Of course, in a particular situation, a subject may purposefully resist the director's intentions, but in this case it is a matter of either different psychological processes or the creative imagination. The peculiarities of creative imagination are connected with the special internal activity of a subject that results in the appearance of some point, image, or position which is different from that in real life. In other words, in one's creative imagination one appears as displaying a different side of his or her personality than usual.

For example, a young boy is sitting in front of the television and watching cartoons. When the cartoon is over, he starts saying, "There will be no more, there will be no more, etc." When his mother, amazed, asks why does he says that, he explains, "The other day I said that and they showed two more cartoons on TV."

---

[3] We use psyche to translate the Russian word «psikhika» which is often translated in English as «mind». We feel that psyche remains closer to the original text (and to Vygotsky who also used the word «psikhika» extensively) in relating the idea of the whole of the psychological domain rather than connotations with «thinking» or «thought» inevitable when using the word «mind». (Translators' remark).

Conscious and Voluntary Use of Memory

What is different about this boy's behavior? First, he is consciously building the situation rather than recreating it. In addition, he tries to look at the situation not from his current position but from the position of the subject for whom the phrase "There will be no more" became closely connected with the continuation of the cartoon show in reality. Second, in the given example the child relies on his actual experience and uses the product of his own memory, but such usage is fundamentally different from re-creative imagination. In the process of re-creative imagination, memory leads a subject, whereas in the situation described above, the subject consciously and voluntarily uses memory and its product.

It seems that re-creative imagination not only has no relation to the development of creativity in ontogeny, but also hinders its formation to a significant degree. We see the proof of this thesis first of all in the expression "the throes of creation" used by Vygotsky to refer to the realization of the products of imagination in real life. In the case of re-creative imagination, the realization of the products of imagination is not a problem at all since the objective reality is the "alpha and omega[4]" of the re-creative imagination.

Creating Worlds Via the Imagination

In the case of creative imagination, realization, of course, requires certain work from the subject since s/he has to relate the imagined object, view, or understanding to the real situation in which it has to be realized. It appears that to a significant measure, this characteristic of creative imagination is the reason for the various difficulties and problems faced by many creative people. It turns out that a substantial portion of creative people to a certain degree are moving within a cycle of internal work with themselves and paying little attention to (and sometimes even ignoring) the external situation in which they are situated. For example, there is some empirical evidence that elementary school students with very high levels of creative imagination may have serious problems in education. The main reason turns out to be connected with the fact that these children are quite content with the world they create with the help of their imagination.

Everyday Reality vs. Creative Imagination

Often such satisfaction with an imagined situation leads to creative children either receiving a diagnosis of autism because of their lack of interest in external circumstances or falling under the label of weak-willed subjects. We believe that the problem is not the development of will or breaking of the connections with the everyday world; rather, the problem is connected with the peculiarities of creativity and creative imagination as well as organization of conditions for the functioning of these peculiarities.

The early education of children—especially if they show some abilities—leads in one case to exploitation of certain characteristics. In the case of creative children, they become cramped into tight frames of one or another real activity. In this case, it appears that they remain genuine creators only in the process of creating an internal image or intention. That is why, as it seems to us, they "hide" like a snails in their shells. They do not need and they are not comfortable with the realization of the objects of their imagination in the external world. They do not want and sometimes even cannot stand the "throes of creation." They are quite satisfied by creating an internal intention and the realizing of it in the plane of imagination. An analogous situation occurs with many creative adults as well. It turns out that it is quite sufficient for them to realize themselves either in the internal plane or in some "hobby[5]". As a rule, they are willing to allow access to this internal plane only to a few other people.

The Importance of Play

One way out of this situation may be connected with an activity that by its very structure and peculiarities suggests a creative character: play. As it seems to us, the creative character of play is connected with its two characteristics. Analyzing the activity of play, Vygotsky notes that this is the first activity in which a child acts starting from intention. This means that subject of play is always realized. Otherwise, it will not be play in the psychological sense of the concept. A second characteristic of play is connected with its realization in objects. Studying play activity shows that it always appears (or may be presented) as something that occurs in a real situation with real objects. Otherwise, this activity may have some characteristics of play but will still not be play with its special psychological content.

Therefore, play in itself combines the characteristics of creativity given by Vygotsky—the presence of the image of imagination and its realization in real life. From this point of view, it turns out that play is not only a leading activity of the pre-school period of development, but is also a mighty means for realization and development of creativity at all the stages of ontogeny. In addition, play ensures the harmonious development of personality and its close connection with the various sides of external reality. Of course, in each period, play is present in a particular form, each with its own peculiarities. However, without play there cannot be what can be called creativity in the context of cultural-historical theory.

---

[4] Quotation marks added. (Translators' remark).
[5] Author's quotation marks. (Translators' remark).

About the Translators

Olga Rowe holds degrees in Mathematics and Psychology from Kharkov State University and in Sociology from Kharkiv National University. She takes a socio-cultural approach to studying identity formation as a part of learning in public identity forums and uses discourse and narrative analysis to study the ideological charge of cultural tools in informal learning settings. She currently works with the Sociology Department and Department of Continuing Education of the Extended Campus of Oregon State University developing and delivering online courses in Sociology. Olga Rowe has co-translated with Shawn Rowe several works in socio-cultural theory.

Shawn Rowe holds a degree in Multilingual and Multicultural Education from Florida State University and a Ph.D. from Washington University in St. Louis. His work draws on socio-cultural approaches to explore the acquisition of social languages and speech genres in both first and second languages. He currently works in the Department of Science and Mathematics Education and an interactive science museum at Oregon State University where he studies free-choice learning. Shawn Rowe has co-translated with Olga Rowe several works in socio-cultural theory.

Imagining the Worst

Nel Noddings

Editor's Note: The following remarks were delivered as an unwritten keynote address at the second annual International Education Research Group Conference in Vancouver, Canada in July, 2004.

This morning, I am not going to be talking about happiness—as you can guess from the title, "Imagining the Worst." My main idea, however, is equally simple and direct.

What I would like to encourage here is that in our schools, there should be an exercise of the imagination in preparing young people for military service. The military, after all, is staffed not wholly, but largely by young people who have not gone to college. They may some day, but they haven't when they first go in: they haven't had the opportunity to read the kinds of things that we are privileged to read when we attend college or university. That is a main theme that will hopefully help unify these remarks. There is, however, a larger theme—one that concerns the exercise of the imagination in education and in the service of self understanding.

Socrates advised each of us, "Know Thyself." But when we try to do that in schools—particularly in the U.S.A.—people protest and say, "That's therapy, that's therapy. Therapy—not education." And yet if we follow Socrates, we see that self-understanding is probably the basis of all understanding. That's what helps us to begin to realize the meaning behind this seemingly simple theme. And then there is a sub-theme: that in our Western Democracies, we're just riddled with contradictions. Contradictions of ideologies, of interpretations. The usual procedure for a citizen is to seize one of the extremes and say, "That's it. That's me. That's right. I know it." And then the people at the other extreme are evil or stupid or ignorant. We don't want to exercise the imagination. It's far easier to say that certain people at the other end are deficient and be done with it. But I would like to suggest something very different—that is, first, I would like for us to imagine ourselves adopting the opposite extreme. Then, we could reflect on ourselves and do some critical thinking.

A Shadow Side

So we've got these three themes—two extremes and a person reflecting on them. But our main concern is still preparing young adults for what might happen to them when they join the military. It is relevant for us to mention contemporary character education, which is mentioned quite often in the U.S.A. at the present. The emphasis there is inspiring the good, teaching the virtues. But I am not at all sure you can say: All right now, in September we're going to teach honesty; and in October, we're going to teach loyalty. In November, we're going to teach perseverance. By the end of the year, everybody will have good character and we can go on to something else.

Still, that approach will probably inspire some people toward the good. But there's another side to human beings and, while I don't consider myself a Jungian, I do think that Carl Jung taught us something extremely important when he warned that every one of us has a shadow side—not just every one of us as an individual, but every group has a shadow side. We suppress or even repress that shadow side at great risk, because Jung said—and I think he was right on this—that the only way to control the shadow is to understand it, recognize it, and say, That exists in me too as a possibility." That doesn't mean that every human atrocity is a possibility for every one of us—I don't think that's true. For example, I can't imagine under any circumstances whatsoever that I would torture a cat. It's just not possible for me to do that. But where did the "me" that I've been talking about come from? And what might that "me" have been like if I had had an entirely different life—an entirely different childhood, an entirely different education?

Contradictions

I said that our culture is riddled with contradictions and here are a couple I would like to mention. Certainly we have contradictions in religion and in our view of democracy, but we even have them in our view of imagination. I was amused yesterday when Kieran [Egan] said, "Who could be against imagination? We're all for it." But historically, there have been people against imagination. They have thought: That is a very bad thing. We don't want kids to imagine. In 2002, Eva Brann wrote a monumental study of imagination which is entitled *The World of Imagination*. When I say monumental, I mean that it is a great, fat, long book. It includes a philosophical history of imagination, a poetic view, and so forth.

But at the very beginning, she lists a whole flock of contradictory views on imagination including what it is, what its sources are, and what are the extreme views on the moral value of imagination. On one hand, we have people who have said, "It invites corrupting passions." Plato worried about that; he didn't want kids exposed to certain forms of poetry because the exercise of imagination in that line invites corrupting passions. On the opposite extreme, it is said to prefigure paradise.

Now those are vastly different views on imagination. What I'm arguing here is that the use of imagination can reveal real possibilities. In doing that, in revealing real possibilities, it may increase the chances of promoting the better, and decreasing the worst—and I think that that's what we're trying to do. Several years ago, the Nobelist Gao Xingjiang wrote an essay on the uses of literature and he said that literature allows a person to preserve a human consciousness. That, to me is quite powerful: "It allows a person to preserve a human consciousness." And Kieran yesterday also pointed out that we're alarmed by the drop in readers in our society. I don't think the statistics are quite as bad as the ones he quoted, but still, if few people ever read a book after high school, it's hard to put a whole lot of faith in using literature to preserve human consciousness.

The Real Me

This is the kind of contradiction that is built into what Harold Bloom has called "The American Religion." We see that it sticks out all over. On the one hand, we have a tendency toward dogma, believing exactly what we're told to believe. On the other hand, our beliefs are riddled with Orphism, Gnosticism, Enthusiasm, and Anti-Nomianism. This is from Harold Bloom and his *The American Religion*. How do we manage with contradictions of that sort? There's an emphasis on knowing, on independence, on something called "soul competence," or a real self hidden from the world. We defend ourselves against the bad things that we do saying, "That wasn't really me; you don't know the real me."

In the U.S.A. today, there seems to be the dangerous notion that the real America is what it says, but not what it does. One of our great seers was Ralph Waldo Emerson, who nevertheless contributed to this problem. Although Dewey called him "The Philosopher of Democracy," there are some oddities in Emerson's views. He said for example, "Every man makes his own religion, his own god." That is typical American rugged-individualism. Next he asked the question "What is God?" and answered it by saying: "It is the individual's own soul carried out to perfection." Then he followed that by saying:

> *Know then, that the world exists for you. For you is the phenomenon perfect. What we are, that only can we see. All that Adam had, and all that Caesar could, you have and can do-build therefore your own world.*

I say that's enormously energizing. It's romantic and it's also enormously dangerous. It generates an almost bipolar energy, and kids—when they hear that—ought to know the two sides. Emerson said to all people, build your own world, you can do anything you want to do. That seems to overlook the terribly oppressive conditions in which many people live. In a similar vein, Socrates said that the unexamined life is not worth living. While that's beautiful from one perspective, it's arrogant from another. How many people have the leisure to spend time examining their lives?

Imagination and War

The suggestions that I'm going to make now aren't the first ones made along these lines. There have been various attempts to engage the imagination for the prevention of war. A very prominent one came from Virginia Woolf and her *Three Guineas*. Those of you who have read it and can remember it know that she was trying to figure out how to prevent war. She suggested that we should exercise our imaginations when we look at photographs and artwork. At that time, there were just horrible photographs of the Spanish Civil War coming out, and she thought that these photographs could be used to turn people against war.

Very recently, Susan Sontag made the same observation in *The New Yorker* and then in a book titled *Regarding the Pain of Others*. She says, "Not to be pained by these pictures, not to recoil from them, not to strive to abolish what causes this havoc, this carnage—for Woolf, these would be the reactions of a moral monster." And, she says, "We members of the educated class are not monsters. Our failure is one of imagination, of empathy. We have failed to keep this reality in mind." So there's that very, very important distinction that I want to make between imagination and reality. When you imagine something that is the reality for others, it can be enormously powerful. But Sontag is not optimistic. Here we have extremes again where some are revolted by these pictures—others are attracted.

I read another recent book by Anthony Swofford, a very thoughtful literate man. (I don't usually read books by ex-marines, but I read this one.) At the beginning, you get a glimpse of what he was like when he joined the marines. He was eager for war. He talked with an attractive language about rape, pillage, burning, destruction, all this. He was a young man just eager to get into it. Swofford pointed out that the great anti-war films of the Vietnam era turned many people into pacifists. In contrast, he said, "But, to the military mind, they're pornography. Enormously attractive! They couldn't wait to get into it!" Now certainly, on one level, that's unfair because not everyone in the military is like that. But Swofford was able to document story after story. So here we have the extremes again. On one hand, that which we would use to prevent war actually sends some people to war with great enthusiasm.

The Illiad Resonates

Where might we begin in schools on this? I suggest here that one obvious place to begin is with *The Iliad*. We usually make children read at least part of it, but of course they don't really study it. They read parts of it and struggle with the language and never get to the essence of the thing. But it's fascinating to me to see how much recent work in literary criticism is directed now to that book. We begin by noticing what kind of man Achilles was before the worst events occurred—a decent man, honorable, strong, a warrior. He did capture enemy soldiers and held them for ransom, but that was the custom in that day. That's what you did: you held them for ransom. So he was merciful, a thoroughly decent fellow.

But what happened to him? Well, two things happened. First of all, there was the perceived betrayal by Agamemnon. That's an important thing to keep in mind because it turns out that a sense of betrayal often turns good soldiers into "berserkers," and Achilles went beserk. Why? First, betrayal and then the death of his friend Patroclus, which really set him off. You would not want to encounter Achilles on the field of battle after that. Where he would have captured an enemy soldier in an earlier time, there is no capture now. Even when a young man is on his knees begging for his life, Achilles still kills him.

Now pause here before we go on to more information and ask the following questions: Can you imagine anything like this happening to you? Can you imagine being this way, doing these things? What might do it? The death of your best friend? A particularly mean, gory type of death. The destruction of your home city? A threat to your mother? What might do this? Can you imagine yourself reacting as Achilles did? Then we go back to seek more information because, again, I think Kieran was absolutely right yesterday when he pointed out that we can't imagine that with which we've had no experience whatsoever. And we at least have to have a vicarious experience, we have to know something before we can exercise imagination on it.

Kids need to know that drastic changes in personality happen, have happened, and will happen in every war—every war, not just in some wars, and they don't just happen to the bad guys; they happen to the good guys as well. Psychiatrist Jonathan Shay wrote a book entitled Achilles in Vietnam. Shay is a psychiatrist who has worked with Vietnam veterans for years. He looks at the psychology of the berserker and he says that in his opinion, soldiers who have become berserkers never really recover. They suffer a lifelong trauma.

Glenn Gray in his book *The Warriors* tells us something that we really don't want to hear. And that is that even in World War II, the so called "Good War," these things happened. Gray is an interesting case because he got his draft notice for World War II, and his Ph.D. from Columbia University on the same day. So he entered the military where you'd expect a Columbia graduate to enter it, in the Intelligence Service. Here's a little excerpt from his journal, written during the war. He says, "Yesterday we caught two spies, making our recent total five. We are getting a reputation as a crack detachment. One had to be severely beaten before he confessed. It was pretty horrible, and I kept away from the room where it was done…though I could not escape his cries of pain…I lay awake until 3 o'clock this morning…I thought of a Hamlet line as most appropriate: "'Tis bitter cold, and I am sick at heart."

That's his journal entry. Gray goes on to say, "A soldier with an awakened conscience who is a member of such a community, coarse, vulgar, heedless, violent, realizes with overpowering clarity the possibility of being alienated from his own kind. This uniformed machine-like monster, the combat unit, drives him back into himself and repels him utterly. Toward individuals who make it up, he can gain many relationships, but the collectivity chokes him without mercy." That's a quote from World War II. We could document loads and loads more to discuss dreadful things that happened in the Pacific War, but you know many of these stories as well as I do.

A Loss of Moral Identity

James Tatum has a new book entitled *The Mourner's Song*. It's one of the most beautiful works of literary criticism I've read; it looks at war poetry memorials and the like. It proves again that these dreadful things happen in every war and not just to the bad guys. And then there's Lorrie Goldensohn's *Dismantling Glory*, for those of you who like poetry and the criticism of poetry. She concentrates on World War I and Vietnam poetry. What sticks out in all of these is that the suffering of the perpetrator is sometimes permanent. In other words, there is a loss of moral identity which is never fully recovered.

What else should we do as we're reading *The Iliad*? Well, we might read at least part of Simone Weil's essay, "The Poem of Force." Weil reads *The Iliad* as an anti-war poem. She points out that many warriors recover and go back to productive and fully moral civilian lives. But she says some do not recover, and she describes such people as "a compromise between a man and a corpse." To send kids out of high school into a situation they don't understand at all, to take the risk that my son or your son may become a compromise between a man and a corpse is a horrible, horrible thing to contemplate. At the very end of that essay, Weil writes in admiration of Homer's genius, "Perhaps the peoples of Europe will rediscover that epic genius when they learn how to accept the fact that nothing is sheltered from fate, how never to admire might or force, or hate the sufferers. It is doubtful that this will happen soon." Weil was writing in 1940.

Weil has been taken to task by other writers because they think that *The Iliad* is not really an anti-war poem. It might be to you or me as we read it. It certainly was to Christa Wolfe and other feminists who have looked at it, and have interpreted it as an anti-war poem. But there's that other side; there are the extremes again. Where Weil sees an anti-war poem, others—such as Seth Schein in *The Mortal Hero*—see nobility, courage, strength, loyalty, the glory of warriors, the glory of being part of the great battle, defending your people, your country—it's a whole ethos of societies. So now the question for young adults is this: What about today, which ethos is dominant? This glorification of war and the warrior, or this revulsion to it? Which is it, and which do you feel, and why do you feel it? And follow right up by asking the question: Is it true that no one wants war?

Before the Iraq invasion, we heard this line from leaders in many parts of the world. Tony Blair used it, George Bush used it, lots of people said it: "No one wants war!" But was that true? Did no one want war? Lots of people want war. I mean some want it for profit, some want it for power, some want it for glory, and some want it just for the excitement of it. And this is the one that appeals to young adults. Chris Hedges published a book entitled *War is a Force that Give us Meaning*. It appeared first as a column in "Amnesty Now," but now is a whole book. It points out that apparently for many people, life is so dull, so boring, so unpromising, that war offers excitement, brings meaning to our lives.

Instantly Heroes

So here's another issue on which to exercise our imaginations: Can you imagine your life so dull, so boring, so unproductive, that war would be attractive beside it? And if that's so, what can we do about it? What can we, as educators, do about it? This is an enormously important question to put to young people. Let me present you with yet another contradiction. This one no doubt bothers you as much as it bothers me. Generally speaking, the young people who go directly from school into the military, are not our favorite students. That may be an odd way to put it, but they're the kids who aren't particularly attracted to academic life. There's no particular job just waiting for them out there; they're not ready to go to college, and sometimes they've even been a pain in the neck in school. As a result, we don't have the greatest affection and respect for them. In fact, generally speaking, we don't have all that much affection and respect for the military—until war comes.

And when war comes, then these questionable young adults become "our boys, our heroes." Instant conversion. And of course this has been pointed out many, many times before, and we still don't seem to get it. Kipling wrote about it in his "Barracks Room Ballads:" It was Tommy this, Tommy that, and the ne'er-do-well was treated with utter contempt. Then the war came about and it was "Mr." whoever he was, our hero. Should our young people hear about that contradiction? You bet they should. Should they hear about the fact that, while kids are being urged to go into the military and go to war now, we're reducing veterans' benefits? 'Cause apparently, once it's over, don't worry about it.

A Powerful Story

A recent article in *The New Yorker* documented the fact that Vietnam veterans who were suffering this perpetrator trauma can't get over the fact that they did certain terrible things. One man even asked, "Why do they do it? Why did I do it? That isn't me!" Well, it would be better to say, "That wasn't me" because once it's done, you're stuck with it for a lifetime. There's no psychiatric help for that particular problem. All right, now, another sort of extended example and then we'll have time for some questions and conversation. Simon Wiesenthal, who is well into his nineties, was a holocaust survivor and a Nazi hunter. A few years ago, he published a little volume entitled *The Sunflower*. It is very, very thought-provoking. The story takes place in a concentration camp and you can't be sure in reading it, whether the protagonist—the young Jew in the story—is actually Simon himself. You're not sure that this is autobiographical. It may be partly fictional. But anyway, it's an enormous and powerful story.

The young Jew is summoned to the bedside of a dying Nazi soldier. Here we have two very young men—one facing imminent death, the other probable death. The man lying on the bed is blind, bandaged, suffering physically, and morally. The Nazi soldier who is about 19 years old recites the story of an atrocity—the burning of a whole village of Jews—that he had been part of. Then he asks for the forgiveness of the Jew. The young Jew doesn't give it. He isn't cruel: he brushes a fly away from the other boy's head, and then just leaves the room without saying anything. Years later, showing that he is a deeply moral person, he calls together a symposium of thinkers to ask the question whether he did the right thing or the wrong thing and what should he have done?

Most of the responses are interesting; some are pompous. In our Christian and Judaic heritage, we have the duty to forgive, so forgiveness is a duty. It isn't something that wells up from natural human feelings: it's a duty. If you don't want to forgive out of a sense of compassion, you do it grudgingly. And then we've got the extremes again. Cynthia Ozick, a writer I admire greatly, had a most horrendous response to this story. She said that the young Jew was right to walk out without forgiving the dying Nazi. "Let the SS man die unshriven. Let him go to hell!" That's her response. But when I look at it, I look at it as a mother and a grandmother and a teacher. I feel pity for the victims for sure, and that should move us to try to prevent such things. But there's also pity for the perpetrator. This isn't a 35-year-old, 40-year-old; this isn't a 55 or 60-year-old professional on whom the weight of guilt should bear heavily. This is a kid, a kid who has lost both his life and his moral identity.

And so I ask myself the question that Gunter Grass asked himself as well. I was a child during World War II and since I'm of German heritage, I can exercise some imagination here. Suppose I had been growing up in Germany, suppose I were a boy instead of a girl, suppose I were exposed as this kid was to the Hitler youth, suppose my whole education oriented me in that direction. As a kid who liked her teachers—and I did adore my teachers—I mean school was more of a home to me than my home was. If my teachers had said, This is the thing to do, would I have had the knowledge, the courage, the sense to say, No, that's not the thing to do?

The use of the imagination in this particular case presents a complexity and a difficulty that is not often seen. It is fairly easy to imagine ourselves as the victims. And to be terribly, terribly angry about that; and that's a good thing. We should have that sort of empathy for the victims. On the other hand, it's very hard for us to imagine ourselves as the Nazi soldier and to ask ourselves: Under what circumstances might I do a thing like that? And then realize that the victim may die, and the perpetrator may live. In which case, the perpetrator lives with this moral wound, this moral suffering all of his life. On this issue, I'm very attracted to the work of Primo Levi. Here you see something really quite wonderful.

For those of you who aren't familiar with the case, Primo Levi was also prisoner in a concentration camp. He survived it, sort of survived it. He lived through it—let's put it that way. And when he was asked to describe his torturers, he refused to call them torturers. He said that he couldn't call them that. The label didn't capture an important truth. He said they were people just like us, with the same ordinary faces, the same ordinary knowledge and lack of knowledge, just like us, except that—he added—they all "had been subjected to this terrifying miseducation provided for and imposed by the schools in accordance with the wishes of Hitler...." He was generous in blaming the educational system for what happened.

I think perhaps, he might be a little too generous on this—that there are other factors entering it as well. But just think of the responsibility that that puts on educators. And when you read Remarque's *All Quiet on the Western Front*, you see the same sort of thing—kids, these young German boys, incited to go and enlist in the army by their teacher. The teacher told them how glorious it would be, how wonderful it would be, the notion that sacrifice for your country is, wonderful, beautiful, glorious. But at any rate, Levi gives us a very important message: Imagine the effects of your teaching. What will they be? Will the result be victims and perpetrators, or will the result be something else? Now as I said, Levi survived it, but years later he committed suicide. And that story, too, is told oftener than we would like to hear.

Conclusion

We know all of these things, that is, the people that Virginia Woolf talked about—we educated people know all of these things, and yet we don't share them with kids who need them so badly. The kids who don't go into the military, who go to a good liberal arts school or university read all kinds of material that will help them with self-understanding. They don't all succeed at self-understanding, but at least there's that effort, it's there. These other kids are sitting ducks sent into situations where they know they may lose life or limb. That they know, but even that knowledge has a way of inspiring them; they will be heroes. They don't know that they may lose their moral selves, their moral identity. And, this is, as I've tried to convince you here, enormously well-documented, in volume-upon-volume documented.

Now there are two things I wish to say in conclusion. Notice how much richer the curriculum might be if we use some of this material. Think of the writers that I have referred to in this brief talk. Socrates, of course. (Socrates wasn't a writer but nevertheless he has been written about.) Harold Bloom, Virginia Woolf, Susan Sontag, Simone Weil, Glenn Gray, James Tatum, Lorrie Goldensohn, Seth Schein, Chris Hedges, Anthony Swofford, Primo Levi, Rudyard Kipling, Carl Jung. To have high-school kids read even excerpts from these people and have discussions about them—ah, now that would really involve raising standards. Our notion of raising standards now is to get people to answer multiple-choice questions, to get them to answer more multiple choice questions correctly, so information goes in long enough to do the test, and then it's gone, totally gone. But the kind of material I'm recommending, reading excerpts from some of these people, I think would not be gone so quickly. It might even encourage people to open a book or two after they've finished high school. So there's that to be said for a richer curriculum, one that matters more, one that addresses issues that are central to human life.

But the most important thing, of course, is that these young people are our kids, they're our children. We should want to protect them from the horrors of war, or at least to prepare them adequately for it. No guarantees, there are no guarantees ever in parenting or teaching, but it's a best bet that if we try this, it might help. People need to be able to understand themselves as individuals and as members of groups. When we see the victims, we should have pity and vow that such events will not occur again. When we see ourselves as perpetrators, we should grieve, grieve and discourage the production of more perpetrators.

Following are questions and answers from the audience.

QUESTION #1: I'm thinking about bullies. A lot of teachers are asking about classroom management plans and many of them seem to be as coercive as the bullying they're trying to stop.

NODDINGS: In writing a more extensive chapter on this kind of behavior, I referred to my asking children if they could ever be bullies? Usually, they'll say "Oh no!" right away. Sometimes, I become more indirect. I say, "Suppose that every time you try to make a friend in this group, you're ignored or left out. Suppose people make fun of one of your physical features, whatever it might be, and that happens over and over again. Suppose every time a team chooses its players, you're the last one chosen. You're just left out of everything. People make fun of the house you live in. Would you ever be tempted to…"

And then I might talk about one of the things a bully does. So even at the elementary school level, we can concoct stories and get kids to use their imaginations—not just imagining themselves as the victims of bullies, but as possible bullies. Often, that leads to a discussion of inclusion, of trying to compose groups in a way that will help to include the kids who are left out. One person's the recorder; one person's the leader; another is responsible for physical items needed in the activity.

I've had more funny conversations with cherished colleague Liz Cohen on this because I wouldn't use small groups the way she would. But anyway, we try to put them together with understanding, with a direction. We work in small groups to help one another, not necessarily to get a better answer or a better product—although that may happen too. In working through one story, I contrasted the problems of parents who understandably don't want their kids associating with bad kids. It's natural for parents to worry when their children begin running around with so-called "bad kids". Teachers have a different situation. They don't have to encourage long-term associations, but they can put bad kids together with good kids and watch for the energy to go in the direction they want it to go in.

There's a wonderful essay that appears in a book called *Smoke and Mirrors* by Klein Chancer. It looked at the kids who committed all these school murders over the last few years. In every single case, the motivating energy was anger. And it was anger over being ignored, mocked, hurt in all sorts of ways—that was what lay beneath it. It seems very important to work on this inclusion, and to invite kids to imagine themselves as the bad guys. You can ask questions like: "How would you get like that?" "What would make you do that?" "How could that be bad? Because the real me is good! So if I did it, it can't be bad." One of the key operative concepts here is the imagination.

SAME MEMBER OF THE AUDIENCE: What you say is helpful in terms of creating an atmosphere in which the bullying or other kinds of victimization will not occur. But when it does occur—which it unfortunately and inevitably does—how do we, as educators, balance the sense of empathy for the perpetrators but also, a sense of individual responsibility for the acts that they have taken?

NODDINGS: That is another enormously interesting question. I have been writing about moral interdependence. It's a very hard thing to write about and to talk about in our Western Individualist culture. I am not suggesting people who do wrong things bear no responsibility: I'm certainly not saying that. I'm not even going as far as B.F. Skinner who insisted that most behavior results from conditioning. Another person who talked that way was Clarence Darrow, the great trial lawyer. And he even got two young murderers off the death penalty by claiming that they were conditioned by their education, they were University of Chicago students, my goodness. Their education was to blame: for instance, they had read Nietzsche! The lawyer had the whole courtroom, including the judge, in tears over the suffering of these young men who committed a horrible murder.

I'm not arguing that way: that people who do these things have no responsibility. But I am arguing for moral interdependence; that is, that we all share some responsibility for things that happen. The parents of children who commit atrocious acts certainly bear some responsibility—not all, but some. The teachers who don't notice that these kids are left out bear some. This next point is very important indeed: <u>The emphasis that we put on trivia in schools instead of on stuff that really matters in life, causes us to bear some responsibility.</u>

But it's a hard notion to push because in our culture we've got these two big extremes. We've got "Existential Philosophy" that says we are essentially and radically free: "You can do anything you want to do." Radically free. Sartre said that we are brought to the point of anguish and even nausea when we realize our complete freedom. At the other extreme, some people claim that there is no freedom at all! Skinner stressed a position that was "beyond freedom and dignity." In my opinion, we have to find another way that is between these extremes. For me, one way of taking this more complicated view involves moral interdependence. We all bear some responsibility for these bad things. People say, "Oh yeah, soft on crime." That's not being soft on crime: that's wanting to get rid of crime!

QUESTION #2: What can you say about getting students to understand the process of mourning and grieving as a cultural event?

NODDINGS: One of the books I mentioned this morning was Tatum's *The Mourner's Song*. There certainly are other things available. For instance, Harold S. Kushner's wonderful book *When Bad Things Happen to Good People*. Kids must understand several important principles. For example, that people do mourn and that memorials help us in this mourning process. They need time to mourn. All that, I think, is important.

Generally speaking, we don't touch that sort of thing unless some sort of tragedy happens right at the school. And then we bring in people called "Grief Counselors" as though we have no way, no capacity, as adult human beings to participate in the grief process and understand it. It's a weird thing to specialize in—"Grief Counseling." I'm not saying we shouldn't have Grief Counselors: I'm saying it's an odd thing that we have them instead of having every adult teacher prepared to do this kind of work.

Then there's a sort of cautionary word that comes right on the heels of that. If we only use memorials to remember, and if we're going to continue to revive the memory, to keep that memory alive, we may become so concentrated on that process that we forget that another real reason for memorials is to prevent future things of that sort. I'm talking mainly about atrocities and violence, not the ordinary tragedies of life. But I think that there are groups making that mistake. Their preoccupation, almost obsession with the memory part keeps them from thinking about the prevention part. When people are in that situation, they're very troubled by my suggestion. It sounds to them like a horrible affront, which it certainly isn't.

QUESTION #3: I was born in South Africa, and I think that most people are aware of Nelson Mandela and the sufferings that he endured in South Africa. He was imprisoned for seven years in Robin Island. And the worst things that could've happened to anyone happened to him, and he made a conscious effort never to hate. He actually lived in his imagination and a sense of accepting the perpetrator as a person—a human being going beyond what they were doing. And when he was released, he became the president of South Africa and has written many books on how to deal with that situation. But a few days ago, I was in Sydney, Australia. And there is an exhibition by Nelson Mandela that has been done now in hindsight of his memories of Robin Island. Not negative, but positive ones in line sketches. He was using his creative imagination to fill in those gaps for people that didn't know what had taken place there. But it's not in maliciousness, and it's not done vindictively: just stating it in coloring and depicting those things that kept his hope alive.

So I think, linking to what you were saying about imagining the worst, there was nothing worse that could happen to a human being. But it's in keeping his imagination alive that he was able to survive. Now I'm just thinking a conference like this could tap into that same kind of energy. And being a teacher and working with children, I was listening to the questions that came up about bad children and good children. Really, it's about self-esteem and honoring each child. We have a program going in South Australia "Program Achieve." It attempts to remove that bullying element because we focus on the action and not the person.

NODDINGS: Thanks, I mean I think that's very helpful. Mandela to my way of thinking, is an exemplary hero if there can be such a thing. I mean it's redundant, but nonetheless an exemplary hero. And the qualities that you've just pointed out, are the qualities I admire so much in Primo Levi. It doesn't overlook his own suffering or the suffering of others, but he looks at this larger picture and can imagine what has happened to the people who were the perpetrators.

QUESTION #4: I'm very interested in this notion of "pity for the perpetrator." Most recently wars have employed technology that removes many soldiers from the destruction they're perpetrating. I'm thinking about "Smart Bombs" that are deployed with the press of a button from miles away. War has always dehumanized the other side, but can you comment on what effect you think it will have on these perpetrators most recently to make war even more impersonal?

NODDINGS: Actually this particular talk was motivated by the recent disturbingly cruel events by "friendly" forces in Abu Graib prison in Iraq. The political leaders pointed out that in such disoriented situations, people sometimes do things that they would never ordinarily do. Now when we're talking about using Smart Bombs and killing from a distance—it is well documented that that is much easier to do. In World War II, it was learned that a significant percentage of men on the front lines never fired their rifles, or if they did, they didn't aim them at human beings. They just couldn't do it. They just couldn't kill another human being. Military training changed after that in order to make it almost instinctive to fire and to kill.

So you see, you have to do something to average good human beings to turn them into killers. I once talked at a conference and mentioned the brutal fire bombings done by the allies in World War II. One man in the audience had been a pilot in those bombings. He just broke down in tears, and I really felt terrible about it. Here was a good man, who was a hero in all the qualities we associate with a hero. Being a good man, however, he never got over what he had done. Was he wrong to be a bomber pilot? You can't say that. Was he wrong to do what he did? You can't say that. But he suffered all his life for it just the same. And that's what kids should be aware of, that maybe you're using Smart Bombs. You don't have to stick a bayonet in someone, but when you know afterward that you were responsible for—like some of these dreadful pictures that Virginia Wolfe wanted us to see—it isn't going to be easy to get over. If they had some of the reflective experiences we read about in literature, if they had discussed Socrates and the knowing of themselves—they might find the Smart Bombs not so difficult and painful to assimilate into their experience of the world.

References

Bloom, Harold. (1992). *The American Religion: The Emergence of the Post-Christian Nation*. New York: Simon & Schuster.

Brann, E. T. H. (1991). *The World of Imagination*. Lanham, MD: Rowman & Littlefield.

Goldensohn, Lorrie. (2003). *Dismantling Glory*. New York: Columbia University Press.

Grass, Gunter. (2002). *Crabwalk*. (Krishna Winston, Trans.). Orlando: Harcourt.

Hedges, Chris. (2002). *War Is a Force that Gives Us Meaning*. New York: Public Affairs.

Homer. (1990). *Illiad*. (Andrew Lang, Walter Leaf, & Ernest Myers, Trans.) London: Macmillan Ltd.

Kipling, Rudyard. (nd). *The Works of Kipling*. New York: Black's Readers Service.

Levi, Primo. (1988). *The Drowned and the Saved*. (Raymond Rosenthal, Trans.). New York: Vintage.

Remarque, Erich. (1982). *All Quiet on the Western Front*. New York: Fawcett Books.

Richardson, Robert D. Jr. (1995). *The Mind on Fire*. Berkeley: University of California Press.

Schein, Seth L. (1984). *The Mortal Hero*. Berkeley: University of California Press.

Shay, Jonathan. (1994). *Achilles in Vietnam: Combat Trauma and the Undoing of Charater*. New York: Scribner.

Sontag, Susan. (2003). *Regarding the Pain of Others*. New York: Straus and Giroux.

Swofford, Anthony. (2003). *Jarhead*. New York: Scribner.

Tatum, James. (2004). *The Mourner's Song*. Chicago: University of Chicago Press.

Weil, Simone (1977). *Simone Weil Reader*. (George A. Panichas, Ed.). Mt. Kisco, NY: Moyer Bell Ltd.

Wiesenthal, Simon. (1976). *The Sunflower*. New York: Schocken Books.

Woolf, Virginia. (1996). *Three Guineas*. New York: Harcourt Brace.

The Math-Story Aesthetic

Cornelia Hoogland and George Gadanidis

EDITOR'S NOTE: *Most of us tend to take words for granted, assuming that for each object or activity, there is a name. The history of language shows us that things are more complicated. For example, in various periods, the meaning of a particular word is stretched. As a result, ideas and usage associated with such words undergo modification. The great value of this process is that it allows us to see things from a different perspective. "Story" as Hoogland and Gadanidis use the word, is a case in point. While not abandoning some of the conventional senses of "a story" or "the story" or "stories," they use "story" in a new way. For them, it is an abstract, non-countable noun not closely related to narrative. This clearly indicates that a relatively new meaning has entered the discussion. Much of the article is concerned with this new meaning and with its implications for "aesthetics," which is also being stretched. At the risk of oversimplification, the authors' "aesthetics" is the condition of deriving pleasure from an intense involvement of the mind. Various aspects of math, the authors point out, provide such pleasure and even excitement. This is a major thrust of the article. An equally intriguing assumption is that "story" can be discovered in "a story." The perspective opened by the authors is new and stimulating as well as challenging.*

AUTHORS' NOTE: *The authors would like to thank Clyde Coreil for the thoughtful and stimulating email correspondence and editorial suggestions he made about this article. Clyde not only assisted in the fine-tuning of the concepts but also in realizing their philosophical underpinnings.*

Our collaboration to explore a research interest in the aesthetic of mathematics has been primarily focused on mathematics experiences within teacher education settings. We are interested in defining the aesthetic, locating it, and noting its effects. From the beginning we expected that "story" would play a central role. Our working title has generally been "Math as Story," and in June, 2003, we hosted an international conference with that title. In this article we want to reconsider the language context in which we are working, to try to locate the meaning of the words we use, and to reconsider where math and story intersect. Most words have different "senses", each with a fairly precise set of meanings that we recognize. For example, "court" refers to an abstract entity concerned with rendering justice. Also consider "to court" which means to treat a person in a special way that often leads to marriage. We note that the two words are used differently in order to avoid confusion. One is in the form of a noun (the court) and the other is in the form of a verb (to court). On the other hand, there is often a reason for using the same word. Here it seems to create—among other things—an association between "justice" and "honor of behaviour and intention" which connotes marriage in popular mythology. Sometimes new words are created to highlight the specific meaning of an otherwise multi-meaning word. An example is the contemporary word "rap."

Cat Burglars

Rap has rhythm, vocalization, words—all of which are parts of music. But the claim might be made that the lack of melody does not really qualify it for the category "music." Instead of long and esoteric debates on the topic, the matter seems to have more or less solved itself by speakers of English who called it "rap music." This conjugation of words is seen as the solution to specifying the popular meaning of rap. The relationship between math and story is not as simple. However, our solution to the problem of what to call that relationship derives in part from a similar procedure of using more than one traditional word in the name. The significance of our observations concerning math and story resides in our noting that there seems to be a high degree of similarity between something in the abstract processing of mathematics on the one hand, and important elements in a story on the other. The semantic features of a word are the various parts of its meaning. Each word can have more than one sense, but each sense consists of a limited number of semantic features. The semantic features of "cat" include "animal, often active at night, often quiet, climbs well, four legs, usually covered with fur, possessing a long tail, with two eyes in the front of its head." To designate a burglar who possesses several features of the cat, the term "cat burglar" has become popular, particularly among the writers of newspaper headlines.

Meaning-Making

As we are discussing them, the pair "story' and "math processing" are similar to the pair "cat" and "burglar" in that they share features. In time, these shared features might well be given a name. It is possible that this name will be "story." To identify this seemingly new connection, we refer to "story" and not to "a story" or "the story." One of the main differences between "story" and "a story' is that the former refers to all of the aspects of narrative and storytelling, whereas the latter includes only those present in a particular story. Also, story has less reference to the differentiation of various genres in which story could be important. It is also possible that "story" will be found to imply the presence of more narrative than is wished for in reference to both "math" and "story." One interesting and important shared feature is the point in the processes in either math or story where meaning becomes felt as present in human consciousness. We can refer to this process more economically as "meaning making."

Math and the Freedom of Thought

Gilbert Labelle, professor of mathematics at the Université du Québec à Montréal, says "I like mathematics because it is beautiful, full of surprises, and gives me complete freedom of thought." Feelings of surprise and beauty are emotional. Doing math is at times emotional. The structure of stories is also often emotional. Students in our research expressed these attributes as well. "Math is just another way of both creating meaning and describing it. It's lovely. I'm lousy at it, but I love feeling my brain tumble over as it understands something for the first time." The feeling of connectedness to stimuli that math provides this professor and student, and that they experience through their bodies, should not be mistaken for sentiment or mere personal expression. Our hypothesis was that there is a substantial connection between math processing (or simply math) and story. Part of this connection is that both involve aesthetics, which help us to interpret and make sense of the imaginable, awesome complexity of reality. The feeling of connectedness to stimuli that math provides the professor and student quoted above rewards their efforts and engages their attention. This engagement of attention is another feature often shared by stories, possibly the most popular and accessible of aesthetic forms. In the coming months and years, it may be found that math and story do share this common ground. At one hitherto unconscious level, each shares with the other several semantic features such as: beginnings, incidents, actions, circumstances, characters, development, time, change, result, loss, gain, and end.

Dissanayake Revisited

Compared to our specific suggestion regarding math and story, Dissanayake, (1992, 25) is concerned with a much broader but related topic when she says that "aesthetic sensibility acts as one of our primary meaning-making capacities in all domains." One of the ways in which meaning emerges in the human mind is through the perception of things as "beautiful." If something is perceived as beautiful, then it can be said to have meaning. This perception would be located near the bifurcation of math and story. Elsewhere Dissanayke adds that the aesthetic, in addition to being a mode of cognition, is an aptitude for life (2000, 101). She says that we derive pleasure from the aesthetic in the same way that we take pleasure from our friendships and families, as well as from specific activities such as cognition and making art. She seems to be suggesting that the human predisposition to aesthetic patterns—sound, number, length, color, details, forms, inherent relationships tensions and harmonies, texture and change—is also located near the bifurcation that resulted in math and story. It would seem that this is near the point where the mind becomes conscious of itself and that one characteristic of this consciousness is the sensation of pleasure not from the senses but from thinking. Dissanayake (2000) notes our human disposition to these aesthetic patterns. We would add that awareness itself can be a source of pleasure.

The Math-Story Aesthetic

A category that would include all of the above elements and the manner in which they function together is somewhat difficult to realize. It becomes easier to conceive once it has a name. We suggest that the cognition involved in our combination of math and story is itself a mode of "the aesthetic." If we look for an identifying usage for this new sense, we will find it in a combination of "the" (which usually precedes nouns) plus the compounded adjective "math-story" plus the adjective form "aesthetic" used as a noun instead of the conventional "aesthetics." Out of this naming process comes a possibly temporary name for the shared features of math and story-the math-story aesthetic. At the beginning of this paper, we suggested a similarity between the elements and origin of math and story. Here, we will add that common to both math and story are a familiar sense of pattern, rhythm and fit, balance, motion and symmetry. This is an important part of our discussion in this paper. If we acknowledge that these elements are present in and perhaps central to both mathematics and story, we can explore further and hopefully find that the light of one illuminates the areas of deep shadow of the other. The structures found in mathematics might well be presented as a linear sequence of metaphors in a specific story. Similarly, the components of what we are calling simple "story" might be useful in math education. Our notion of "aesthetics", then, as the condition of deriving pleasure from an intense involvement of the mind, can be found in various aspects of math that provide such pleasure and excitement, and which we have found to be often linked to both the narrative and meaning of story.

References

Dissanayake, E. (2000). *Art and Intimacy: How the Arts Began.* Seattle, WA: University of Washington Press.

—— (1992). *Homo Aestheticus.* New York, NY: Free Press.

Gadanidis, G. & Hoogland, C. (2003). "The aesthetic in mathematics as story." *Canadian Journal of Science, Mathematics and Technology Education* 3(4) 487-498. Toronto: OISE/University of Toronto.

Gadanidis, G., Hoogland, C., & Hill, B. (2002a). "Critical Experiences for Elementary Mathteachers." The 24th Annual Meeting of the North American Chapter of the International Group for the Psychology of Mathematics Education. Athens, GA: University of Georgia.

—— (2002b). "Mathematical Romance: Elementary Teachers' Aesthetic Online Experiences." The 26th Conference of the International Group for the Psyhology of Mathematics Education. Norwich, UK: University of East Anglia.

Images at the Core of Education

Elliot W. Eisner

Note: These remarks were delivered as the keynote address at the 2003 IERG (Imaginative Education Research Group) Conference in Vancouver, Canada. They were tape recorded and edited for print by the editor, after being transcribed by William Lake. This is the first time the address has appeared in any publication.

It is imagination, not necessity that is the mother of invention.

E. Eisner

I want to talk about images and imagination this morning. We live and work at a time in which imagination and its development is not high on the list of our educational priorities. Education today, by which I mean schooling, is buffeted by pressures to boost test scores by focusing attention on a narrow range of particular skills. Reading and performance in math are, for example, center stage. The pre-specification of outcomes are then to be measured and compared to predetermined standards in order to guide our efforts and to meet accountability requirements. To devote time to imagination is regarded my many as frivolous—a luxury that is nice but not necessary. This view of the place of imagination and education is ironic since imagination is precisely what we need to enrich our experience and to advance the quality of our culture. It's imagination, not necessity that is the mother of invention. What drives artists and scientists is lust not greed. Imagination is a trip whose satisfactions are pursued with passion.

We're here at this conference to examine the meaning and educational functions of imagination, and I am here to talk to you about the image as the core of imagination and education. And now to do this, my remarks will be in nature of the image and how it functions. The second part is a short nine-minute video of an art teacher promoting his students' imaginative processes. I'll have something to say about what both he and his students are up to after the video is projected. My hope is that our own educational practices as teachers and curriculum developers can be enriched. It is with deliberate intention that my renewed interest in the imagination comes at a time when standardization seem so important to so many as a way to improve our schools.

The Possibility of Images

To talk about images at the core of education requires some analysis of the features of images and the conditions that make them possible. For example, the term "image" can refer to the images that populate our private mental life—that are the stuff of our consciousness. Images can be produced at will. They can also emerge against our will. Images can also have a social currency. For example, those that we see in advertising such as "McDonald's golden arches." These public images are made by others and appropriated by us. Among other things, sharing a culture means sharing images as a form of social currency. I mention this because when we talk about images and imagination, it's useful to have some sense of what we're referring to. Eventually, what we want to be able to do is create the conditions in which the imagination is nurtured through the process of education. As I said, to illustrate how this process can be promoted, I'll show you a short video of a teacher encouraging his students to see and create images through language.

Auditory Images

But first, let's talk about the features of the image, and let's start with some basics. The first idea I want to share with you is that images can be formed in any sensory modality. We tend to think about images as being visual, but images can also be auditory. They can be tactile. They can be olfactory. In fact, images can take shape in any sensory modality that operates in an individual. So the use of the term "image" is not restricted to what people can see or imagine in their mind's eye: although certainly that is extraordinarily important and the one that we typically refer to. But I think it's important to remember that people can also have musical images. What we are able to conjure up for ourselves through a process of recollection takes place in any combination of sensory modalities that humans have the capacity to experience. I repeat this because I do not consider the following trivial: Images can be cultivated for the purpose of using them in classrooms.

Enriched Possibilities

We can think about these alternative ways in which images are developed. The public expression or representation of an image is influenced by the degree to which we are able to observe and by what we are able to represent. The emphasis I want to leave you with, with respect to that idea, is that the articulation of an image—in some public medium—requires certain skills. The better the development of those skills—the more refined they are, the more sophisticated they are—the greater the likelihood that images will be able to be represented in a public way. It's one thing, for example, to sit on the edge of your bed and imagine whatever you want to imagine. That is very possible and is done by a great many people. Sometimes we do it while driving. We "daydream." We see images that we don't represent publicly, but we might enjoy privately. But the public representation of an image is a result of what has been conceptualized. It's not strictly a matter of mimesis. In the articulation publicly of what has been imagined, there is always some kind of change in the image itself. But the extent to which that can take place—the extent to which that image can be made public—depends on the sorts of skills that youngsters or adults possess. So the development of representation—in writing or in painting or in dance or in whatever the medium happens to be—is necessary if the images are to have a social status. If you can read minds, you don't need anything made in public. But if you can't read minds, then something has to be made in public. When representation is made public, there are skills involved that have to be acquired. If they are acquired, then schools can do something about promoting that kind of ability.

Reading the Frigate

Images can also be engendered by what are not imagic: words and stories, for example, perform this function. If I say that there is no frigate like a book, I'm using a kind of metaphor to get an idea across. Does anybody know what a frigate is?

AUDIENCE: It's a ship.

Of course, a ship. You weren't supposed to be so quick to respond. There are some people who would not know what a frigate is, and that is related to another point: if you want to ensure meaningless verbal learning in your classroom, make sure kids don't have images for what you're trying to get them to understand.

A Symbiotic Lexicon of Words and Images

Images have been articulated in philosophical discourse. They have an enormous power to represent very complex ideas. For those of you who had, in the course of your education, the opportunity to read Plato's *Republic*, you will remember the end of Book Six. Socrates was trying to explain to Glaucon, something about the nature of knowledge with the help of a line. Remember? He draws a horizontal line. The part above the line is the world that is accessible to the mind; and the part below the line is the visible world. Then he divides that line with a vertical line to articulate various degrees of knowledge that could grasped by moving up the line to the sun. Then Socrates realizes that Glaucon doesn't get it, that the illustration is somehow too abstract. It's not sufficiently concrete. So what does he do at the beginning of Book Seven? He talks about the parable of the cave. Socrates moves from an abstract illustration into something which is concrete. Why does he devote so much energy to express an idea? Because that idea had been extraordinarily important to Western Civilization—the way of thinking about the nature of knowledge. So we can see that Socrates uses language as a vehicle to get through images the meanings that in some sense transcend the language itself. Images are capable of expressing meanings that have no words, and words are capable of stating meanings for which we have no images.

Science and Art

In the book that he wrote in 1934, John Dewey advises us to make the distinction between what a science does and what art does. Art, he says, expresses meaning. Science states meaning. And by the former, he means that an experience, so to speak, contains a certain quality of humanness which is run through with meaning. So that the creation of an image—be it musical or visual—can represent meanings for which we have no words.

Let us recall what happened on 9/11, when people were building the little religious sanctuaries with flowers, candles and notes to express their grief. Why do people create such images in the first place? Why not just write a text? They do this because they recognize, I think, that certain kinds of human experiences require a certain form of representation that will transcend what is literal. A propositional discourse will do a great deal, but it doesn't do everything. And so we appeal to images made—whether it's in music or in poetry, whether it's in dance or in visual arts—to represent what we cannot say. One of the great ironies is that poetry was invented to say what words can never say. The meanings of poetry transcend language itself. The poem is used as a vehicle to get someplace else. But words can also be used to say things that images can't get at. I don't want to take the position that for every word we use, we have an image, and that we're seeing pictures for everything we are able to articulate.

There are things for which you could never get an imagistic equivalent: "He came to pick me up after 7 p.m. the day before yesterday, which was three weeks before I came here in the first place." That's hard to represent visually. So we have a deep grammatical structure which allows us to construct and recover meaning in ways that are not just images, but are part of the resources through which imagination takes flight and through which meaning is made.

Images and Time

Images can function both synchronically and diachronically—which is simply a fancy way of saying that images like the flag offer an immediate presentation of a meaningful configuration—provided, of course, that you're a part of the culture in which that image participates. But we can also think about images diachronically as functioning over time, as is the case for example in film, video, music and in stories. In a certain sense, you "get it" at once. You see the configuration and grasp its meaning immediately. That's one of the reasons why many teachers—certainly at the university level—ask students to make concept maps. These teachers wish to display relationships simultaneously. The alternative is listening to someone talk about those relationships over time. A visual display makes possible comparisons that would be quite difficult to express without the stability and the immediacy of that which is seen. So there's a diachronic character of images, and a synchronic character of images. Images can be recalled, or they can be imaginative creations. The difference between the recalled image and the imaginative one is one of degree. Even recalled images are to some degree imaginative.

The Recalled Image

What do I mean by a recalled image? If I ask you to think about a can of Coca-Cola, you can engender or reproduce that image in your consciousness. You can imagine it. You can recall that image.

Then I can ask you to put wings on it or to modify it in some other way in order to make it more interesting. There is some degree of imaginative activity taking place. So the past can be structured in school which invites youngsters not only (1) to recall but (2) to treat imaginatively what they have recalled, and (3) to acquire the skills necessary to transform that experience into something which is public.

To have a social value, images need to be made public. Representation is the process that transforms the private into the public. Images represent through expressiveness, through mimesis, and through convention. What does it mean to talk about expressiveness, mimesis and convention? One of the ways in which meaning is constructed is by creating or encountering an image whose character expresses a certain quality of life. There is something in the display that has kind of an analogic character in the quality of experience. Think about your experience and the words we use to describe it. There a person can be upset, be down, be blue, be high, be up. All of that metaphorical terminology is designed to represent. Think about the metaphors we use in visualization. We say things like: "Oh, I see. It dawned on me. I'm completely in the dark on that one. Can you shed some light on this? He's very bright." Or you could say: "I worked around the clock last night." If you don't treat that metaphorically, you'd think somebody was working near a clock. It's obvious that we have a metaphorical grasp of the meaning of things. Images collectively constitute our imagic store, and allow us to make connections among the images that we can generate. For example we can generate a bank of images associated with the Civil Rights Movement or Tienamen Square.

Expanding Our Store of Images

Education can be considered, at least in part, as a process of expanding our imagic store, and helping students make connections among its contents. I don't want to get into a static conception of imagery, and there are problems with the idea that images constitute a bank of resources, but there are also advantages. For example, I might say, "I'd like you to imagine a Romanesque church." Unless you have the idea of Romanesque-ness as a visual, architectural form, I might as well pick something completely nonsensical, and you wouldn't know the difference. So, there is a set of resources for making those connections. In a certain sense, as my students go through this program, they are going to be introduced to an increasingly dense array of ideas. Some of these ideas are going to be connectible with each other at some point. The connections that are made between the concepts they're familiar with and those that they're encountering for the first time will become increasingly complex and often puzzling. I also tell my students that "I'm here to complicate your life," by which I mean that we engender images that allow us to make meaning from what we have heard or what we are hearing.

Saying the Unsayable

Poetry traffics in images in order to reach the imaginary. In poetry, the imaginary is put in the service of meaning that will not take the impress of logically structured propositions. That is to say that there is a cognitive function performed by poetry that makes it possible to express and recover meaning that cannot be conveyed through propositional discourse. So this is a resource that humans have generated over the millennia to be able to say—in a certain sense—the unsayable.

The Central Question

Why then aren't images and the imagination at the core of education? This is a central question because we rely on images to represent what we cannot articulate, and we rely on imagination to conceive of new possibilities. The ability to frame purposes depends on being able to imagine a future that is different from the present. Thus, images shape our actions, they influence our values, and they allow us to express and grasp what we cannot put into words. Grasping the meaning of metaphor depends upon them.

My comments so far, were designed to help sort out some of the qualities of images to both clarify and complicate. But what really matters to those of us who have practical needs and who work where the rubber hits the road—the classroom—is what can be done with images in the context of our teaching. In order to get an idea of how this plays out in one classroom, I'm going to show you a nine-minute video of a high-school art teacher, working in the inner-city, apparently in Los Angeles. He is teaching aesthetics, something that seldom gets taught in high schools or anyplace for that matter. What I would like to do afterwards is "Unpeel" what's going on in that video. [The video is played.]

Analyzing the Video

Let me try to give you an analysis of what's going on here. This teacher's name, paradoxically, is Mr. Harsh. As you saw, he asked his students to distinguish between two types of activities they routinely engage in, one practical and the other, aesthetic. In effect, in helping them grasp this distinction, he wished to show them that there are different ways in which the world can be experienced. He proceeded to illustrate this distinction not by resort to some exotic of fine art of philosophical theory, but by calling their attention to a common activity: pouring cream into a cup of coffee. He first selected a styrofoam cup, poured a little coffee into the cup, added a little cream, tasted it, and pointed out that the primary function of pouring the cream into the coffee, is practical.

He then used a transparent plastic cup and carefully poured a little coffee into it and then, a little cream, while describing the way in which the white cream seemed to explode in the cup for a brief two seconds, after it was poured. He delighted in the beautiful burst of cloud-like formations that the cream in the dark coffee created. That kind of activity, he told the class, was an activity experienced for its own sake: it was an aesthetic activity, not simply a practical one.

Choice and Perception

The example was something that students were familiar with, but not in the way Mr. Harsh addressed it. The larger point of the lesson was that perceptual attitude is a choice—there is more than one way to see. This point was reinforced by giving students terms— "practical" and "aesthetic"—with which to frame the distinction. Mr. Harsh moved from the coffee example to the task that students were to engage in. This "spectator activity" was writing about what they saw. Mr. Harsh wanted a form of writing that has literary qualities. He didn't use the word "literary" but that's what he hoped they would create. And to increase the probability that they would, he tried to make sure that they had a sense of what literary language entails.

This was accomplished two ways: First, he modeled the use of language by giving them a picture of what it looks like. Second, he gave them an example that former students had written in the past, thus making it clear that the task was do-able, and that it did not depend on special forms of expertise. In fact, he also gave them a negative example that is what their language should not look like. He moved on by giving them examples of experiences they had, or could've had, in their own life. These practical experiences were transformed into aesthetic ones—watering the lawn and being lost in the experience of beauty. He made it clear that this did not involve some exotic material outside of their experience.

Red Ink and Water

Mr. Harsh then introduced the materials with which they were to work. These materials, water and red ink, are significant. Each student not only got his own cup of water, but Mr. Harsh came around to drop red dye in their cup individually. Personal attention was being provided here. The red dye in the water allowed projection. The fluid quality much like a cloud made it possible to see in the unfolding burst of form images. These would receive, without difficulty, the meanings each student wants to confer that's what is talked about simply upon them. The unfolding clouds of red opened the door wide to individual interpretation. Unlike many tasks in school, this exercise has no single correct answer. On the other hand, not any response will do: the key word is single. It had to have a literary or poetic feel.

Thus what we have here is an open-ended task that invites the individual response, and that yet is not simply an instance of anything goes. Not anything goes here. The heart of the problem resided for Mr. Harsh's, students in the relationship between seeing and expressing. Seeing is necessary in order to have a content to express. Expression is necessary to make public the contents of consciousness. What we have here is an imaginative transformation of a perceptual event that is imbued with meaning. The features and significance of this activity is what the students try to transform into language capable of carrying that meaning forward. This transformation is, of course, what writing is about. Somehow, the writer must find a way within the constraints of a linguistic medium to create the structural equivalent of the experience.

Emergence of the Unexpected

Often, in the very process of representation, new ideas will emerge. These ideas were not themselves the target of expressive aim. This is exemplified in a student's narrative about the destruction and contamination of the Native-American population. When asked to write a brief reaction to the cream exploding in the coffee, this is what she wrote:

The clear crystal water looks to me like the landscape the native Indians loved to live in. The land that was given to them from the Great Spirit. As the dye drops, Columbus lands. The Europeans not only destroy it, but pollutes their beautiful land with diseases. The red dye spreads throughout the souls of innocent Native Americans, The red dye destroys their people, their tribes, their culture, their beliefs. In good hearts, these beliefs will never die.

It seems to me that these ideas were close to the surface of her consciousness, and were triggered by the color and form of the ink. Note, however, that the narrative that she wrote had itself a powerful, expressive quality, not only because of the imagery, but because of the form. Think about the coda she used to bring her narrative to closure: "In good hearts" she says, "These beliefs will never die." It is in relationship of image to form—or more precisely, the forms that images take—that we are moved as Mr. Harsh was by her words. This situation is one in which students use qualitative forms of thinking to do a number of things. First, perception, not mere recognition, is employed, Mr. Harsh is asking the students, not merely to look in order to categorize, but to look in order to see.

Second the student's imagination is engaged in part because of the supportive relationship Mr. Harsh has with his student, but also because of the exploding forms of ink creates and invites such a response. In a sense, the free-floating cloud of red dye becomes a Rorschach-like experience. Third, the students must find a form; a form crafted in narrative that conveys their experience: that is to say, they become writers. Their writing begins with vision and ends with words. We, as readers or listeners, begin with their words and end with each our own visions. The circle is complete. The artful crafting of language so that it expresses what sight has given birth to is what the short episode is about. Finally Mr. Harsh's students bring closure to the episode by sharing their work with each other.

The Desperate Need for Imagination in Education

I began my remarks by describing the hyper-rationalized approach that we are taking to schooling and its improvement. It is unfortunate that schools are guided by an industrial image. What I am suggesting is the need for a new, more generous image—one that nurtures the spirit, that is not fearful of surprise, that has a place in its aims for the cultivation of the imagination. For such an image to reside at the heart of education requires not only advocacy: it requires imaginative pedagogy. We too, in the end, need a new image for what we do in classrooms. Perhaps this conference will provide some leads for those images.

The First Lady of the Imagination: An Interview with Maxine Greene

Clyde Coreil

COREIL: This recorder isn't brand new.

GREENE: So what is?

COREIL: Certainly not me. Sometimes I wake up and think that I might be in heaven. Then I get hungry. People in heaven don't get hungry.

GREENE: The only thing I thought, and I still think that is relatively new or at least needs repeating is the neglect of imagination in education.

COREIL: Hear, hear. That should be very, very clear. No Windex needed. Yet when you manage to see through that window, all you find are folks pondering A, B, C, or D.

GREENE: If we spent half as much time on the imagination as on testing, the scores would shoot up. Or at least at least more of the focus in the classroom would include the imagination and creativity, and less on trying to teach the kids how to second guess the test writers.

COREIL: That has been one of the main purposes of my life in the past twelve years-to make educators aware of the importance of the imagination.

GREENE: You know, Dewey said, "Facts are repellent things, unless you use your imagination, and open up intellectual possibilities." And people hear that, but they don't believe it. This is off on a tangent but anyway. At first, I found it ironic when the commission on nine-eleven gave as one of the main reasons for the catastrophe: "We didn't have any imagination." Then the depth of that observation hit home. The spokesman for the investigative commission was not being darkly facetious. He was telling it exactly as his commission had found it. If various officials had been more imaginative, they might have noticed some of the warning signs and it would not have been so bad. That statement should have reverberated throughout American education. It has not, as far as I know.

And where do officials learn to use their imagination? In elementary and high school and college. The line from singing "Frere Jacques" to the World Trade Center is certainly not direct, but the general implication is or at least seems to be that the imagination can be developed as a fundamental mental faculty. When that is done, then you will find a lot of people trying different approaches to problems at work as well as in the visual arts and music studio. We must recognize the imagination as a major faculty in people, where it certainly is enormously more than having an inclination to sing a song after dinner. That's what the man, the spokesman for the nine-eleven investigation was referring to, whether he knew it or not.

At the moment, we seem to think that if we test students more, they will improve. That's absurd. But it is the prevailing wind, so a lot of supervisors and school board members are constantly asking about the performance of young people on this test or that test. If it's too low, then we need a couple of billion dollars to provide after-school training in how to take a test.

COREIL: And so sad. I wonder if the Boards of Education heard that.

GREENE: Very probably. They heard it, but it doesn't sink in.

COREIL: I agree. Obviously, that is closely tied in with a few of the things I'd like to talk with you about today.

GREENE: Shoot.

COREIL: Let's start with Dr. Elliot Eisner. You said you and he have done professional things together.

GREENE: AERA [American Education Research Association], Qualitative Research things, and we're friends. In fact, they did a Festshrift on Elliot. And I never got around to writing my articles so they interviewed me at the end. When I saw the book, I said, "Oh my God, did I say all that about Elliot." I do have the highest respect for him.

One of our differences is that I don't believe in what he calls "art-based research." You know why? For one thing, I don't think you can define art like that, you know. That's one. Another is—and I kid him all the time about this—I say: "You don't ever face the mysteries." You know what I mean? It's as though he thinks that it can all be explained. And I don't. You can think about aesthetic experiences; you can talk about them, but you can't explain them. So I tell my students at Lincoln Center where I work, "I want to make an aesthetic experience more and more likely. But how am I to know whether you've had an aesthetic experience as part of teaching—that's the mystery. But Elliot thinks you can—and he doesn't believe in testing, and I don't either. But he still has this funny idea about that.

COREIL: Yes. It's the experience itself that is primary.

GREENE: He just wrote a book on art and the creation of mind. I don't think that mind is created. I think it emerges. Who creates it? So we have those differences. You can have them and still be friends.

COREIL: "Emerges" as in a process. That is in keeping with current theory about the imagination, I believe. I wish it were created at birth. Like an eye in the back of the head. You couldn't look at people standing around and pretend it didn't exist. Howard Gardner said people had multiple intelligences and teachers seem to be taking it seriously. Now how high that goes up the supervision chain is another matter.

GREENE: Yes. Gardner. Do you know him?

COREIL: I've just edited an anthology about him. A piece by him is the lead article.

GREENE: What's the book about?

COREIL: The title of the anthology is *Multiple Intelligences, Howard Gardner and New Methods of College Teaching*. About 40 college teachers show how they can address different intelligences in their classrooms. The place where I work, New Jersey City University, published it.

GREENE: What was the occasion? There doesn't have to be one of course.

COREIL: We had a conference at my college. He was the keynote speaker. We transcribed his speech and used it as the lead article.

GREENE: He's a psychologist. Are you in that field?

COREIL: No, I'm a linguist of sorts. I'm a playwright first. But I had to keep my job so I became a linguist.

GREENE: One group invited Howard to a meeting on independent schools. And they also invited me. Secretly. "We won't tell the audience that you're coming, it'll be a surprise." So, I came to respond to him. His whole speech was about all the important professors he had. It wasn't really about teaching like they wanted it to be. It was much more interesting to hear him talk about his education. But you could tell that they were a little disgruntled. So when I went up, I said "Howard Gardner stands on the shoulders of the almighty, and if I was up there, I'd slip right off." He wrote me a letter later. He said, "Thanks for humanizing me." He's such a funny guy. A little short on charisma maybe. But he's an author. Has his book, the one you edited, been well received?

COREIL: Yes and no. I think it's very interesting. But it's about teaching methods for college teachers. That's not exactly something they're interested in. Not all of them, by any means. But a lot. They tell their students how to teach, but they don't want anyone telling them about their own teaching. It's interesting, curious and sad that there are virtually no courses for college teachers on how to teach, how to get their students interested, how to work the imagination into the courses many of them will teach later. Into the curriculum. Anyway, Gardner's theories have touched a lot of elementary and second school teachers.

GREENE: And he's making art at least respectable, you know.

COREIL: It's incredible, I mean there are virtually no school teachers in the USA—elementary, high school—who haven't heard about his ideas that we all have seven or eight kinds of intelligences and not just those "measured" in IQ tests.

GREENE: You know, my problem—I mean I would agree with everything you said, but there is one idea that bothers me because I think I don't know if you can put a grid on every child.

COREIL: I agree. I think intelligence is variable. Teach a kid about math, and he is different. He knows about math. Teach students about a lot of things, and they get smarter. I've even got my acronym: PRI—"Present Range of Intelligence." The PRI of a kid from the ghetto might be low. But he's not locked into a whole system based on that low score. Instead, the score itself can change. A system based on that automatically gives them somewhere to go.

GREENE: You ought to write a book on it.

COREIL: Thanks. I think I like the idea of Multiple Intelligences better.

GREENE: He's had a lot of influence. It's better to talk about multiple intelligences than just a couple. I pointed this out on the podium when I was responding to remarks he had just made. Howard is unflappable. He's marvelous that way. He just smiled and said, "There is an existential intelligence that you might be interested in." I said, "Thank you, Howard, for letting me in."

COREIL: Yeah, what he lacks in charisma, he more than make up for in being so darned bright.

GREENE: Oh my God, look how much he writes. And his wife, Ellen, she wrote one book called *The Inventive Word*. Her uncle was a well-known aesthetician. He used to be at Columbia [University]. So you never know, it might be genetic.

COREIL: Anything's possible.

GREENE: We've been digressing all afternoon.

COREIL: You've been handling yourself with aplomb. If necessary, we'll call this interview "Digressions with the Lady."

GREENE: You're very diplomatic.

COREIL: My favorite is my wife's calling me a "snooty dud." She's Chinese but also controls a potent English. I was angry about something and then I heard her come out with that—out of the blue. I couldn't help but laugh.

GREENE: That a good one. Is that a list of questions you have there?

COREIL: Something to fall back on. Okay, here's the first: How is the imagination of a nuclear physicist different from the imagination of an artist?

GREENE: I think a nuclear physicist begins with what they claim is known. And then they look at the permutations of what might, or might not follow. And I don't think the artistic imagination, or the artist, begins with what is known. I think he might begin with a question, or with wonder. He or she doesn't begin with a certainty. They keep being in search of themselves with all those images on the wall. So that, to me would be one difference.

COREIL: That is astute. I'm not drawn to conceptual artists, who don't seem to start with wonder. The opposite seems true. Often then seem to get a small idea, and they do forty paintings with that.

GREENE: If that's so, it would seem to be unfortunate.

COREIL: When I was one of the speakers at Kieran Egan's conference in Vancouver [International Education Research Group], I brought up the possibility of organizing a couple of courses that would be entitled "Imagination I" and "Imagination II". The course or courses would bring together many ideas that are presently considered impressionistic. That led me to consider offering a "Bachelor of Arts in the Imagination." Any reactions?

GREENE: I think that would be wonderful. I mean after all, a Bachelor of Arts in Science, a Bachelor of Arts in Empirical Studies, there's already quite a few. I think anything to restore imagination to its proper place is worthwhile. It's still a new concept, but we don't believe in fantasy, we don't believe in fairy tales. But we need to restore it. I taught a class once; I called it "Changing Styles in Philosophy and Literature." And I started with the modern and then I went back to William Blake and looked at the changing notions of the imagination of Blake and Wordsworth and so on. It was fascinating. I would still like to do that. The different visions of imagination, it still would make a good course. You know, from Blake to Wordsworth to Baudelaire to Malarmé, into the post-Rilke. I'd love to do that. Are you still teaching?

COREIL: Yeah, I banged around the world in my younger years. So my retirement is not earned.

GREENE: They can't make you retire now.

COREIL: I wouldn't want to retire. Compared to a lot of places, a university is not a bad place to be working.

GREENE: I definitely agree. But then, I got sick. But for many years, I've worked at the Lincoln Center Institute. And they call me "The Philosopher in Residence." So, for twenty years, I've been lecturing on what we call aesthetic education. And relating it to the performances we've had. When we started, it was possible to go to plays because we could afford them. It's difficult to do that now. Especially for students. I remember there was a production of *The Cherry Orchard* at the Lincoln Center. It was marvelous. A Jewish band that kept playing off-key. Members of the audience could go on stage and look at the cherry trees after the performance. Good productions make a lot of things magical, both things in the plays and things long after the show has closed…And then to hear it from the point of view and the director. We have nothing at Teacher's College [Columbia University] in the line of staged drama. We used to, but we don't anymore. I go to NYU [New York University] a lot. I am fortunate enough to have friends there.

COREIL: I'm surprised they don't have drama at Teacher's College anymore.

GREENE: They're very backward in some ways because now they don't even have a professor of dance. Teacher's College was once well known for dance. The faculty was down to one professor, and the president let her go because he said: "We can't have only one, and we can't afford two." I was on a tenure committee at that time. They were all psychologists and mathematicians and the like. It was all discreetly arranged. They kept saying, "She didn't publish enough." And I said: "A dancer dances. If she can write excellently about dance, then probably she doesn't dance." They didn't understand that. And there aren't so many journals of dance. But they're so stubborn.

COREIL: They're stubborn in so many universities in America now! There are more than 4,000 four-year colleges. Where are all those people going to publish? Who will read it? It's not realistic. The emphasis on publication seems far more relevant where you have much fewer universities. I think that it should be brought to the forefront now. I suspect that the lack of publications becomes relevant when a deficiency is needed for final termination.

GREENE: It's not realistic…

COREIL: Anyway, I had thought of a Bachelor's, and then a Master's, and then a Doctorate's, and then I said "Why not a Department of Imagination?"

GREENE: Or a Department of Creative Imagination.

COREIL: Yes. Exactly.

GREENE: Because the imagination can be used to do terrible things. Like 9-11.

COREIL: And the Holocaust. Your point is very well taken. Which is another reason why it is necessary to begin thinking of the imagination as a real function of human cognition and not simply as a characteristic of clever activities. Eisner makes related points repeatedly.

GREENE: Yes. Once he was on a panel with Howard in the AERA. They were arguing about whether you should get a doctorate for writing a novel. Elliot thought you should, and old Howard thought you shouldn't. I think you should. Of course, you would have to have a jury or committee of novelists. You know, not college professors.

COREIL: No, no, you've got to have to the right people.

GREENE: Yes. That's where holding a prestigious office can be useful. You can use it to do the right thing. And sometimes it works. Often your meaningful introduction reverts after you leave office. In 1984 I was president of the AERA. You know, a man called me, from the nominating committee. He said: "You've been nominated as the president of AERA." So I said, "Oh my God." He said, "Don't worry, you'll never be elected." But I was. I've made a lot of speeches for so many things. I set aside a whole part of the program for the arts. I had a David Mamet play, with the original actors called Duck Variations. I thought, "Maybe this will change." And the next year, it was never mentioned.

COREIL: I'm selfish. When I am onto something, I usually don't want anyone else involved. If I had confidence in them and could trust them, but that kind of person is rarely around. At those times, I write every night, from about 11 p.m.to 3 a.m. Until the sun rises if I can. After a couple of months, the ideas that had kept evolving were nothing like those I had begun with. I won't say I was in a trance, but I was slowly getting there. Have you experienced anything like that?

GREENE: I think so.

COREIL: Would you like to talk about it?

GREENE: You know, I know it sounds foolish now, but I think of imagination having to do with an alternative reality. You know, and a creative reality. But—and this is going to sound strange—but when I got sick in January, I didn't know how to explain it, nor did the doctor. I fell into the deepest depression you can imagine. Terrible. And then, you know, they said arthritis. Then, I met a doctor a couple of months ago, and he said: "Sometimes, when you think of your memory, you think of it in a linear way." He said: "Sometimes, the losses in your life collect." Like my father's death, my daughter died. And he said: "There's no temporality in it." That hit me as so true. And then I started thinking "How do we make use of that in teaching, in creating?" You know, because everybody thinks of memories as, "in 1922 I did this," So he said: "That causes a trauma." Because maybe I never faced that my father killed himself, or my daughter died of cancer. You can't face it all together. So it's left like an open question. And that made me think, "How do I talk about that to people?" And somebody said, maybe the best thing to do is to try to write what I remember. And that's what I'm gonna try to do. You understand.

COREIL: Do I understand? I had a brother who killed himself. And my eldest brother died about three weeks ago.

GREENE: Oh, I'm sorry.

COREIL: Thank you.

GREENE: There are four in our family and for such a long time and I thought that by some magic, we'd always be four. You know, and then my youngest sister died, and then two years later, my brother. Now there are two of us left and it seems so strange, you know? We were supposed to be four. And it doesn't matter how old you are. At moments like that, you regress, you return to childhood or to some other period.

COREIL: And to get back to these sorrows that lead to the depression or whatever it was that you experienced. Would you care to talk more about that or not particularly?

GREENE: Among other things, even to the people who took care of me, I said, "I don't want to live. There is no reason." I was very suicidal. And they would say, "Oh, wait a few weeks." I said, "I can't wait a few weeks." But I did. I have to start again now. And now I think I must be terribly lucky because I didn't have a compelling idea. I don't know if I would've gotten better. Now, I want to do something else. Existentialism says, "You are what you are not yet," and if I believe I'm finished now, or just sit in the corner...I couldn't do it. So I'm going to try to write about that.

COREIL: Have you read William Styron?

GREENE: About the mental hospital?

COREIL: Yeah.

GREENE: That's the best example...

COREIL: He came to our college to speak once, and I was fortunate enough to hear him. And all he did is read from his writing. He delivered about 3 or 4 sentences before that. Then he started reading. It was spellbinding. There's no other word.

GREENE: I sent his book to the psychiatrist who was taking care of me. He didn't give it back yet. He said,"It's a remarkable book."

COREIL: *Darkness Visible: A Memoir of Madness.* That's the title, I believe.

GREENE: Yes. I remember I'd been sick years ago at some surgery or something. And I was in critical care for a while. You know Calvin Trillen? He called me, because I knew his wife, and he said, "You have to write about it because very few people who can write have gone through that." And I didn't do it then. But now, I think he's right. Styron was the only one I could think of.

COREIL: We write so that we can find out who we are so we can find out who we want to become.

GREENE: Exactly, that's how I feel. You create yourself as you write, or paint. Have you had plays that one can read or see?

COREIL: I've had a few small productions. But, I have written about 20 longs plays and four or five short plays.

GREENE: Would you send me one or two?

COREIL: I'd be happy to do that.

GREENE: I'd love to see them.

COREIL: What I am doing in my older age—I'm 64—is having a website constructed for myself.

GREENE: Oh you have?

COREIL: And they are in the process of taking the old plays—some of them written on a typewriter, faded masterpieces, born to blush unseen in the desert air…

GREENE: And putting them on the web.

COREIL: Otherwise, I would have to go back, and retype all that. I can't do that sort of thing.

GREENE: No, I wouldn't think so.

COREIL: But the technology of scanning is so good that they can be scanned. Even the older typewritten ones.

GREENE: Do you get responses when it's put on the web?

COREIL: I don't know. I haven't yet. But then it's still under construction.

GREENE: Do you have to pay for that?

COREIL: Several hundred dollars—not bad. It makes you whole again if a lot of your things are in boxes. I also threw in my dissertation for good measure.

GREENE: Oh, that's wonderful. Do you have the address?

COREIL: A little stroking of the ego. Yes: www.clydecoreil.com. Have you ever done anything like that?

GREENE: Sure I have, on the web. I started a foundation. It was going strong for about a year. It was called "The Foundation for Art and Imagination." I made some speeches. We had seminars in the house. We taped some of the sessions. And then we had a big event in a formal theater. And then after that, the young woman who was really running it called me and said: "We didn't have enough money to have a regular foundation." And she dropped out. I haven't been able to start it again but I kept the board. If you can start a free-standing foundation, maybe it will last. But then, I got sick so I couldn't. But we're trying to keep it up and make it smaller. And one reason I started it, is because, like you, I'm obsessive about getting attention. The other reason is that I don't spend a lot of money. So I thought I could invest in a foundation. So that's my experience with the web. We are trying to get a new designer.

COREIL: Well, it's not a very expensive enterprise.

GREENE: I realized that.

COREIL: This couple in New Jersey agreed to put up about 25 plays and several other short books I've written…

GREENE: That's great! So you don't have to publish your dissertation.

COREIL: Exactly!

GREENE: What was it?

COREIL: My dissertation?

GREENE: Yeah.

COREIL: In a nutshell, I think syntax is one side of the coin. The other is preformulated language that basically don't change. "Start sleeping" seems grammatical. But no one says that. Everyone says, "Go to sleep." I formally characterized such phrases. And the beat goes on and on.

GREENE: So it wasn't about the imagination.

COREIL: At least not on the surface. But then where does the imagination end?

GREENE: I agree.

COREIL: Let's get back on task. For example, would you care to say something about the relation between the imagination and education?

GREENE: For one thing, neither the imagination nor education is about facts and information. Of course, they're involved but not centrally. Education is not something put on you. I think of it as a process of becoming. You know, and, becoming different. And for me, it has to do with a feeling of agency. And selecting from the literature or the numbers, what will feed into your becoming in terms of your choosing, and your identity. And I think that education in one way to help you shape your identity. For example, I don't think the self is ready made. I think you keep creating, and keep creating. And I think all the richness of literature, or Greek tragedy, or whatever it is you are reading and thinking about become food for that identification.

Many Americans don't read anymore. I think that partly explains the horror that we're in now—that people believe things without context. They tend to buy these messages and have no way to understand them. A lot of people are for the Iraqi war. I'd like to say to them, "Read the Trojans!" Get a different slant. And it's just frightening to me because that's where imagination comes in. They should realize that there are alternatives to war. You know, there are alternatives to the stupid things they do. I had a student of mine who is a Mexican dancer. And she wants to do a performance of her feelings about violence. So she asked me to think of some words. So like, she'll dance for four minutes, and I'll speak about violence and violation for three minutes and she'll move.

We were talking later about the television side of the bombs on Baghdad. And nearby there were people saying, "Oh, how beautiful; how sublime." You know, the red and the clouds. How do you get people out of that mindset? That's what's so frightening.

COREIL: We seem to need to destroy.

GREENE: You didn't happen to see *Fahrenheit* yet, did you?

COREIL: Not yet.

GREENE: You have to see it. It's not perfect, but thank God Michael Moore did it. Sending 19-year-olds to die over there. Kids who came in because they needed money to go to school. You feel so powerless. We have these big marches all over the world, but it didn't make a bit of difference to Bush, it just got worse and worse. It's so hard to understand…I'm sorry. I didn't mean to ramble.

COREIL: You are on target, not rambling. In the possible expansion via the imagination, is it the consciousness itself that grows and becomes larger?

GREENE: I think so. I'm big on phenomenology—that consciousness is a way of grasping, you know, it's intentional, it reaches out. And it just seems to me that what consciousness grasps by imagination in a way has to be infinite compared with the physical imagination, the chemical imagination, I think there are boundaries around those. But how could there be boundaries.

COREIL: Who knows where possibility ends.

GREENE: You're thinking about alternative possibility? Because I teach that. I'm interested in the possible and not the predictable. Or, I quote Emily Dickenson. "Is it imagination that feeds the slow fuse of possibility?" she says. I don't want to think there's a limit to possibility. I mean, you know, I could say, "It's not possible for me to be a surf-rider," but other people can ride surf. So I think that that what you say is so; the expansion of imagination, of consciousness itself, of what we can grasp…

COREIL: And you know, if you look at contemporary physics, they are reaching such astute levels, that they have to go into poetry to frame their new concepts.

GREENE: Yes. Every year, the physics teacher and the philosopher and the literature person have more and more to talk to each other about on the higher levels, of course.

COREIL: Often, I try to understand exactly what the imagination is. And one of the possibilities I came up with was that it's the formation, or the relating of component parts of two entities. Or like two parts of the brain. And when you do that, it…

GREENE: Something comes out.

COREIL: Something comes out. Like a solution to a problem that before could not be solved.

GREENE: That's good, I think. I think, was it, Virginia Wolfe, who referred to the severing that comes together when you imagine?

COREIL: That's a well articulated idea.

GREENE: Has it helped you to think about what they say the left brain and the right brain?

COREIL: Well, you know, indeed it has. When I was 14, I had an accident. I was fooling around with a air rifle and I shot myself right square in the eye.

GREENE: Oh boy…

COREIL: And so because I was that age, I think many of the functions that are normally performed by the left brain, had a chance to migrate to the right side.

GREENE: Oh how interesting.

COREIL: Something happened. I have minimal impairment on my left, my right shoe wears out first 'cause I drag it a bit. I think that my right brain and my left brain have been put together as unlikely bedfellows.

GREENE: That's very interesting. Are there experiments about that?

COREIL: Not that I am aware of.

GREENE: Like I saw a program on—I forget the word, typical (laughs) of, you know, when you lose your memory. Dementia, what do you call it again?

COREIL: Amnesia?

GREENE: Oh then worse than that. Older people get it.

COREIL: Alzheimer's.

GREENE: I saw a program on that and how the nerves break apart. You know, at first they're together and then it's forever, and you can't do anything about it. It's such a tragic, tragic thing. And I think all of us are afraid of it.

41

COREIL: Every now and then I sort of run a little check on myself. But it's hard checking yourself.

GREENE: Like when you can't find your keys.

COREIL: I keep mine on a chain. With a watch that tells me it's time to go. But I do have a couple of more questions. If teachers are evaluated in terms of their students' scores on multiple choice tests, what are some ways of keeping those teachers from turning most of their classes into techniques of test-taking?

GREENE: That whole myth of test taking…It's a way of afflicting children with the idea that there's one correct answer. And there's no better way to discourage imagination…And now they have portfolios.

COREIL: That's a sorry alternative.

GREENE: I don't know how they evaluate them.

COREIL: Is it possible to teach teachers how to be imaginative if the professor himself, or herself, is not imaginative?

GREENE: I always tell students if the teacher comes to class with Hamlet all solved, she shouldn't come in.

COREIL: Last semester was one of the best in my life. I walked in and saw that they were about to riot at the idea that they were in an ESL class. So I began explaining all types of ideas, some from my dissertation. We talked about everything under the sun. All relevant, but spontaneous. I had great fun. And so did they.

GREENE: You respected them.

COREIL: When they didn't understand, they'd ask…And every now and then, they would come up with something new. I would say, "That's a great idea."

GREENE: And they'd beam. I think it's the obligation of the teacher to make demands of his or her students. And students will often value highly their working under such demands. That is the existential dynamic of the teacher-student relationship in kindergarten through college. The teacher demands and gives approval; the student executes.

COREIL: I have a friend who sends beginning drawing students to the Met to copy masterpieces. Other classes are still drawing sliced lemons. It's incredible the level these beginners leap up to. Not at all in keeping with the outcomes and assessments that currently have all the buzzers buzzing.

GREENE: From one point of view, outcomes sets limits on what the student can work for and achieve. Like so many widgets. The way I think about it and said before—and Dewey would say—that it's a process of becoming and there's no product. You know, somebody made a documentary about me. And at the very end, I'm walking in front of the apartment saying: "I am what I am not yet." So there's no outcome. How could there be an outcome of person's life? And who would assess it.

COREIL: Maybe St. Peter at the Pearly Gates. Like you said, it's all a complex process. I think it's awfully narrow to try to reduce it to outcomes.

GREENE: That's probably what those students in your class were objecting to. Recently, I was invited to be on a panel on education at a local university. Everyone talked and talked. Finally, it was my turn. I said, "I've been listening to all of you and I haven't heard one word of outrage at the Iraqi War. Not one word." And I thought that was a crime. To have a big conference in the war, they're bombing. And here we are, talking about assessment. There were maybe 200 people at this conference. And nobody wanted to talk about the war. They were there to get their name in the program. If you ask a kid what he wants to be when he grow up, often he will say, "Anything, as long as I'm rich." What a society. The only ambition is to be rich.

COREIL: Someone once said, "It's not too difficult to be rich, if rich is all you want to be.

GREENE: Touché.

COREIL: It's all changing very quickly, especially since 9/11.

GREENE: I know I sound crazy. But, you know with The Patriot Act, and censorship, and security.

COREIL: Yes. If you recall, right after, before and after the attack of Iraq, no one was talking about the tragedy of Vietnam.

GREENE: The same lack of reason.

COREIL: I had wanted to talk more about story, but I don't believe we have enough time.

GREENE: Charles Taylor has a book called *Sources of the Self*. And he begins talking about narrative as a search for meaning. You know, and it's like you were saying before; "You write to find out who you are." And Bruner. He talks about narrative and storytelling as a way of knowing. And I think that's very important. And that's not—and he opposes that to all these linear, logical efforts to make sense.

So I think lately, the trouble with that—you know, there are a lot of articles about storytelling and it becomes a lot—it sounds so easy to some people, that they make it sort of sentimental. You know, that bothers me. There's a certain purse and he grabs it. It's like a sweet story, but is has to involve understanding of yourself and reaching into yourself. And no story is without, I think, without contradiction, without ambiguity. And I think a lot of people think it's got a beginning, a middle and an end. And, most stories shouldn't have that, beginning, middle and end. It's not that simple. Sometimes, I have teachers come here on a Sunday afternoon. I give them wine, and we have a text every time. And this time—and I was surprised how they responded to it because I know how people are complaining about the canon, you know and white male writers. But I chose *Death in Venice*. You know, it was a wonderful discussion, wonderful. There's a new translation of it which is beautiful. This writer who lives like a clenched fist and then kind of falls apart when he goes to bed as he falls in love with a little boy. And it ends—he dies looking at the ocean. And there's no beginning, middle and end, it just opens everything. And the students were—not students—some were teachers. Ohhh, I liked this at the end after they talked about it, you know. So I believe again in not just their own stories, but in a book like that.

COREIL: You make good things happen.

GREENE: In Jersey City, do they talk about post-modernism and such?

COREIL: Yeah, a little. I think that an excellent way to assemble a curriculum is to ask for one suggestion for one level from one fairly well known writer in each field. Assemble them, sort them out and you'd have a curriculum for the next ten years.

GREENE: Yes, You can do so much in curriculum. At a conference I attended, a man said, "Before you teach a child a computer, give them experience in writing plays." I thought that was really good.

COREIL: Fascinating. What was his point?

GREENE: I think his point was: Before you get them involved in one-way, linear, you try to make them see that there are a great many ways. I think that's what he meant.

COREIL: One last question. Answer if you choose: In the course of your life, has there been one realization that has continued to evolve?

GREENE: In about the fourth grade I met a French teacher who gave me the impression of being very, very cosmopolitan. She'd been everywhere. Her father died in the first World War, and she had tragedy and languished. But I thought she was my ego ideal, she was my model. You know, I didn't want to be like my mother. I wanted to be like her and take chances. So that was one.

And then the other day at Lincoln Center, I was remembering one of my first—it seemed to me—aesthetic experiences. And I started—I don't know if it's the first one but—I was remembering going to Chartres Cathedral in France. And I said there was a blue window in that cathedral. It just, you know, hit me, and on top of that, made me see so many connections. I've been deeply affected by Wallace Stevens. And I named a book I did for Lincoln Center, *Variations on a Blue Guitar*, after his poem.

COREIL: Yes.

GREENE: I think that was one of my first really aesthetic experiences. It was so beautiful and it opened so much. And I said: "I'm not a Catholic, I don't know about cathedrals." Those are the two experiences, strangely, that I remember now.

COREIL: The blue cry of the peacock. Stevens and Yeats. My choice for a desert isle.

GREENE: Thank you. We must do this again sometime.

Regular Daily Writing & the Creative Process

Stephen Krashen

Editor's Note: This article has an immediate value in its close study of the habits of many writers. It is also of considerable interest in the insight it provides on the relationship of the conscious mind to the imagination. In searching for a correlation between the practice of writing and the operative principle of the imagination, Dr. Krashen presents an exemplary treatment of that faculty as being capable of a significant and meaningful role in the real world. It is in support of such a principle that this anthology is assembled.

In personal correspondence, the author reported that he is a night person and does much of his writing after midnight. He added that an informal survey he conducted indicated that the number of night people and of day people were equally divided. I am certain that that bit of information would be of formal interest to some researcher on the imagination.

Some experts advise blocked writers to simply plunge ahead, and get into the business of writing without delay or nonsense. Patrick McGreath agrees. Writers block, he claims, "doesn't exist. Stay at your desk and something always occurs to you" (in Winokur, 1999, 194). To cure writer's block, Emma Bombeck recommends that the writer "put the paper in the typewriter, stare at it a long time, get snow-blindedness if you have to, but write something"(Winoker, 1999, 194). But Daly and Miller (1975) believe otherwise: "The procedure commonly used of forcing students to write is very likely the wrong choice of treatments. All one is doing is reinforcing the punishing nature of the writing act in these situations" (248).

Should writers force themselves into regimented, planned writing sessions, or should they take a more relaxed approach and wait for inspiration? The answer, I will argue, is that both recommendations are correct. There is strong evidence supporting the practice of regular, planned writing sessions, but there is also a need for rest. The evidence for regular daily writing comes primarily from two sources. The first is what writers themselves say about their writing habits. This evidence is supportive of the practice of regular daily writing, but it has obvious drawbacks. First, we must take the writer at his or her word. Second, we don't know if a particular writer's insights can be generalized to other writers. Nevertheless, the writers themselves present a strong case for regular writing. A second source consists of studies in which blocked writers were "forced" to write in order to help them reduce their writing blocks. These studies also provide evidence in favor of regular planned writing, but they also suggest that there are limits to regimentation.

What Writers Say

When one looks at the "anecdotal" literature on writing, that is, what writers say about their work habits, there appears to be near universal agreement that one must approach writing as a job, that planned writing sessions are necessary, and that inspiration is the result of writing. Some writers make sure they put in a certain amount of time, others set goals in terms of quantity. Here are some descriptions of those who punched their own time clock and treated writing like a job with set hours. Rosellen Brown states this philosophy clearly: "It's a job. It's not a hobby. You don't write the way you build a model airplane. You have to sit down and work, to schedule your time and stick to it...If you're going to make writing succeed you have to approach it as a job" (in Winokur, 1999, 188). Walker Percy has the same advice: "You've got to sit down and follow a schedule. Unless you do that, punch the time clock-you won't ever do anything" (in Murray, 1990, 60).

Irving Wallace tells us that "...most successful writers invest their work with professionalism. From Balzac, who worked six to twelve hours a day, and Flaubert, seven hours a day, and Conrad, eight hours a day, to Maugham, who worked four hours a day, and Aldous Huxley, five hours a day, and Hemingway, six hours a day, these authors were uniformly industrious, and when they were once launched on a book they wrote regularly, day in and day out...In short...the vast majority of published authors have kept, and do keep, some semblance of regular daily hours..." (Wallace and Pear, 1971, 518-9). According to Wallace,

Victor Hugo had a unique method for regimenting his writing: "While the story may be apocryphal—I should like to believe it is not—it is said that Victor Hugo sometimes forced himself to work regularly by confining himself to his study. To do this, he had his valet take away every stitch of his clothing, and ordered this servant not to return his attire until the hour when he expected to be through with his writing" (Wallace and Pear, 1971, 519).

Molly Keane describes her work habits as follows: "I try to write for three hours in the morning, and if I don't write anything I sit and stare at the paper-otherwise, nothing would ever be written" (Murray, 1990, 56). Standahl regretted not establishing a regular writing practice earlier in his life: "If when I was young I had been willing to talk about wanting to be a writer, some sensible person might have said to me: 'Write for two hours every day, genius or not.' That would have saved ten years of my life, stupidly wasted in wanting to become a genius" (Quoted by B. F. Skinner, 1981, reprinted in Bolker, 1997, 80). Keeping regular hours is not limited to writers of fiction. Scientists work regular hours: "Scientists such as C. Darwin, Pavlov, and Skinner adhered to a rigid daily schedule where the first major activity of each morning involved writing for a couple of hours" (Ericssson, Krampe and Tesch-Romer, 1993, 392).

Quotas: Pages, Words

Other writers keep track of how much they write, and set quotas for themselves. Some count pages, others count words. Irving Wallace recorded the number of pages he wrote each day (Wallace and Pear, 516) and informs us that other well-known writers also kept such records, including Anthony Trollope and Ernest Hemingway. We have specific details about quotas for several writers. John Updike's goal was three pages per day (Murray, 1990, 64), Morris West's was one page per day (Murray, 1990, 65), Ray Bradbury's four (Murray, 1990, 48) and Robert Coles' three to four (Murray, 1990, 49). Arthur Haley set a goal of 600 words a day, "regardless of the weather, my state of mind or if I'm sick or well. There must be 600 finished words-not almost right words" (Murray, 1990, 54). Joseph Wambaugh's goal was 1000 words per day (Murray, 1990, 65). Stephen King counts pages and words, aiming either for ten pages a day or 2,000 words. He tells us, "…only under dire circumstances do I allow myself to shut down before I get my 2,000 words" (King, 2000, 154). (See Poff, 2004, for additional reports.)

Don't Wait for the Muse

The reason for the use of daily, planned sessions, writers agree, is that their ideas come as a result of writing. Stephen King advises: "Don't wait for the Muse. Your job is to make sure the muse knows where you are going to be every day from nine 'till noon or seven 'till three. If he does know, I assure you that sooner or later he'll start showing up, chomping his cigar and making his magic" (157). Irving Wallace notes that the timekeeper writers he described were not always inspired when they sat down to write, "but if they were not, they simply wrote as well as they could…and hoped for the best" (Wallace, 1971, 519). Peter Elbow, the author of the classic treatise on writing, *Writing without Teachers*, concludes that in writing, "meaning is not what you start out with but what you end up with" (Elbow, 1973, 15). Other writers agree: "Any productive writer learns that you can't wait for inspiration. That's the recipe for writer's block." (Susan Sontag, Murray, 1991, 62; Brodie, 1997, 38) "Inspiration usually comes during work, rather than before it."((Madeleine L'Engle, Brodie, 1997, 35; Murray, 1990, 57) "You don't wait for inspiration. The muse does not do your work for you" (Rosellen Brown, Murray, 1990, 49).

Regular, Daily Writing, not Binge Writing

The popular novelist Anthony Trollope anticipated Robert Boice's conclusions (Boice, 1994; see below) that modest regular writing was superior to "binge writing": "A small daily task, if it be really daily, will beat the labors of a spasmodic Hercules" (Trollope, 1946, cited in Wallace and Pear, 1977, 518). Woody Allen agrees: "If you work only three to four hours per day, you become quite productive. It's the steadiness that counts" (Murray, 1990, 46). As suggestive as these insights are, it must be pointed out that they are selected; it is possible that many writers disagree. Here are three who take a different view: "All this advice from senior writers to establish a discipline—always to get down a thousand words a day whatever one's mood—I find an absurdly puritanical and impractical approach. Write, if you must, because you feel like writing, never because you ought to write" (John Fowles, in Winokur, 1999, 189). "Writers say two things that strike me as nonsense. One is that you must follow an absolute schedule each day. If you're not writing well, why continue it? I just don't think this grinding away is useful" (Edmund White, in Plimpton, 1999, 72). "I…never acquired the discipline of regular hours for creative work. I write irregularly, and perhaps in that I get more subconscious development of the theme" (Thornton Wilder, in Kellog, 1994, 195).

Successful and Unsuccessful Professors: A Post-Hoc Study

The focus in this section is on two studies by Robert Boice, selected from his extremely productive series of experiments, all of which support the effectiveness of regular daily writing. Boice (1996) studied 16 junior university faculty members considered to be "regular" writers and 16 "binge writers" over a six-year period. The regular writers displayed a "regular, moderate habit of writing" while the binge writers had "a clear preference for writing only occasionally but in binges (that is, more than ninety minutes of intensive, uninterrupted work)" (64). The differences in accomplishment between the two groups were remarkable.

1. None of the regular writers failed to get tenure or promotion with ease. Only two of the binge writers got tenure.
2. Binge writers were far more likely "to display binges of three or more uninterrupted hours of writing during which they

resisted my attempts to interrupt them" (69). Regular writers binged, but much less frequently, at about one-fourth the rate of the binge writers.

3. Binge writers produced less. The regular writers averaged 5.3 papers accepted for publication over the six year period, while the binge writers averaged less than one (mean = .81). The regular writers also had a higher acceptance rate for papers submitted, about 70% compared to 50%.

4. Binge writers showed three times as many signs of "blocking": When binge writers actually wrote, "they more commonly did nothing or very little (for example, recasting a first sentence or paragraph for an hour; staring at a blank screen)" 68.

5. Binge writers "were three times more likely to be rushing at their work…during scheduled writing periods" (68), and were three times more likely to put off scheduled writing in favor of "seemingly urgent, more important activities" (67).

Boice also studied the opposite of bingers: "Quick starters" among new faculty, estimated to be the top one-tenth of faculty in productivity. They appeared to work at tasks like teaching preparation and writing without rushing or anxiety" (73) and displayed "few signs of business" (73). Despite the failure of their approach, binge writers still believed in it. One subject, for example, said: "You can't get enough good writing done in little pieces; you need big, undisturbed block of time "(70).

DRW: Quantity, Creativity

Boice (1983) is the most important of the studies of this kind: It probes the impact of regular daily writing (DRW) not only on the quantity of output, but also on creativity. Subjects were three groups of nine college faculty; none reported having a writer's block, but all "complained of difficulties in completing written projects" (538). All subjects met with the experimenter one time per week and kept track of the number of pages written and the number of creative or novel ideas that emerged that week that were relevant to their writing project. Those in the first group were first asked to write they "only when they felt like it" for ten days (baseline stage). After this, they entered a new phase in which they agreed to produce three pages per session, and a strong motivator was introduced: If subjects did not meet the goal on any day, they would have to donate $15 to a "despised organization." They stayed in this phase for 30 days. I refer to this condition as "forced writing." A second group wrote only when they felt like it for 15 scheduled days. After this time, for an additional 20 days, they were asked to write daily, whether they felt like writing or not, but no quota and no reinforcers were used.

A third group acted as a control group, agreeing to do no writing for 50 days or ten weeks and also kept track of any new, creative ideas they had. For ease of exposition, Boice's results are presented in terms of four writing conditions. Conditions 2, 3 and 4 represent increasing amounts of management in writing.

1. No writing: the control group.
2. Spontaneous writing, writing when one "feels like it.": the baseline conditions for groups 1 and 2.
3. Regular writing: the second phase activity of group 2, asked to do regular writing without incentives.
4. Forced writing, those who had to send a donation to a despised organization if they did not meet their writing goals. This was the second phase activity of group 1.

Tables 1, 2, and 3 present the results, in times of quantity of writing (pages per day), number of creative ideas reported per day, and number of creative ideas per page, an analys is added by this writer.

TABLE 1: AMOUNT OF WRITING REPORTED	
Treatment	Pages/Day
No writing	.1 (control, baseline); .2 (control, post-baseline)
Spontaneous writing	.4 (group 1, baseline); .3 (group 2, baseline)
Rdw*	.9 (group 2, post baseline)
Forced writing	3.2 (group 2, post-baseline)
Regular daily writing from: Boice (1983)	

As seen in Table 1, there is no question that tightening the writing management conditions resulted in more writing. Encouraging writers to write regularly tripled output (from .3 to .9 pages per day) and imposing a punishment increased output eightfold (from .4 to 3.2 pages per day). This result is consistent with the results of other studies (Boice, 1982, 1987, 1989), as well as case studies such as Passman (1976) and Rosenberg and Lah (1982). (For additional studies, see Poff, 2004.)

Production of Creative Ideas

Boice presented his results on the quantity of novel ideas in the form of graphs. Table 2 presents this information in numerical form, measuring the output of creative ideas for each condition. Table 2 shows that writing itself resulted in more creative ideas (compare the "no writing" and "spontaneous" writing conditions), and that the number of creative ideas increases sharply with increased management, with forced writing producing the largest increase.

TABLE 2: OUTPUT OF CREATIVE IDEAS	
Treatment	Pages/Day
No writing	.01 (control, baseline); .06 (control, post-baseline)
Spontaneous writing	.21 (group 1, baseline); .32 (group 2, baseline)
Rdw	.63 (group 2, post-baseline)
Forced writing	1.39 (group 2, post-baseline)

*Regular daily writing from: Boice (1983)

Table 3 presents an analysis not included in Boice's paper: The results in terms of creative ideas produced per page of writing. The results for the spontaneous and regular groups are remarkably similar. Under both conditions, writers produced about three-fourths of a creative idea per page. The efficiency of writing in generating new ideas was nearly cut in half in the forced writing condition, however; the forced writing group produced more writing and more ideas, but they were less efficient.

TABLE 3: CREATIVE IDEAS PER PAGE	
Treatment	Pages/Day
Spontaneous writing	.8 (group 1, 2, baseline)
Rdw	.7 (group 2, post-baseline)
Forced writing	.43 (group 1, post-baseline)

*Regular daily writing from: Boice (1983)

Results

These results suggest that there is an optimal level of management that encourages writing and the creative process. Encouraging writers to write regularly, with the modest reinforcer of their recording their output and reporting it to someone else, was the most effective level of management among all the conditions used in this study. "Forcing" writing produced more writing (but note that forced writers produced only what they were required to produce, averaging 3.2 pages per day), but it did not pay dividends in new ideas. After working with 52 writers over many years, Boice (1994) recommends that writers should always employ the "least pressure sufficient" when using external means to maintain (or reinstall) a regular schedule of writing (108). In fact, Boice concludes that extreme punishments (such donating money to a despised cause) are to be used only "as a last resort, temporarily; with longer use, their aversiveness can generalize to the act of writing itself" (108).

Regular Daily Writing and Incubation

According to Wallas (1926), problem-solving occurs in several stages. First, we have to present the problem to our mind clearly. Wallas states, "Our mind is not likely to give us a clear answer to any particular problem unless we set it a clear question" (44; see also Elbow, 1973,129, 133). In the next stage, incubation, the mind actually solves the problem. Incubation appears to require that the mind be relaxed and not focused on the problem; it takes place during "an interval free from conscious thought on the particular problem concerned…the stage of incubation should include a large amount of actual relaxation" (Wallas, 95). Some incubation takes place during writing time, when writers take short breaks. Irving Stone, for example, reports that "when I have trouble writing, I step outside my studio into the garden and pull weeds until my mind clears" (Winokur, 1990, 325). The champion of regular daily writing, Robert Boice, recognizes the need for breaks during writing, to "reduce tension and fatigue" (Boice, 1982; 201). Incubation also takes place in the time between writing sessions: Creative individuals interviewed by Csikszentmihalyi and Sawyer (1995) all reported that insights often occurred during idle time, and several mentioned that they occurred while they were doing something else, during a "repetitive, physical activity" such as gardening, shaving, taking a walk or taking a bath" (348).

It may be the case that the DRW provides the optimal stimulus for between-session incubation, allowing the writer to keep the project at just the right level of awareness. Waiting too long between sessions drags the project below this threshold, and overwork prevents incubation from taking place. Incubation, in other words, requires that the problem be on your mind but not dominating it. Boice (1994) suggests that regular daily writing results in "more noticing of things that relate to the writing, noticing that adds ideas and connections because the writing stays fresh in the mind each day" (106). When I do regular daily writing, the world seems to conspire to help me: I find ideas for the current project everywhere, in casual conversation, light reading, movies, etc. This is because the project is at an optimal level of awareness.

Apparent Counterexamples

Some writers deny that inspiration is the result of writing, claiming that new ideas emerge when they are away from their desks: Henry Miller's view was that "most writing is done away from the typewriter. it occurs in the quiet, silent moments, while you're walking or shaving or playing a game or whatever, or even talking to someone you're not vitally interested in. You're working, your mind is working, on this problem in the back of your head. So, when you get to the typewriter it's a mere matter of transfer" (Kellogg, 1994, 193). Jospeh Heller also mainstained that "I don't get my best ideas while actually writing" (Kellogg, 1994, 195). For Heller, writing "is the agony of putting down what I think are good ideas and finding the words for them and paragraph forms for them. A laborous process." Heller says he gets his best ideas when not writing, "A bus is good, or walking the dog" (Kellogg, 1994, 195).

Miller and Heller are clearly talking about incubation (as was Thornton Wilder, when he noted that he gets more "subconscious development" when he writes "irregularly," as discussed earlier). It is likely that their ideas would not have emerged without considerable time spent preparing the subconscious mind for problem-solving by writing, writing that set the stage for the emergence of solutions and ideas. Inspiration is, as Boice claims, the result of writing, but the ideas may require incubation to emerge.

Warming Up

One major cause of writing blocks may be the difficulty "warming up." "I have the peculiarity of a camel: I find it difficult to stop once I get started and hard to start after I've been resting" (Gustave Flaubert; Murray, 1990, 31). "I'm always reluctant to start work, and reluctant to stop" (Gore Vidal, in Kellogg, 1994, 192). The warm-up problem may be the result of waiting too long between writing sessions. When we wait too long, we "lose our place" and often our enthusiasm. Hughes (1999) noted that if Charles Dickens missed a day of writing, "he needed a week of hard slog to get back into the flow" (Hughes, in Plimpton, 1999, 247). Stephen King wrote that "If I don't write every day, I begin to lose my hold on the story's plot and pace. Worst of all, the excitement of spinning something new begins to fade. The work begins to feel like work" (King, 2000, 153). Regular daily writing, Boice notes, "helps…by eliminating most or all the need for a warm-up in each new session" (Boice, 1994, 106).

Efficiency

The results of the experimental studies have interesting implications for efficiency in writing. and in creative work in general. There is no doubt that those who have achieved eminence produce a great deal and devote a huge amount of time to their creative efforts: "As compared with the average individual, distinguished creative thinkers have usually possessed, among other things, an astonishing capacity for hard patient work" (Simonton, 1988, 57), a conclusion consistent with that of Ericsson, Krampe and Tesch-Romer (1993) that time spent practicing is a good predictor of attainment in several different fields, including music and athletics. Similarly, Boice, Shaughnessy, and Pecker (1985) reported that academics with lighter teaching loads devoted more time to research and published more than those with heavier loads. But time on task is not the whole story. Correlations between time on task and academic productivity are positive, but they are not dramatically high. Boice and Johnson (1984) found a .33 correlation between academic productivity and time spent writing, and Hargenes (1978) reported only a .18 correlation between hours devoted to work and number of publications among 549 faculty members in chemistry, mathematics and political science. Hartley and Branthwaite (1989) reported that the most productive writers among the professors they studied spent only slightly more time per week writing than the least productive (most productive = 4.84 hours per week, medium = 4.64, least productive = 4.31). Of course, this modest difference in hours per week totals up over time (about 75 hours over three years), but it is unlikely that it fully accounts for the difference in productivity.

The insights of actual writers and the experiments reviewed here suggest that given equal time, those who do regular daily writing are better off than those who binge. Having free time is necessary, but it is not sufficient. A productive writer has to know how to use that time. As Frank Smith has noted, the secret to success in writing is not "grim determination" (Smith, 1994). The secret is having better strategies.

Conclusions

The advice given by writers at the beginning of this paper, i.e. McGreath's view that writers should "stay at their desk" and Bombeck's advice to "write something" is consistent with the case histories and studies presented here. But Daly and Miller's view that excessive "forcing writing" is the "wrong choice of treatments" is also correct. There appears to be an optimal amount of regimentation for the creative process to work most efficiently. The optimal prescription appears to consist of (1) planned, regular sessions of modest length, without excessive forcing, as Boice's 1983 study suggests, and (2) sufficient rest and relaxation to allow incubation to take place, the dividend of regular, daily writing.

---

1. Surveys of university professors produce results mildly supportive regular daily writing: Hartley and Branthwaite (1989) reported that more productive psychology professors reported less binge writing ("sporadic" writing) than less productive professors. Kellogg (1986, 1994), however, reported a very weak positive correlation between frequency of regular daily writing and productivity (r = .11) among science and engineering faculty. The more productive writers in Harley and Branthwaite (1989) appeared to agree that inspiration is the result of writing and not the cause. Fewer productive faculty than nonproductive faculty agreed with the statement "I wait for inspiration/clever ideas."

References

Boice, R. (1982). Increasing the writing productivity of "blocked" academicians. *Behavioral Research Therapy*, 20: 197-207.

— (1983). Contingency management in writing and the appearance of creative ideas: Implications for the treatment of writing blocks. *Behavioral Research Therapy* 21 (5), 537-543.

— (1987). Is released time an effective component of faculty development programs? *Research in Higher Education* 26(3): 311-326.

— (1989). Procrastination, busyness, and bingeing. *Behavioral Research Therapy*. 27(6): 605-611.

— (1994). *How Writers Journey to Comfort and Fluency*. Westport: Praeger.

Boice, R. and Johnson, K. 1984. Perception and practice of writing for publication by faculty at a doctoral-granting university. *Research in Higher Education* 21(1): 33-43.

Boice, R. Shaughnessy, P., and Pecker, G. (1985). Women and publishing in psychology. *American Psychologist* 577-578.

Bolker, J. (1997). *The Writer's Home Companion*. New York: Holt.

Brodie, D. (1997). *Writing Changes Everything*, City: St. Martin's Press,

Csikszentmihalyi, M. and Sawyer, K. (1995) Creative insight: The social dimension of a solitary moment. In R. Steinberg and J. Davidson (Eds.) *The Nature of Insight*. Cambridge, MA: MIT Press. pp. 329-61.

Elbow, P. (1973). *Writing without Teachers*. Oxford: Oxford University Press.

Daly, J. and Miller, M. (1975). The empirical development of an instrument to measure writing apprehension. *Research in the Teaching of English* 9, 245-249.

Ericsson, K.A., Krampe, R., and Tsech-Romer, C. (1993). The role of deliberate practice in the acquisition of expert performance. *Psychological Review*, 100(3), 363-406.

Hargenes, L. (1978). Relations between work habits, research technologies, and eminence in science." *Sociology of Work and Occupations*, 5(1), 97-112.

Hartley, J. and Branthwaite, A. (1989). The psychologist as wordsmith: A questionnaire study of the writing strategies of productive British psychologists. *Higher Education*, 18, 423-452.

Kellogg, R. (1986). Writing method and productivity of science and engineering faculty. *Research in Higher Education*, 25(2), 147-163.

—— (1994). *The Psychology of Writing*. New York: Oxford University Press.

King, S. (2000) *On Writing*. New York: Pocket Books

Murray, D. (1990). *Stoptalk: Learning to Write with Writers*. Westport, CT: Boynton Cook.

Passman, R. (1976). A procedure for eliminating writer's block in a college student. *Journal of Behavioral Therapy and Experimental Psychology* 7: 297-298.

Plimpton, G. (1999). *The Writer's Chapbook*. New York: Modern Library.

Poff, S. (2004). *Regimentation: A Predictor of Writer's Block and Writing Apprehension*. Ph.D. Dissertation, USC, School of Education.

Simonton, D. K. (1988). *Scientific Genius: A Psychology of Science*. Cambridge: Cambridge University Press.

Wallace, I. and Pear, J. (1977). Control techniques of famous novelists. *Journal of Applied Behavior Analysis*. 10, 515-525.

Walas, G. (1926). *The Art of Thought*. London: C.A. Watts.

Winokur, J. (1999). *Advice to Writers*. New York: Pantheon.

China's English Corners: The Learning Revolution?

Kevin Gaudette

> *The fatal drawback in Confucian education was its inflexibility and its commitment to the status quo…This dedication to an established order paralyzed the imagination of the people. Thus progress came to a halt.*
> (Cowles Encyclopedia, 1967)

The widest attempt ever undertaken to learn a language outside of a school system presently exists and is doing exceptionally well in China it is called "English Corners" (ECs). The spontaneous activity has no formal syllabus, curriculum, admission policies, graduation ceremonies, placement tests or any of the other policies and procedures we in the West have come to think of as indispensable to language learning. But it does seem to work, and work very well.

English Corner China yields 18,900 websites—relating to various (usually weekly, sometimes daily) corners in public parks, university campus spots, private schools, tea houses, KFCs etc. English Corners (ECs) began informally in China after Deng Xiao Peng's "Opening up" to the world in 1980, and they sprouted up all over the country as English learners and curious observers came together. After the trauma of the Cultural Revolution, it was a liberating experience for people to have freedom of assembly and limited speech with strangers. ECs were closed for some time after the 1989 Tienanmen incident. At the typical public EC, learners of various levels-ranging from a handful to over one hundred-gather together in small clusters, talking about whatever interests them, or whatever they are able to say. As at a vibrant cocktail party, English Corner folks often circulate from cluster to cluster, checking out for interesting individuals, attractive group dynamics and suitable English levels. Such high-energy non-formal English language environments are in sharp contrast to typical English classroom dynamics.

> *Archimedes said, "Give me a big enough lever, and I will move the world." China's English Corners offer an Archimedean opportunity to promote whole-brained theory and practices to China's English learners and English teachers, and hopefully into China's schools.*

My first experience with an English Corner was in Hong Kong in 1982. During the past five years I've been teaching in various Chinese cities from north to south, and I have become a regular participant at English Corners wherever I've lived. In public parks and university campuses throughout China, weekly English Corners offer freedom of assembly and speech (with discretion) to English learners and curious observers. In many major cities, there is an active English Corner somewhere every day or evening of the week. As Non-Formal Education environments, English Corners can be in natural harmony with Krashen's prescriptions for successful laguage acquisition acquisition:

1. Low affective filter
2. High intrinsic motivation
3. Real messages of interest are transmitted and understood.

However, there's room for continued evolution in the English Corners. One limitation

50

is that the process lacks whole-brained context and content. Advanced English learners typically can talk and complain quite intelligently about current events, without imagining creative alternatives; less-advanced learners, like folks on a first date, can struggle nervously to find a topic they can discuss. Frequently the talking can become dominated by a few (male) advanced English speakers/thinkers, while a small crowd listens passively. The use of movie-based Role Play, and other approaches described in *The Journal of Imagination in Language Learning and Teaching* (JILL), can significantly expand both the attraction and the effectiveness of China's English Corners. The key factors, however, are the nitty-gritty ones:

1. How can we promote whole-brained evolution in China's nationwide English Corners?
2. How best can the English Corners help promote a China-wide educational transformation-from bored and stressed students of English to whole-brained and intrinsically motivated learners of English?

Atkisson's Strategies

Atkisson's (1999) suggests three strategies for motivating Archimedean Transformation:

1. *Promote the new.* Or…"increase the perceived value of the new idea. This is the principal work of the Change Agents, but they certainly depend upon the work of the Innovators, who make a 'cool' product initially."
2. *Critique the old.* Or…"decrease the perceived value of the status quo by attacking it, either directly or subtly, in short, making the old way of doing things seem uncool. This is generally the work of the Iconoclasts, though Change Agents also help."
3. *Facilitate the switch.* "This is the most important and the least obvious strategy for making change happen. It is also where many change efforts fail, because they forget to reduce the perceived cost of making the change. (Atkisson, pp. 193-194)"

Promote the New

China's official national policy states: "Encourage people to be creative and inventive. (Wang and Yu, pp. 98-99)" Certainly Chinese learners of English see many movies as being "cool," and they already use movies extensively for learning English. China's book/audio tape publishers (all government-run) have responded to the market demand. Bookstores-both government-run and private—throughout China offer a wide range of movie-based English-learning materials, containing a bi-lingual film script with grammar/vocabulary/culture explanations, and an audio tape/CD of the movie dialogue. DVD movies for $1 (USD) are easily available throughout China at the difficult-to-control DVD movie-piracy shops. Those without a DVD player or a computer can be seen throughout China, throughout the day and night, watching movies at Internet Bars-where they can either view their own DVDs, or they can download a wide selection of movies from unofficial student-run websites.

In my classes in China over the past 5 years, I have used DVD movies with excellent results. For classes at all levels—K-12, university, etc.,—experienced native-speaker English Conversation teachers can often design their own courses, and movie-based TPR/Role Play and other activities can be easily used by them to promote whole-brained learning. In the spirit of "promote the new" paradigm an international non-profit movie-discussion project was recently launched, called Spiritual Cinema Communities (which, in China, I am renaming "Movie Magic"). A movie review from the website (www.mysticalmovies.com) demonstrates the project's commitment to the power of the imagination: "When an old paradigm dies, a void in time is created and that twilight space becomes a magical opportunity for all those who have been born into it. The new paradigm is still but a ray of sun on a distant horizon and it is that light that sustains us in the unknown of that suspended moment in time." As a volunteer China Representative for this network, I shall be developing community activities for English learning by using movie-based Community Language Learning/TPR/role play/imagination/discussion activities for learners of (1)English and (2)Chinese.

Precedent as Dictator and Liberator

The phrase "promote the new" resonates with unique dynamics in China, which has for millennia been a nation profoundly influenced by precedents, tradition and custom. As a common saying regarding China states: "No dictator ever ruled with greater power than 'Precedent in China.'" This Movie Magic English Corner project is building upon two precedents in China—(1) English learning and (2) English Corners. Over the past 20 years they have been increasingly perceived as a valuable asset for China's "Opening to the World" initiated by Deng Xiao Peng. The status of English in China has shifted from that of a scorned pariah (intensely so during the 1966-76 Cultural Revolution) to one of high prestige today. Centuries ago, during the early days of the Canton settlements, only the despised 'linguists', social outcasts to a man, were permitted to learn the barbarians' tongue. In contrast, English is nowadays a prerequisite for both academic development and political advancement, as it would appear from the growing numbers of competent English speakers among top-ranking leaders in the Chinese Communist Party.

Currently 250 million Chinese are trying to learn English via English language television programs. The figure for those studying English in their spare time is as high as 1 in 3 workers in Shanghai. In 2001, English language learning was brought even further into the spotlight through Shanghai's hosting of the APEC (Asia Pacific Economic Conference). A great upsurge in learning occurred amongst civil servants in preparation for the meeting. The People's Liberation Army (PLA), for example, reported that: "English Corners were set up and daily usage of the language was taught to ensure over 80% of them can answer questions in English." By way of contrast, it is worth noting that following the 1989 PLA-enforced Tienanmen Incident, the English Corners were closed by the government for several years as potential sources of anti-government activity.

Movie Magic and China's English Corners

This non-profit Movie Magic project (not yet begun) in China will seek to offer Internet-based materials and training to expand the content and process of English Corners throughout China, by promoting the use of movie-based Role Play. Before coming to the English Corner, participants around the country will be able to prepare for the process, by viewing the theatre games (performed by fellow learners and native English speakers), movie segments, and JILL article (with translation) available for the week, while reading selected segments of movie reviews (such as those from www.metacritic.com and www.imdb.com), and preparing Role Plays based upon the movie segments. Internet-cameras, available at Internet Bars throughout China, can be used to promote nation-wide Role Play competitions. In addition, a special effort will be made to attract international visitors to China, including readers of JILL. These folks will be able to access the Internet and learn about the location, days, times of English Corners anywhere in China, as well as the history and processes of China's English Corners. Hopefully we will be able to link up with universities and secondary schools which will provide free accomodation to international visitors to their English classes.

The Website will especially seek to educate both learners and teachers regarding the value of imagination training in both English languge learning as well as corporate/national development. To demonstrate to skeptical Chinese educators that this approach has historical precedent, that it is not merely the "latest fad from the USA," a bi-lingual history of research findings will be available on the Website, such as the one below (from Swisher and Dehle, 1989):

A. Imagery assists creativity since it is the preferred human processing mode when tasks are abstract (Paivio, 1969), or require increased information processing in a novel situation (Kaufmann, 1980).
B. Initial research in imagery and creativity implies that they are closely related (Gowan, 1978).
C. Pylyshyn (1981) reports that imagery accesses an underlying matrix of information in the unconscious mind which can explain the insight or "aha" phenomenon that accompanies the creative process.
D. Creating improvisational rhythm vivifies the imagery (Rider, Floyd & Kirkpatrick, 1985).
E. Horng and Torrance (1987) report that measures of flexibility, vividness and richness of imagery predict high creativity scores.
F. Rhythm acts to stimulate the limbic system of the brain which also activates the imagery process (Nelson, 1987).

Chinese Traditions and Sheldrake's Morphic Field Effect

In addition, bi-lingual information will be available linking this body of modern research with ancient Chinese Taoist theory and practices, such as Tai Chi Chuan, Qi Gong and Acupuncture. Of particular relevance to this focus upon the ancient Chinese—modern Western link is the pioneering "morphogenetic learning" theory and research of biologist Rupert Sheldrake, who was influenced by the insights of William McDougall, author of *The Group Mind* (1920/ 1972). In the 1930s, McDougall theorized that a group mind existed which included all members of a society and which had its own thoughts, its own traditions, and its own memories. China, with its thousands of years of culture, could be expected to have a high-context, multi-dimensional group mind—"the Chinese Tao of Doing Things." As Sheldrake suggests;" If we think of such a group mind as an aspect of the morphic field of the society, it would indeed have its own memory since all morphic fields have in-built memory through morphic resonance."

Sheldrake has hypothesized a field of morphic ("pattern-related") resonance in which patterns of knowledge, structure or behavior of a certain kind of thing (whether a salt crystal or a human mind) become increasingly embedded as a "habit," an ingrained pattern of information which influences and is accessible to other members of that category of thing.

In commenting on rat experiments, Sheldrake has said: "If rats are taught a new trick in Manchester, then rats of the same breed all over the world should show a tendency to learn the same trick more rapidly, even in the absence of any known type of physical connection or communication. The greater the number of rats that learn it, the easier it should become for their successors." Here throughout every part of China, English Corners bring together intrinsically motivated English-speaking/listening participants-whether engaged in vigorous discussion, male-female friendship-making, or (yet-to-come) dynamic/creative mind-body activities and creations. English Corner participants have an enthusiasm for learning far greater than that of rats "trained" according to Behaviorist principles. It could seem logical to conclude that the "morphic resonance" of the vital and loquacious English Corner students could be qualitatively different than that of the under-stimulated, under-motivated, alienated, Behavioristally-trained, rat-race rodents. Unfortunately, these motivated English Corner active learners constitute less than 1% of China's English students, the vast majority of whom are under-stimulated and under-motivated, with high affective filters due to neo-cerebral and cultural stress. Though disorganized and disfunctional, the morphic resonance of these bored and even passive-aggressive students could be expected to be massive in comparison to that of the English Corner learners.

TV and Mass-Morphic Resonance

What Archimedean lever can be used to "promote the new" for China's English learners-on a mass scale? TV. DVD. Internet downloads. In 1983 Sheldrake showed two difficult-to-discern patterns to a group of test subjects to establish a base line for how easily the hidden picture in each could be recognized. Next he showed 2 million viewers of British TV what one of the hidden pictures was. He then tested thousands of people all over the world. By significant percentages, they recognized the image shown on television; the percentage recognizing the control picture didn't change. China's English Corners and the Movie Magic project can offer an extraordinary opportunity to explore the morphogenetic dynamics of whole-brained English learning. Sheldrake's theory would suggest that as more Chinese actually acquire English as a useful skill (rather than stressfully "study" for the English tests), then English acquisition should be significantly easier for other learners in China. China official policy states: "Eliminate ignorance and combat feudal and superstitious activities." "Improve our ability to understand the world and change it" (Wang and Yu, p.98). In China, criticizing the current English etc. pedagogy is so widespread that it is passé. From the early days of the People's Republic of China, policy makers spoke of a firm determination to break free from the process of feudal-Confucian education. As Mr. Lu Ting-Yi, Chief of the Propaganda Department of the Chinese Communist Party's Central Committee indicated in 1960, the goal of education reforms was nothing less than the total overturn of "old traditions in educational work that have persisted for thousands of years" (Hu, 1974). The reform process involved large-scale experimentation on reducing the number of years spent in education, raising the standards, controlling the study hours, and increasing physical labor to a suitable extent in the full-time middle and elementary schools (Hu, 1974).

Confucian Pressure-Cooking

Fast forward forty years to contemporary China. The traditional exam-oriented, pressure-cooker process of "Confucian education" seems to be far from overturned, and there is concern in the society as a whole—students, parents, teachers, school officials, government officials. A recent story from the official, government-owned China Daily News seems to verify the saying "The more things change, the more they remain the same." Sun Yunxiao, deputy director of the China Youth and Children Research Center, states in the article: "Though children nowadays enjoy a much better living and study environment than their parents did, they are overwhelmed by a kind of invisible pressure which can not allow them to feel the pleasures of life." Statistics support the concerns expressed:

- Students with psychological problems make up 21 percent of primary schools and 32 percent of secondary schools nationwide.
- The ratio at universities and colleges range from 16 to 25 percent.
- According to a sample survey in Nanjing, "after-school training courses take up an average of 57 percent of a child's spare time, while children in some developed countries spend over 90 percent of their spare time on sports or activities of their own choosing."

Perhaps it is not appropriate or even necessary to critique the old in China at this time. In theory, students, teacher, parents, school administrators and government officials agree that English pedagogy reform is necessary. In terms of the actual process of reforming English teaching, however, the difficulty is that China's education system is excessively exam-oriented, with intense competition for scores which can qualify students for places in China's woefully low supply of universities. As English conversation ability is not tested on the national exams, the "teach for the test" syndrome can easily prevail. Lacking confidence in their own English conversation skills and untrained in the communicative approach pedagogy, Chinese teachers typically focus upon vocabulary and grammar. Students in English Conversation class often can be seen studying in class for a test in another subject. Students who have had many years of English classes typically lack the confidence or the ability to engage in a simple conversation in English. Certainly China's English Corners are a major improvement upon the typical overcrowded/stress-filled/boring English classroom in China. With the Beijing 2008 Olympics approaching, the Chinese national and local governments are increasingly focused upon the need to promote cost-effective mass English training. The context and content of English Corners can be expanded and deepened.

Facilitate the Switch

"This is the most important and the least obvious strategy for making change happen. It is also where many change efforts fail, because they forget to reduce the perceived cost of making the change" (Atkisson, 112). "Cultivate an atmosphere in which the whole of society learns from the advanced" (Wang and Yu, p. 134). Atkisson (195) emphasizes that an innovation's potential for success typically is related to five factors: 1. (Perceived) Relative advantage; 2. Simplicity; 3. Trial-ability; 4. Observability; 5. Compatibility with lifestyle/values. In terms of the English Corners, all five factors can promote the success of this project. There will be, and there will be perceived to be, an actual advantage in learning English within such a whole-brained and vibrant environment. Unlike complex pedagogical approaches such as Suggestopedia, which require careful teacher/student training, this Movie Magic project will be user-friendly. Individuals and groups will be able to visit and try out the Movie Magic learning environment at the English Corners. As the English Corners take place in public parks and on university campuses, with many different people visiting and passing by, the lively and entertaining Movie Magic approaches will certainly be observed by many. As well, active participants will be able to observe their progress from being part of the Movie Magic process. Watching/talking about movies and doing role plays will be compatible with the lifestyle and values of many people. A key element is that the individuals at the English Corners will be able to choose which various groups and activities they wish to participate in while at the English Corner. As experience with these techniques is developed and refined with a core group of English Corner participants, we will be ready for mass-morphic methods, such as workshops at English Corners and schools, and eventually a TV program.

Conclusion

China's English Corners already can be described as a truly extraordinary phenomenon, and we have the Archimedean opportunity to introduce whole-brained learning dynamics on a nation-wide scale. The next steps are: (1) To continue to develop core members at the public English Corner at Sichuan University and the small-group English Corner at my on-campus residence; (2) To develop our first Summer Camp for English/Chinese/Tibetan learning, in a Tibetan village in pristine JiuZhaiGou nature preserve in northern Sichuan county; (3) To get TV publicity for our Summer Camp; and (4) To see what sprouts. We welcome ideas and hands-on assistance from the JILL network, especially in response to the questions:

(1) How can we promote whole-brained evolution in China's nationwide English Corners?

(2) How best can the English Corners help promote a China-wide educational transformation-from bored and stressed students of English to whole-brained and intrinsically motivated learners of English?

References

Andors, S., (1976). The Dynamics of Mass Campaigns in Chinese Industry: Initiators, Leaders, and Participants in the Great Leap Forward, the Cultural Revolution, and the Campaign to Criticize Lin Biao and Confucius. *Bulletin of Concerned Asian Scholars*, Vol. 8, 1976

Atkisson, A., (1999). Believing Cassandra: An Optimist Looks at a Pessimist's World. Melbourne, Scribe Publications China Daily, August 15, 2002. A Generation under pressure. http://www.china.org.cn/english/NM-e/40923.htm

Cowles Comprehensive Encyclopedia, (1966). New York, N.Y., Cowles Educational Books, History of Education, p.20

Gowan, J. C. (1978). Incubation, imagery and creativity. *Journal of Mental Imagery*, 2, 23-32.

Horng R., & Torrance, E. (1987). Imagery abilities, sex and intelligence as predictors of creative thinking abilities. Presented at the 3rd International Imagery Conference, Fukuoka, Japan.

Kaufmann, G. (1980). *Imagery, language and cognition: Toward a theory of symbolic activity in human problem solving.* Olso, Norway: Universitetsforlaget.

Krashen, S.D., (1983). The Din in the Head, Input , and the Language Acquisition Device. In Oller, J.W., Jr.&P.A. Richard-Amato,1983. *Methods that Work.* Cambridge, MA., Newbury House.

McDougall, W., (1920). *The Group Mind.* Cambridge University Press

Nelson, A. (1987). Accelerating memory through imagery and rhythm. Presented at 11th American Imagery Conference, New York, NY.

Paivio, A. (1969). Mental imagery in associative learning and memory. *Psychological Review*, 76, 241-263.

Pylyshyn, Z. (1981). The imagery debate: Analogue media versus tacit knowledge. *Psychological Review*, 88, 16-45.

Rider, M. S., Floyd, J. W., & Kirkpatrick, J. (1985). The effect of music, imagery and relaxation on adrenal corticosteroids and the re-entrainment of circadian rhythms. *Journal of Music Therapy*, 12, 46-58.

Sheldrake, Rupert. Society, Spirit & Ritual: Morphic Resonance and the Collective Unconscious http://www.stuartwilde.com/Learn/SW_learn_Society_Spirit_Ritual_Part2.htm

Swisher, K., & Deyhle, D. (1989). The styles of learning are different but the teaching is just the same: Suggestions for teachers of American Indian youth. *Journal of American Indian Education*, August, 1-14.

Wang, Yiduan and Yu, Songxi (1999). *A Glossary of Contemporary Chinese Politics and Economics.* Beijing, China: Foreign Languages Press.

Language Arts & the Education of the Imagination

Geoff Madoc-Jones

Editor's Note: This is not an easy article, but it makes a very strong case for the centrality of literature in the curriculum as well as in the relationship between the individual and the world. It is the author's premise that each of us has the opportunity and the obligation to become what he or she is not yet. This growth of the self is possible in large part because of the powers of the imagination. Make no mistake: the following is a seminal article and deserves our full and undivided attention.

One of the key responsibilities of the language arts teacher is to initiate students into the realm of imaginative thinking through the study and use of poetic language. In this paper I make the claim that poetic thinking is linked to a much larger realm than mere acquaintance with literary works. It is a central part of how we as human beings make sense of the world both on a personal and social level through the use of metaphor. Getting students to use metaphoric language in order to understand the self and interpret the world requires a theory of the way in which what Paul Ricoeur calls "linguistic imagination" works. I will investigate aspects of Ricoeur's thought in order to suggest such a theory that is of import to the pedagogy of language arts teaching

Metaphor and Making Meaning

Metaphor is a universal, constitutive property of all natural languages. The philosopher, Ricoeur, sees metaphor as having two functional traits: (1) economy at the level of code, and (2) contextual dependence at the level of the message, which leads to combination of finite means and infinite use.

> *The simplest message conveyed by means of natural language has to be interpreted because all words are polysemic and take their actual meaning from the connection with a given context and a given audience against a background of a given situation.* (from Word, Polysemy and Metaphor in Ricoeur, 1991a, 125)

Ricoeur distinguishes between polysemy and ambiguity by showing that while polysemy is a feature of words, ambiguity or equivocity is a feature of discourse. While polysemy is an inherent phenomenon, a feature of all words, ambiguity is not necessarily a normal feature of discourse because it may lead to misunderstanding of the sentence and thereby distort the inter-subjective process of communication. Thus an art of interpretation or hermeneutics and its related strategies capable of meeting the challenge of the possibility of misunderstanding is required.

Scientific Language, Poetic Language

Ricoeur suggests that these strategies may be different for ordinary language, scientific or artificial language, and poetic language. He maintains that ambiguity cannot be eradicated in ordinary language: it can only be reduced. The fact that ordinary language is polysemic has led, historically, to a number of strategies which attempt to eradicate or reduce it. One such strategy is found in scientific language, however, any attempt to replace ordinary language with scientific language for normal discourse, according to Ricoeur, is bound to fail, because they have different aims. The aim of ordinary language is to communicate and interpret; the aim of scientific language on the other hand is descriptive. This can be seen when

> *we read a scientific paper, we are not in the position of an individual member of a speech community...All readers are, in a sense, one and the same mind, and the purpose of discourse is not to build a bridge between two spheres of experience, but to insure the identity of meaning from the beginning to the end of the argument.* (129)

The link with natural language is broken and the ultimate stage of abstraction using mathematical and other formal systems with strict rules for translating them or interpreting them in relation to empirical fields by excluding ambiguity become the norm.

Preserving Ambiguity

Poetic language, on the other hand, instead of reducing or suppressing polysemy uses metaphor as a way of preserving and extending ambiguity. Ricoeur is critical of rhetorical theories of metaphor which classify it as merely a trope or a figure of speech and which do not give an account of the generative process that accounts for its formation. This is because "the metaphorical process occurs at another level, at the level of the sentence and of discourse as a whole" (131), and not just at the level of the word. Ricoeur argues that as one moves from description to interpretation, "the imagination is considered less in terms of 'vision' than in terms of 'language.' Or to put it more exactly, imagination is assessed as an indispensable agent in the creation of meaning in and through language" (from "Paul Ricoeur and the Hermeneutic Imagination" by Richard Kearney in Kemp and Rasmussen, 1989, 1).

Ricoeur emphasizes the linguistic functioning of imagination, where there exists "…not just epistemological and political imagination, but also, and more fundamentally, a linguistic imagination which generates and regenerates meaning through the living power of metaphoricity" (3). Ricoeur affirms the poetical role of imagining, that is, its ability to say one thing in terms of another, or to say several things at the same time, thereby creating something new.

Eidetic Phenomenology

This he calls "semantic innovation" and it gains its validity by seeing that the productive unit of metaphor is not the word but the sentence. This power of imagination to transform given meanings into new ones enables us to see the future as an opening of possibilities. "We have thought too much in terms of a will which submits and not enough of an imagination which opens up" (4). Ricoeur thus claims that the productive power of imagination is not primarily visual but verbal. This means that if images are thought to be spoken before being seen, they can no longer be reduced to quasi-material residues of sensual perception, that is to objects for merely empirical study or modifications or negations of direct perceptions. This configuration of ideas constitute eidetic phenomenology ["Eidetic" pertains to the detail and vivid recall of visual image.] Thus if the image exists in a verbal dimension prior to becoming the focus of perception, then linguistic imagination is originary and is a productive force while the non-verbal is reproductive.

At the heart of the linguistic imagination is the verbal metaphor where figurative meaning emerges in the interplay between identity and difference. It is the meeting place of two semantic fields, the literal and the poetic, where the action of metaphoricity brings different meanings into a state of identity. That which is predicatively impertinent at a literal level becomes predicatively pertinent at a new level that is, the poetic. For example; take the statement, "The life of ignorance is a dark cave." We have here a dissimilarity, a state of semantic shock, and because the predicate does not follow literally from the expectations set up by the subject, it seems initially impertinent. There is a moment of rupture in the semantic field—an aporia of meaning, because we know that "ignorance" is not "a dark cave" at the literal level. The issue then becomes, how are they to be reconciled so as to produce a new meaning? This takes place through the imagination working with the generative power of language, so the "cave" is seen as "ignorance", but only after its semantically impertinent state has been realized. Thus imagination is the act of responding to the pressure for new meanings which life throws at us because we are future-facing beings; we live formed by the past but also are always futural.

Creation as Discovery

The linguistic imagination has a further dynamic which transcends the logic of discovery found in semantic fields. Gaston Bachelard, (1958, xix) says "By its novelty, a poetic image, sets in motion the entire linguistic mechanism. The poetic image places us at the origin of the speaking being." Thus "seeing as" implies also "being as"."This exhibits the ontological paradox of creation as discovery. "Through the recovery of the capacity of language to create and recreate, we discover reality itself in the process of being created….Language in the making celebrates reality in the making." (xix)

But the imagination needs images otherwise it would remain invisible, and the visual image is the moment where the verbal turns sensible. Seeing one thing as if it were another is the key to the sensual aspect of poetic imagination. Here, sense and image are held together in an intuitive manner, so that from the quasi-sensory mass of tacit imagery, a semantic order is formed by imagination, which also has the capacity to move back from intuition to conceptual meaning. These two ways of moving—from the intuitive to the conceptual and back again—form a creative tension between expression and interpretation that can be helpful in the Language Arts classroom.

The seeing-as activated in reading ensures the joining of meaning with imagistic fullness, (and) that conjunction is no longer something outside language since it can be reflected as a relationship. Seeing-as contains a ground, a foundation, this is precisely, a resemblance. It is a schema which unites the empty concept with the blind impression…Thanks to its character as half thought and half experience, it joins the light of sense with the fullness of the image. In this way, the non-verbal and the verbal are firmly united at the core of the image-ing function of language. (Ricoeur, 1978, 199-200)

The function of imagination in poetry or myth is defined accordingly as the "disclosure of unprecedented worlds, an opening onto possible worlds which transcend the limits of our actual world" (5-6). An interpretive approach to imagination thus differs from a structural or existentialist one in its concentration on the capacity of world-disclosure yielded by poetic texts. In short, "hermeneutics is not confined to the objective analysis of texts, nor to the subjective existential analysis of the authors of texts: its primary concern is with the worlds which these authors and texts open up" (5-6).

This opening up of possible worlds by the imagination assists in our understanding of the concept of 'being-in-the-world'. First, because the human subject cannot come to know itself through any direct path, but only through the detour of interpreting signs and works and by the deciphering of the products of the imagination in myths, dreams and symbols, In Ricoeur's words, "the shortest route from the self to itself is through the images of others" (5-6). Second, this kind imaginative thought is not confined to the circle of interpretation. The projection of possible worlds that is seen above through semantic innovation is an essential ingredient of the dynamism of action. Semantic innovation points towards the transformation of the social world because of the freedom inherent in projecting possible worlds; there is "no action without imagination" (6). What is interpreted in a text is the proposing of a world that I might inhabit and into which I might project my own inner most desires. Thus,

the world is the whole set of references opened by every sort of descriptive or poetic texts I have read, interpreted, and loved. To understand these texts is to interpolate among the predicates of our situation all those meanings that, from a simple environment (Umwelt), make a world (Welt). Indeed we owe a large part of the enlarging of our horizon of existence to poetic works. (Ricoeur, 1984. Vol.1, 80)

As language arts teachers, we are most interested in the creating of the capacity of language to create and recreate, to discover reality in the process of being created. Language in the making celebrates reality in the making; literal meaning is shattered as metaphor is formed, and as language is recreated and increased, our sense of reality is likewise. In other words, it is in metaphor that we experience the coming together of both language and reality.

Triple Referenced Forms

One of the key functions of language is that it refers to the world. It says something about what is happening in the world. The poetic form, however, complicates matters by also referring to itself as language. As well as its role in the creation of new meaning through metaphor and thereby opening up the possibility of a new reality, the poetic form also instantiates three referential functions at once, which are of import to the language arts. First-order reference is in, the immediate world of perception (empirical reality), the author's and the reader's, as contained in the ordinary literal meaning. Second-order reference is a world where the meaning contained in the metaphor is possible. In the poetic work, the first-order reference is suspended while the semantic innovation plays its role, that of disclosing new ways of being in the world. Therefore, in its most fundamental sense, it is an ontological event. Thus linguistic imagination is committed both to the role of semantic and ontological innovation. The third-order reference comes from the notion that language in its poetic form also refers to itself. I include it in this analysis because it has an important pedagogic role to play in the language arts classroom: The teacher may use it to highlight students' realization of the "languaged" nature of their thought. Thus the poetic imagination creates meaning by responding to the desire of being human—the desire to be expressed, to form and understand the world.

Referential and Poetic Functions

Roman Jakobson in *Linguistics and Poetics* (1958) outlined a number of functions of language. The two of interest to us here are the referential and poetic functions. The referential function of language is what is being spoken of, what is being referred to in a statement. In the expression "Please hand in your assignments on time!" the referential focus of the message is "I am requesting that the written documents which you have prepared for this course be placed in my mail box by Friday 13 at 4:30 PM". It is referring to a social world where there are teachers and students and written assignments. The poetic function, on the other hand, has to do with the focus on the medium of the message for its own sake. Such a focus includes associative repetitions of sound values, and word and phrase boundaries. In the imaginative use of language these two functions can be combined and language becomes what Ricoeur calls "double referenced." This quality of language of being able to face two directions at once is further complicated by the fact that someone is saying or writing that double referenced bit of language. This may not be of great import for many situations of language use, e.g. "Help, I am drowning" but it is of particular importance to the language arts teacher, who is attempting to develop not only the competence of the student in language, but also a heightened awareness of both conscious language use and the linguistically constituted nature of thought and being. The question of reference posed is thus more complex; for certain texts—the poetic ones—seem to constitute an exception to the reference requirements of descriptive language. Ricoeur explains this in the following way:

The literary work through the structure proper to it displays a world only under condition that the reference of descriptive discourse is suspended. Or to put it another way, discourse in the literary work sets out its denotation as a second-level denotation, by means of the suspension of first-level denotation of discourse…Just as the metaphorical statement captures its sense as metaphorical midst the ruins of the literal sense, it also achieves its reference upon the ruins of what might be called its…literal reference. (Ricoeur, 1975, 221)

Thus poetic language has the capacity to perform these functions in a way that other linguistic modes do not: it can sweep back to the being that is revealed and leap forward to the language that is revealing both itself and a world. However, language does not merely refer to the world: it also has the capacity to form a world by opening up new horizons of meaning for the speaker, the writer and equally important, the reader. The poetic imagination liberates the reader into a space of possibility, suspending the reference to the immediate world of perception—both the author's and the reader's—and thereby disclosing "new ways of being in the world." This is the function of what we have seen that Ricoeur (1991,173) calls "semantic innovation", which is how he maintains that metaphor is related to imagination in its most fundamental sense as an ontological event. Imagination above all else is the process of restructuring semantic fields instead of being seen as either a problem of our perception (reproductive imagination) or as the raw material out of which are wrought our abstract ideas, our concepts (productive imagination).

Imagination and Language

The question then is how is imagination derived from language? Ricoeur (172) maintains that the poetic image is a paradigmatic case of such a field of semantic innovation and that it emerges as a result not of things seen but as the result of a reverberation of things said. He invokes Bachelard's work on poetics as revealing the depth of this process. Bachelard (1964) claims a deep rapport between imagination and language, and situates the desire to attune oneself to ones being itself at the root of imagination. It combines an awareness of our own creative idiolect while at the same time opening up the possibility for the discovery of the logos of the human world. A most important principle of language arts education is making sure that as the emergence of a student's personal creative use of language takes place: it is seen not merely as a subjective act but also as an instance of the re-emergence of the logos within a linguistic tradition.

Bachelard sees a particular relation between poetry and being human: "the poetic image has an entity and a dynamism of its own; it is referable to direct *ontology*…The communicability of an unusual image is in fact of great ontological significance" (Bachelard, 1964, xii- xiii). The importance of the imagination and the poetic image lies in their capacity to break through the habits of ordinary perception, of scientific and philosophical thought. The poetic image creates a privileged space through its reverberation in which being discloses itself. Bachelard claims, "The poet speaks on the threshold of being" (1964, xiii), and that the originality of the poetic imagination exemplifies human freedom by being independent of causality: "The causes cited by psychologists and psychoanalysts can never really explain the wholly unexpected nature of the new image, any more than they can explain the attraction it holds for a mind that is foreign to the process of its creation" (Bachelard, 1964, xiii), because the

poetic act itself, the sudden image, the flare-up of being in the imagination, are inaccessible to such investigations. In order to clarify the problem of the poetic image philosophically, we shall have to have recourse to a phenomenology of the imagination. By this should be understood a study of the phenomenon of the poetic image when it emerges into the consciousness as a direct product of the heart, soul and being of man, apprehended in his actuality. (xiv)

Bachelard had been a philosopher of science for most of his life but states that when he came to study the imagination, the detachment and prudence of the scientific approach was insufficient to account for the phenomenon, in great part because the "prudent" attitude itself is a refusal to obey the immediate dynamics of the image" (xiv). He calls this a minor cultural crisis on the simple level of a new image, for it,

contains the entire paradox of a phenomenology of the imagination, which is: how can an image, at times very unusual, appear to be a concentration of the entire psyche? How—with no preparation—can this singular, short-lived event constituted by the appearance of an unusual poetic image, react on other minds and in other hearts, despite—all the barriers of common sense, all the disciplined schools of thought content in their immobility? (Bachelard, 1964, xiv)

The problem which Bachelard raises lies at the heart of the trans-subjectivity of language and has important implications for language arts teachers in particular. For if the image cannot be understood through the notion of subjective reference alone—i.e., if it cannot be determined once and for all, and does not have the constitutive longevity of the concept, how is it to be studied? Bachelard claims the approach must be one of "microscopic phenomenology". That is, because of the ephemerality and variational nature of the poetic image, this means that it must be studied at its onset in an individual consciousness. The reader

of poems is asked to consider an image not as an object and even less as the substitute for an object, but to seize its specific reality. For this, the act of the creative consciousness must be systematically associated with the most fleeting product of that consciousness, the poetic image. At the level of the poetic image, the duality of subject and object is iridescent, shimmering, unceasingly active in its inversions. (xv)

A Becoming of Being

For Bachelard, the resonances and reverberations which the image sets off in the "poetry-lover" go immediately beyond the descriptions of the psychologist or the understanding of the psychoanalyst and becomes a "new being in our language, expressing us by making us what it expresses; in other words, it is at once a becoming of expression, and a becoming of being. Here, expression creates being" (xix). This is the revealing of the ontological depth of the poetic imagination, where the image is not considered as an object to be critically considered or causally explained, but raises the question of the speaking being's creativeness. "Through this creativeness, the imagining consciousness proves to be—very simply but very purely—an origin" (xx). Bachelard emphasizes the powers of wonder, astonishment, and innocence. The reader must be receptive and "reverberate" with the poem in order to experience "the very ecstasy of the newness of the image" (xi). This newness places us at the origin of the speaking being where a sort of original naming discloses beings in their primordial presence.

Bachelard's lyrical reveries on images of "felicitous space such as houses, closets, cupboards, drawers, suggest the "human value" of places and objects (Bachelard, 1964, xxx). Such spaces—idiosyncratic and contingent—make such revelations of being always paradoxical, as they are both hidden and disclosing, absent as well as present. Furthermore, reveries of this kind are experiences that reveal the creativity of language, and students may wish to have their own and interpret them for the purpose of developing an understanding of the ontological aspect of their own languaged selves.

Language Arts and Interpretation

One of the central activities of the Language Arts classroom is the interpretation of written texts. While these texts may present themselves in a number of forms, the poetic text is our concern. By "poetic," I mean those texts which not only attempt to communicate a message but which also consciously draw attention or refer to their own artistic "languaged" mode. Take for example the following fragment of a poem by W.B. Yeats:

> The unpurged images of day recede;
> The Emperor's drunken soldiery are abed;
> Night resonance recedes, night-walkers' song
> After great cathedral gong;
> A starlit or moonlit dome disdains
> All that man is,
> All mere complexities,
> The fury and the mite of human veins.
> (from "Byzantium" by W.B. Yeats)

This could, I suppose, be read as the telegraphic epistle of a war correspondent wiring his evening report to the local daily newspaper; but if it were, it would miss the point. The abundance of the music of the sound of the words, the repetition of "n's" and "r's" of line three coupled with the central trope—the personification of nature's disdain for man's triviality—are all clues that the intent of this fragment is not the simple transmission of some content.—Language leaps out, showing what is particularly the case in all poetic speech: that language is always present even if it is at times temporarily hidden in the flow of ordinary dialogue.

The verbal arts are, of course, not restricted to written literary texts: there are also oral forms, the first forms of verbal art. But in both cases of production and reception, the signifier emerges as equal to and at times more important than the signified. Of all the various literary forms the one which is most concerned with language is poetry. This is what Paul Ricoeur refers to as "language in all its fullness". Of course, many features that are found in poetry are also found in other language forms. The difference is that in poetry, reference to language as language is a constitutive part of its mode. In other words, to write or to speak with constant attention to language in all its fullness is to write or speak poetically. Even in the following piece by William Carlos Williams (1949, 30) which, despite its seeming lack of "poetic" patina, is poetry because it is concerned with language in all its fullness:

THE RED WHEELBARROW
> so much depends
> upon
> a red wheel
> barrow
> glazed with rain
> water
> beside the white
> chickens

If the object of study of the language arts classroom is language, then the form of literary art which has language as its most important concern must be central to its curriculum, as well as to its teaching and learning activities. I do not mean to imply that literature is the only form that should be studied in a language arts program. There must also be a place for studying various forms: expository essay writing and letter writing for example; or an array of opportunities for personal expression, such as, diaries and journals. Just as in a mathematics program, while the content may have various applications, the central concern of the mathematics teacher should be to teach those necessary and unique aspects of mathematics as a mode of understanding, which may or may not have practical application, but which the student needs to learn in order to think and express herself mathematically.

Three Aspects of Language Study

If the central concern of a language arts program is the study of the literary text, how should it be studied? There are three aspects to language and literary study: first, learning about them; second, learning how to best study them; and third, having an experience with them. All three of these aspects play a part in coming to an understanding of a literary text, which means being able to interpret the text in a manner so that its meaning is understood as fully as possible.

It is necessary here to distinguish between the two kinds of work of art. First, there are arts where the existence of the work coincides with its creation such as painting and sculpture. Second, those in which the existence of the work requires a second performance or recreation, such as plays, musical compositions, choreography, a score, a script, a novel or a poem. "One could then ask what is the status of a ballet, or of a musical score when they are not played, while awaiting their performance. It is perhaps here, in this indefinite capacity to be reincarnated, and in a way each time historically different, but substantially and essentially" founding, that the profound signified of the libretto or of the score occupies the status of the sempiternal. (Ricoeur. 1996, 3) The question then raised is where is this work of art? Ricoeur's answer is that it exists only in its capacity for reception or reinscription.

> There is doubtless something specific in the work of art: its prophetic character, in the sense that, breaking with the values of utility and commercial values, the transcendence of the work of art is affirmed in opposition to the utility that itself is exhausted in the historical. It is the capacity to transcend immediate utility that characterizes the work of art in this capacity for multiple and indefinite reinscription. One could say that in the arts of two times the moment of the sempiternal is in the hiding place (retrait) of the libretto and the script, but the temporal test is in monstration. The capacity for a "monstration" renewed endlessly, as being always other although the same, constitutes the link between the sempiternal and the historic; perhaps here is the most pregnant temporal mark of the work of art. (Ricoeur. 1996, 3)

Thus a key part of the language arts teacher's job is the recreation, the reinscription or performance of these "second order" works.

Literature and Interpretation

One of the roles of education, in Charles Taylor's (1995) terms, is to instantiate both a "horizon of significance" and a certain quality of dialogue from which an authentic self may emerge. One of the key elements in this dialogue is the provision of an appropriate interpretive dialogue with carefully selected canonical literary texts. These texts can be used positively for this purpose because they possess two important qualities: (1) a higher degree of internal organization, and (2) a greater value in the social and cultural treasury. All language reduces and orders the potentially endless stream of events in the world as we make sense of the world with its mediation.

Literary art works or "literature" is like any other utterance in that it provides order to the world, but it does so to a much greater degree. Furthermore, its internal organization enables a high degree of ordering of the world to emerge without overly restricting the range of possible meanings. This range, of course, is not infinite, yet these meanings may be obscure and require an interpretive competence on the part of the reader. For example, how can a reader work out what is happening in John Donne's poem, *The Computation*, without first of all navigating the various rhetorical positions that the poet posits between himself and the reader, including a speaker of the poem who is not the poet and an implied listener who is not the reader. Is the poem an actual Petrarchian conceit or a feigned one? And, if so, how is the reader supposed to know that and, thereby, acknowledge the poet's wit? Or is it the speaker's ladylove who is meant to be in on the irony and, thereby, correctly answer the poet's final question by jumping into bed with him? Further examples of such structurally palimpsestic works abound, particularly in the modern novel, the magic realism of Carlos Fuentes or Borges or Salman Rushdie, the imagined histories of John Barth or Milan Kundera or Umberto Eco, and Thomas Pynchon's tales that wrap reality in hallucination. These all play with the conventions and idioms of the realist novel and knowledge of this play is crucial to understanding the meaning of the novels.

Possibilities of the Imagination

Certainly the study of literature may enable a high school student to discover a new self which he or she can become, in part, through a dialogue with literary texts that both bring a high degree of order to the world while remaining open to the possibilities of the imagination. But if they are not educated readers and are left alone with the text and their reflective journals, without good teachers to guide their reading, all they may become is confused or filled with misunderstandings. Eco (1990) makes the same point when he distinguishes between interpreting and using the text,

> I can certainly use Wordsworth's text for parody, for showing how a text can be read in relation to different cultural frameworks, or for strictly personal ends (I can read a text to get inspiration for my own musing); but if I want to interpret Wordsworth's text, I must respect his cultural and linguistic background. (Eco, 1991, 68-69)

The reader should have a "competence in language as a social treasury" (67) that includes "the whole encyclopedia that the performances of that language have implemented, namely, the cultural conventions that language has produced and the very history of the previous interpretations of many texts" (67-68). The act of reading is a difficult transaction. Thus how can a student, if he or she lacks such a competence, interpret the line, "A poet could not but be gay" from Wordsworth's I wandered lonely as a cloud; she needs to know that at that time "gay" had no sexual connotation.

We need to learn to think about the interpretation of texts in the opposite way from which it has been so often taught to students. With so much stress today on personal response and personal opinion, the clarifying of the student's own opinion is often the main purpose of the study of the work. However, if the work being considered is of any importance in itself, or if it is to be any value in the authentic formation of the self, then it cannot be regarded as merely an extension of the reader's own will. If the work is regarded as such an extension, then its value is narcissistic and its study will merely lead the students back to what they were. We need to teach students to interpret what the literary work is saying in its terms. That is, we need to get students to understand the text, not just in our own terms, but through a careful reading of what the author had fixed in the writing.

The Hermeneutic Circle

The development of self-understanding is not restricted to a process of an informed dialogue with literary texts, but can also be seen as part of a more general development of understanding within the historically constituted culture. On this relation between culture and self, Gadamer says,

> *Long before we understand ourselves through the process of self-examination, we understand ourselves in a self-evident way in the family, society and state in which we live. The focus of subjectivity is a distorting mirror. The self-awareness of the individual is only a flickering in the closed circuits of historical life.* (Gadamer, 126)

Thus in order to "understand" one always "fore-understands", that is, one has a stance, an anticipation and a contextualization which cannot be acquired monologically. We find ourselves at the dawning of self-consciousness already in a world constituted by a language and a tradition which in great part form us prior to our "choosing them". However, their meaning requires that we learn how to interpret the texts even as we find ourselves in dialogue with them. Thus we find ourselves in what is known as a "hermeneutic circle," where one can only know what one has been prepared to know. The hermeneutic circle can thus be taken to be an inherently limiting, self-binding process. Yet because of the symbolic and self-reflective nature of our being, the hermeneutic circle does not close us off but opens us up. Thus, the self is always and already in a state of pre-understanding while at the same time struggling with the challenge of the future to form new meanings and new understandings. The hermeneutic experience—the encounter with the other, the contextual, linguistic, historical, fusion of horizons—is the one which liberates us from the contingencies of our birth and the limitations of our own subjectivity.

This has been part of what Ricoeur has referred to as the long detour through culture,

> *Perhaps it is at this level of self-understanding that the mediation effected by the text can best be understood. In contrast to the tradition of the cogito and to the pretension of the subject to know itself by immediate intuition, it must be said that we understand ourselves only by the long detour of the signs of humanity deposited in cultural works. What would we know of love and hate, of moral feelings and, in general, of all that we call the self, if these had not been brought to language and articulated by literature? Thus what seems most contrary to subjectivity and what structural analysis discloses as the structure of the text, is the very medium within which we can understand ourselves.* (Ricoeur, 1991b, 143)

Ricoeur (1975) remarks, "To bring (experience) into language is not to change it into something else, but, in articulating and developing it, to make it become itself." This is a point I wish to stress again, in particular because of certain popular post-structural ideas currently in vogue in education. Experience is neither just language, nor can language be reduced to experience, because, they are intertwined. The limits of language, however, are always being stretched, through the ongoing attempt of human expressivity to grasp the real, and the surplus of meaning is, therefore, located both in our being-in-the-world, as well as in language.

Thus, the most important concern of the language arts educator must be the conditions necessary for understanding, i.e. the ontological state of always being in understanding. Is the student appropriately open to the possibilities embedded in the text? How does the teacher mediate the conversation, the dialogue, which is the necessary condition for educative learning to take place? Is the imagination of the learner ready? If we are always in understanding, what stance, what anticipation and contextualization is necessary for its educational development? In the "hermeneutic circle" the learner can only know that which he or she is prepared to know. The circle is not necessarily closed, however, because of the relation of meaning to being, the polysemic nature of language and the "semantic impertinence" of original metaphor. "Semantic impertinence" is a concept used by Ricoeur to account for the creation of new meaning in the act of metaphor. Ricoeur argues that metaphor exists most potently at the level of the sentence and not the word. It fuses two previously unrelated semantic elements, which previously were not seen as being pertinent to each other. Once the fusion, an act of semantic impertinence, has occurred there then exists a new semantic element containing new meaning. Intimately associated with this is the imagination. From this point of view, the imagination can be conceived of as an act of fusion. By fusion, I mean the coming together of previously unconnected concepts in the creation of new meaning. The literal dies and a new metaphoric meaning emerges from its ruins.

Conclusion

The innovative power of linguistic imagination is not some decorative excess or effusion of subjectivity, but the capacity of language to open up new worlds. The function of imagination in poetry and myth is to disclose unprecedented worlds and create openings onto possible worlds which transcend the limit of the actual world. Metaphor epitomizes this process by creating new connections rather than mere congruence and by making a similarity out of what was previously dissimilar. The degree of "semantic impertinence" of the dissimilar elements is related to any gains in new meaning. Clichés are old metaphors which once created a new pertinence but no longer do so. These are then available for renewal through a new metaphoric relation where the "is like" element and the "is not" element are intrinsically connected. This is the way in which language deals with the indeterminacy of the future and enables the speaker or writer to create new meaning.

This is the creative imagination at work poetically and represents one of the most important aspects of language arts education. Children who are schooled in metaphoric thought learn to become semantically impertinent thinkers who are not just capable of producing an apt metaphor for a verse writing exercise, but who have as a constitutive feature of their thought the capacity to think that which is not the case. This connection between seeing that which is not the case, and educating the imagination shows that these elements are not merely the frills acquired in the literary classroom but are essential components of being able to make sense of a world that is both finite and indeterminate.

References

Bachelard, Gaston. (1958) *The Poetics of Space.* (Trans. Maria Jolas). Boston: Beacon.

Jakobson, R. (1958). *Linguistics and Poetics.*

Kearney, Richard (1984). *Dialogues With Contemporary Continental Thinkers: The Phenomenological Heritage: Paul Ricoeur, Emmanuel Levinas, Herbert Marcuse, Stanislas Breton, Jacques Derrida* Manchester, UK; Dover, NH, USA: Manchester University Press.

—. (1998). *Poetics of Imagining; Modern to Post-Modern.* Edinburgh: Edinburgh University Press

Ricoeur, Paul. (1974). *The Conflict of Interpretations: Essays In Hermeneutics,* Edited By Don Ihde. Evanston: Northwestern University Press.

—. (1991a). *From Text To Action;* Translated By Kathleen Blamey And John B. Thompson. Evanston, Ill.: Northwestern University Press.

—. (1991b). *Hermeneutics and The Human Sciences: Essays On Language, Action, And Interpretation;* (J. B. Thompson, Ed & Trans). Cambridge [Eng]; New York: Cambridge University Press.

—. (1967). *Husserl: An Analysis of His Phenomenology,* Translated By Edward G. Ballard and Lester E. Embree. Evanston: Northwestern University Press.

—. (1976). *Interpretation Theory: Discourse and the Surplus Of Meaning* Fort Worth [Texas]: Texas Christian University Press.

—. (1992). *Oneself As Another;* (K. Blamey. Chicago, Trans): University Of Chicago Press.

—. (1996). *Paul Ricoeur: The Hermeneutics of Action* (R. Kearney, Ed.). London; Thousand Oaks, Calif.: Sage Publications.

—. (1989). *The Narrative Path. The Later Works of Paul Ricoeur.* Cambridge, Mass: MIT Press.

—. (1978). *The Philosophy of Paul Ricoeur: An Anthology of His Work* (C. E. & D. Stewart, Eds.). Boston: Beacon Press.

—. (1991). *A Ricoeur Reader: Reflection and Imagination,* Edited By Mario J. ValdÈs. Published Toronto: University Of Toronto Press.

—. (1977). *The Rule of Metaphor: Multi-Disciplinary Studies of the Creation of Meaning in Language.* (R. Czerny, K. Mclaughlin & J. Costello, Trans). Toronto; Buffalo: University Of Toronto Press.

—. (1984). *Time and Narrative* (K. Mclaughlin & D. Pellauer, Trans). 3 Vols. Chicago: University Of Chicago Press.

Valdez, M.J. (1987). *Phenomenological Hermeneutics and the Study of Literature.* Toronto: University of Toronto Press.

—. (1982). *Shadows In The Cave: A Phenomenological Approach To Literary Criticism Based on Hispanic Texts.* Toronto: University of Toronto Press.

Firing the "Canon"

Unconventional Approaches to Literature in the ELT Classroom

Claudia Ferradas Moi

What is the role of literature in second and foreign language education? Is there a place for literary texts in the learner-centered, communicative English Language Teaching (ELT) class? If so, what is meant by literary texts and how should they be approached in the classroom? Such questions have been the focus of publications and conference presentations in the ELT field in the last few years. Literature, once related to traditional text-centered approaches, has started making its way back into language classes, now within the context of reader-response theory and humanistic approaches. But why should ELT practitioners be concerned with literature if, as it is often claimed, it has little practical application, is connected too closely with a specific cultural context, and it can be idiosyncratic, even subversive? It is my contention that these features of literary discourse can contribute to language acquisition, first, by involving the imagination and thereby revealing the creative and expressive potential of language; and second, by giving learners access to new socio-cultural meanings and thus contributing to the development of intercultural awareness.

Representational Language

On the grounds that materials should aim at communicative competence, the expressive and poetic functions of language have often been disregarded in ELT, due to the emphasis laid on what is supposedly more practical or useful. Learners are often taught how to communicate in international contexts through language meant to be as culturally "neutral" as possible. However, once they have gone beyond that "survival" level, once they need to express their own meanings and interpret other people's beyond the merely instrumental, representational language is needed. By representational language we mean "language which, in order that its meaning potential be decoded by a receiver, engages the imagination of that receiver….Representational materials make an appeal to the learner's imagination: they can be any kind of material with imaginative or fictional content that goes beyond the purely referential, and brings imaginative interaction, reaction and response into play" (McRae, 1991). Besides, the claim "that literature is not 'relevant' to learners is easily quashed. Natural curiosity about the world, and about any text to be read, means that a learner is always willing to make some attempt to bridge the relevance gap which the teacher may fear separates the learner and the text….The relevance gap is bridged by identification of (if not necessarily with) different ways of seeing the world, and the range of ways of expressing such a vision." (McRae, 1991)

Different Ways of Seeing the World

Can a video, some photographs, a song, the students' written production be considered literature? Surely not, according to what is traditionally considered Literature, with a capital "L." That involves the recognition of a canon, the existence of an intellectual field around it, and laws that allow inclusions and exclusions within a certain tradition. But while a long-established text-centered canon dominates the teaching of literature, a parallel system develops side-by-side with school literature and its restrictions and prejudices as to what can or should be read (Bombini, 1989). This literary system has its own laws of production, reception and distribution; its own criteria as to what should be included or excluded. In it, the concepts of "text" and "reading" are stretched to include not only texts of non-conventional circulation (underground magazines, the production of adolescent writers) but also graffiti, comics, computer games, video. This advocates a strong synergy between text culture and image culture.

Beyond Referential Language

I strongly believe that there is room in our language classes for unconventional literary materials as well as for Literature traditionally understood as such. After all, as Brumfit and Carter (1986) have stated, "it is impossible to isolate any single or special property of language which is exclusive to a literary work…it may be more productive for us to talk about language and literariness rather than "literary language"…what is literary is a matter of relative degree, with some textual features of language signalling a greater literariness than others. "And as Henry Widdowson put it in an interview for the ELT Journal in 1983 (in Brumfit & Carter, 1986): "In conventional discourse you can anticipate, you can take shortcuts….Now you can't do that with literature….because you've got to find the evidence, as it were, which is representative of some new reality. So with literary discourse the actual procedures for making sense are much more in evidence…If you want to develop these procedural abilities to make sense of discourse, then literature has a place…." Such training in deciphering the communication, in working how language means, is a crucial factor in the development of language learning abilities. The use of visual and verbal texts, characterized by their literariness, or to use McRae's terminology, by the use of representational language as opposed to a purely referential one, can help our students succeed in this respect, for "where referential language informs, representational language involves" (McRae, 1991).

Let's then extend this involvement from the Literature class into the foreign language class. If the focus is on the learners' response, this can be done at different levels of proficiency—tailoring the task to the level of the learner rather than vice-versa. The modest proposal in this article is, then, the inclusion of unconventional literary materials (notice the small "l") in the language classroom. Unconventional in two senses: (a) texts that would easily fit conventional definitions of what is called Literature are selected for purposes other than traditional literary analysis, and (b) the materials themselves are chosen because of their "literariness," though they defy traditional classifications.

Basic Assumptions

The approach is based on certain basic assumptions:

- The focus is on what language can do, on how language means, highlighting its expressive and poetic functions.
- The text (whether verbal or non-verbal) is a stepping-stone for the learners to develop responses (which need not always be verbal).
- The teacher does not provide "model interpretations": s/he contributes to making different levels of reading transaction possible.
- It is exploitation of the text that matters: the teacher will design activities based on the text aiming at language awareness as well as cultural awareness.
- The approach is intertextual and intercultural, encouraging a fluid dialogue between each reader and the text, each reader and other readers, the text and other texts, the L2 culture and the learners' culture, the text used as stepping-stone, and the text(s) produced in response to it.

In short, creative, critical reading of representational texts easily leads to responding/writing/thinking creatively. Designing textual intervention activities for the classroom (Pope 1995)—rather than merely aiming at analysis—can demystify the literary text and facilitate the process of appropriation. We must also be aware that any thesis—including my own—remains open to support or opposition by students who must however, present an argument with objective supports or evidence.

A. **Working with the Canon in an Unconventional Way:** Here are some ideas that seemed to work in my language classes and those of teacher trainees in different contexts. Take the case of Shakespeare's "Sonnet 130": a highly traditional, prestigious and rigid poetic form, the sonnet, can lend itself to somewhat disrespectful but rewarding uses:

> *My mistress' eyes are nothing like the sun;*
> *Coral is far more red than her lips' red;*
> *If snow be white, why then her breasts are dun;*
> *If hairs be wires, black wires grow on her head.*
> *I have seen roses damasked, red and white,*
> *But no such roses see I in her cheeks,*
> *And in some perfumes is there more delight*
> *Than in the breath that from my mistress reeks.*
> *I love to hear her speak, yet well I know*
> *That music hath a far more pleasing sound.*
> *I grant I never saw a goddess go;*
> *My mistress when she walks treads on the ground.*

And yet, by heaven, I think my love as rare
As any she belied with false compare.

1. Cut the poem into pieces (individual lines or couplets, depending on the level of the course and your aims).
2. Ask the students to reconstruct it (useful to learn the distribution of lines according to the rhyming scheme, if that is among the objectives in your class, and to see in what way textual organization works. Remember there isn't a single "right answer" but one original and many different versions).
3. Go through Shakespeare's poem and get students to draw a list of the poetic clichés mentioned and the way in which he demystifies them: e.g. "soft, silky hair" vs. "hairs like wires"
4. Get students to generate a list of modern clichés, taking top models as a referent: bring fashion mmagazines to class and get them to cut and paste!
5. Discuss how the parameters of beauty have changed and how they are imposed.
6. Invite students to write a text in groups describing someone they admire though s/he does not fit the "model image" at all, or have a try at an "anti-love poem."
7. Discuss the possible displeasure caused by this approach itself. Students can debate whether (a) everyone has the right to respect whatever he/she chooses to respect, and (b) teachers do not have the right to impose their theoretical and possibly personal beliefs regarding the sanctity or lack of sanctity on different texts they might encounter.

When students discover that Shakespeare himself openly parodied the sentimental clichés of his time, they generally feel tempted to do the same, and they discover that great literature has a lot to do with transgression—something teenagers easily identify with! The "anti love poem" is particularly popular among teenage boys, tired of the sentimentalism of the girls in the class, who generally prefer to write sentimental poems themselves. Of course, students do not need to write poems if they don't feel like it—but they generally do, and they explore ways of using language for humorous and ironic purposes.

B. Working with Unconventional "Literary" Materials

1. Comic strips are a rich source of metaphor and a useful tool to develop cultural awareness.
2. Graffiti, at times disrespectful, can also be cleverly epigrammatic and can therefore activate interpretation skills and act as useful warm-up "anchors" to start a complex topic. So can proverbs and publicity slogans. Start collecting them! One of my teenage classes once had a lot of productive fun changing (or matching "wrongly") the second half of proverbs and writing them on a large bulletin board that they referred to as their 'graffiti wall': statements like "A rolling stone is not a beatle," "A new broom gathers no moss," or "Don't put all your eggs before the horse" led to meaningful language use (and fun!) when a "logical" interpretation had to be offered for the new proverb. Whole stories were often written to exemplify the meaning and use of a creative proverb or graffiti.
3. Rock lyrics can be highly motivating representational materials. A song that lends itself beautifully for the dramatization of implicit dialogues (a textual intervention technique which consists of getting students to imagine the conversations not developed in the song) is Billy Joel's "Piano Man." You can also ask students to write interior monologues for each of the characters in the song, and the presentation of a "typical piano bar" in the lyrics allows rich comparisons with other "typical" bars in the learners' culture, encouraging the building of intercultural bridges.

A more recent hit, Red Hot Chili Peppers' "Californication," can offer students from diverse origins the opportunity to reflect on their own perception of stereotypes and their prejudices about what it means to live in California (and on the American way of life in general). Such reading of the song, aimed at intercultural awareness, can also give rise to a productive discussion on the globalization process, the way it affects their lives and the role Hollywood movies and rock and pop music play in it, for example. (For a more detailed discussion of "rock poetry" see my article in Volume II of this Journal l—Ferradas Moi 1994—and especially Ferradas Moi 2003).

C. Getting the Canon to Meet Texts Outside It

The Truman Show (dir. Peter Weir, 1998) is a film that allows you to bring to class issues such as virtual reality, the manipulative handling of the media, and reality shows. Both the script and the film itself can be exploited as representational materials in their own right, but they can also offer interesting links into "canonical" texts such as George Orwell's novel *1984*.

Intertextual relationships between Richard Marx's Song "Hazard" and John Steibeck's *Of Mice and Men* can throw light on issues such as discrimination against the most vulnerable members of society and lead to class projects on this broad topic, which can also mean bringing more representational texts into play and encouraging students to produce their own (by using textual intervention techniques like changing the ending, omitting or adding characters or changing the plot at a crucial point and deciding on the impact of such changes on the story as a whole...).

Conclusion

It goes without saying that the activities above will need to be adapted to suit your aims and your students' needs, as well as the characteristics of the particular teaching context in which you work, but they are intended as a sample of the kind of awareness-raising that literary materials can develop in the language classroom while contributing to language acquisition. Stretching the concepts of "text" and "literature," while remembering that a text can grow with every reading, can offer attractive challenges to the imagination, empowering students both as readers and as producers of new texts and helping us teachers in our efforts to build a learner-centered classroom.

References

Bombini, G. (1989), La trama de los textos, problemas de la enseñanza de la literature, El Ouirquincho, Buenos Aires.

Brumfit, C.J. & Carter, R.A. (1986), Literature and Language Teaching, Oxford University Press, Oxford.

Ferradas Moi, C. (1994), "Rock Poetry: The Literature our Students Listen To," in the *Journal of the Imagination in Language Learning*, Volume II, New Jersey City University, Jersey City, NJ.

— (2003), Rocking the Classroom: Rock Poetry Materials in the EFL class", in Tomlinson, B. (ed.), *Issues in Developing Materials for Language Teaching*, Continuum, London and N.Y.

McRae, J. (1991), *Literature with a Small L*, Macmillan, London.

Zephaniah, B. (1992), *City Psalms*, Bloodaxe, Newcastle upon Tyne

Singing Together: Personal History in the Classroom

Sylvain Nagler and Sarah Springer

This article first appeared in All About Mentoring, *Issue 26, Fall 2003 and is under their copyright (2003). The present anthology appreciates the cooperation of the authors and of the publication.*

We came together as mentor and student, both seeking to learn more about our social conscience. Through coincidence, we learned of our common passion for folk music, especially as it is a vehicle for the expression of our political energy. What follows is our account of the impact the study's final project—compiling a musical CD—had on each of us. Nagler's description of the experience is followed by Springer's.

Sylvain Nagler

I recall with some nostalgia sitting in an undergraduate advanced psychology course being awed once again by one of my very favorite teachers. He would frequently digress from the formal syllabus and engage us in animated discussions about more personally relevant topics, a pattern that, no doubt, contributed to his popularity and which introduced me to an approach that I embrace today with considerable enthusiasm. On this particular occasion, he asked how many of us sitting in the class were considering a career in clinical psychology, and particularly preparing to be trained as psychotherapists. I joined the overwhelming majority of my fellow students and raised my hand. He announced after the count that the survey results had served to confirm his prediction. He then proceeded to challenge us to inquire into the motives that may have shaped our decisions. What emerged was, not surprisingly, a general consensus that our interest in clinical psychology was in no small way fueled by a personally compelling interest we shared to learn more about ourselves. Presumably, the hope was that our clinical psychology studies would not only train us to be psychotherapists but also indulge our wishes for self-exploration.

Sitting with a student and planning a study, I find myself returning to memories of those wonderfully illuminating classroom interludes, now more than forty years ago. Is there something to be learned from those discussions that can inform my work with students? Of course, the answer is yes. I share with you a recent encounter with a student, which I believe illustrates the connection that was, for me, such an important topic of conversation in that psychology class. The question concerned the extent to which our personal needs/wants find their way into decisions affecting our work with patients or, in our case, students. I invite you to substitute your own stories.

For much of my adult life I have struggled with what it means to develop a social conscience. I suspect there are many of you who might make a similar claim. For me, there are many facets to the question. Among the most compelling for me is: How do you go about joining feelings and theory with behavior and praxis? This is not the place to engage in greater detail about the subject. Instead, I propose to inquire into how my own personal struggle with this issue may affect the role I assume in planning learning contracts and working with my students. Given the centrality of the topic to my identity, it ought not be surprising that at times I have taken the occasion to share different aspects of that internal debate with students, sometimes in response to a point they raise, and sometimes as a point of departure to chart a direction for us to pursue. I am wary of my motives at times like this and also sensitive to what I began to learn in that psychology class. I harbor the wish that

68

my decision to extend myself in this way is born out of a pedagogical assessment that the student will benefit. While I recognize it may be quite easy to fool oneself in arriving at such a selfserving conclusion, I remain fairly secure, contending that the feedback typically has been quite positive. On the one hand, students appreciate hearing about the experiences of others, especially their teachers; and, secondly my sharing establishes a precedent for them to follow, a license, if you will, for them to probe and surface their own personal history. Given the strong emphasis I place on inviting students to find ways to join what they are studying with their own personal histories and life circumstances, this encouragement certainly serves that objective.

Pete Seeger

So, here I am meeting with Sarah. She has been referred to me because of her interest in doing a study on "Developing a Social Conscience." It is a particular treat to have students express an interest in pursuing a subject, which has a strong personal relevance for me. From my perspective, it presents an opportunity to advance my own learning, both by teaching the student and by being taught by her. Sarah has enjoyed considerable success at the college and comes highly recommended. It does not take long for me to feel comfortable with her once we begin a general conversation about what we mean by social justice and what she might wish to learn from the study. Our early discussion turns to talking about heroes and what roles they play in the framing of social values. To my delight, we shared one from the world of folk music—Pete Seeger.

Music for me, particularly political folk music, is a growing passion. I have a rather substantial collection of such music and—as I am sure is the case with many of you—have been inspired by the likes of Joan Baez; Peter, Paul and Mary; Sweet Honey in the Rock; Tommy Sands; The Weavers; and, of course, my only real hero, Pete Seeger. Most recently, I have developed a hobby of sorts making compilations of such political music, having finally acquired sufficient computer skills to burn my own CDs. It is an exciting and intriguing way for me to search into my personal politics while enjoying the lovely melodies and being stirred by the powerful lyrics that spell out a social justice agenda with which I can easily resonate. I am not a musicologist and can say very little about the music theory and the like. My connection is nearly exclusively visceral—the music makes me feel really good and inspired.

Classic Literature on Moral Development

Sarah and I begin working on designing what will be her final college study before graduation. This fact alone makes the study something special, as does her obvious commitment to making it into something personally meaningful. Other than expressing her general interest in the topic, Sarah does not propose any specific learning activities. She leaves that to me. So, I set about the process of designing an Empire State College learning contract. I reflect on my own past readings on the subject matter. I consult with colleagues who might provide additional resources. I search the Internet. These are fairly routine activities for me. In this case, my goal is to provide her with a set of readings that will familiarize her with the classic literature on moral development in works by Lawrence Kohlberg and Carol Gilligan, and personal accounts of social activism in works by Laurent Daloz and Robert Coles.

Whatever Sarah might be able to derive from the readings about the theories of moral development and social conscience building, I believe the study would be less successful if it did not in some way get linked to some sort of individual, autobiographical analysis as well. What can Sarah learn about Sarah's social conscience? How does she define it? How did this definition evolve? Where might it take her? In the course of our early conversation, I refer to my own history as one instance for her to examine in considering her own. In telling my story, I hope to encourage her to probe her own. I am aware of the danger in pursuing this approach because it does serve to lead the student, to focus her compass in a direction that falls into place for the teacher, but perhaps not necessarily for the student. As noted above, choosing to be trained as a clinical psychologist was not only a route to learn how to help others, but an avenue to learn more about myself. Is there a parallel in my encouraging Sarah to narrow her interests to ones that fit in comfortably with my own?

In the course of a subsequent conversation, I tell Sarah about my new passion for burning CDs, my love of folk music and what it represents, and how it has moved and excited me. I imagine out loud to her what it is like for me to burn a CD that captures some core feelings about matters of social justice and activism. I keep reminding myself to remain conscious of the power and authority I have in this engagement and how easily I can exploit Sarah into doing what I would like to do, were I in her place. In fact, this dilemma is not really all that different from the one confronting classroom instructors who must also ask themselves whether the materials and assignments they have set in front of their students are not only what they believe are the essential contents of the subject matter but nuanced to integrate their values and the place they would like their students to end up. So at least I am not alone.

A Final Project

With these issues in my mind, I invite Sarah to contemplate undertaking a final project that she might find personally meaningful and informative. How about burning your own CD, Sarah? I now had some direct experience with such a project myself. I share with her how in compiling my favorites, I weighed the relative power of the lyrics and the pull of the melodies. Beyond the aesthetic pleasures I derived, the process of making the selections brought with it a rekindling of personal memories, as I worked to make the connection to the first time I heard the piece or to a particular period or events with which I associated it. When I share the prospect of undertaking a similar venture with Sarah, she seems quite excited. I lend her several of my collections to provide a model for what I have in mind. I choose not to engage in any personal analysis of the individual selections or the nostalgia that I associate with them. We agree that she will have the freedom to select her own criteria to determine the selections, and that a significant component of her work will be to surface the reasoning that shaped her decisions.

I leave it to Sarah to share her recollections of the project. For me, the activity was a wonderfully rewarding one. As I retrospectively assess the experience, I feel a bit exploitative in that I derived so much pleasure from her project. I wonder whether that can legitimately be a reasonable and justifiable outcome of our professional work. I am reminded of the star athletes who wonder why they are being paid for doing what they so enjoy and which they would gladly do for no compensation save the personal satisfaction. Sarah's project has emboldened me to continue making such collections and I remain more open to encouraging other students with similar interests to undertake a comparable adventure. Music, for me, is a powerful expression in its poetry and in the force of its melodies, which get you to sing along. I feel extremely fortunate that I had the opportunity to apply it in working with Sarah, and I am grateful for having this opportunity to thank her for the partnership.

Sarah Springer

Throughout my studies at Empire State College, I have utilized a variety of instructional approaches. My degree is a Bachelor's of Science in human services with a concentration that I called families and children's services. Study groups were, initially, my instruction of choice because I always enjoyed having other students with whom to discuss the issues of the study. I did take several courses through the SUNY (State University of New York) Learning Network when my home schedule demanded the presence of two parents on a consistent basis. Prior to signing my learning contract for the independent study titled "Developing a Social Conscience," I had only one other experience in an independent study and I did not enjoy it. This independent study was the final course of my degree plan. I was eager to be finished. Of course, I had no way of realizing that this study was going to have such a powerful impact on me.

For an opening discussion topic, Sylvain chose the concept of heroes. To be asked who my hero was (and why), and then to be told to go home and take a survey of family members and friends and ask them who their heroes were, was quite an eye opener. After only a moment of contemplation, I said my hero was my father. Sylvain mentioned Pete Seeger as someone he respected. This led to the subject of music and then to the idea of having as a final project a musical compilation. Because I grew up with music as a central part of my life, I was very excited to have a musical collection as a final project. But to continue to explain the powerful impact this study had on me, I need to digress and explain my background.

Growing up Catholic and in a very large family in the '70s were two major influences that shaped my personality. Being a Catholic was not just a religion: it was a way of life for us. As children, we were instilled with a deep sense of right and wrong. As we were being brought up, being "Christ-like" was the goal for all of us. Music also played a central part in our household. Folk music, mixed with some Irish and religious music, made for an eclectic mix. The Chad Mitchell Trio, The Kingston Trio, the Clancy Brothers, and Tommy Makum were my personal favorites. The importance of music to my parents was linked to the time they came of age. They were raising a family during the Vietnam era and the time of the civil rights movement. I know these issues shaped their choices and consequently shaped ours. We have always been a close family, and despite the physical miles between my parents and me, we still remain close. As my husband and I go through the daily process of raising three middle-school aged children, we are trying to instill in them the same values and moral/social conscience that was instilled in us.

Heroes in the Wake of 9/11

As I look back on this tutorial and the impact it had on me, I think of several parallel lines running together. The initial concept of heroes and what they mean to me and to my family was timely in the wake of 9/11. Forefront in the media and, therefore, in our minds are the heroes, both dead and alive, of 9/11. I see the topic of heroes addressed in classroom assignments within the school system. I hear the term heroes used in songs on the radio. We all see the latest books on heroes in the bookstores. Thus, when Sylvain introduced the topic of heroes, I couldn't help but think of the parallel lines to current social issues. It was during my initial discussion with him that I realized that I held my father as my hero. My father is a kind and generous man, totally unselfish, with a very dry wit. He is well educated and instilled in us a deep belief in education, pushing all six of his children to get a college education. He has democratic ideals combined with stiff Catholic values. I admire his political savvy, and throughout working with Sylvain, I spoke with my father frequently and discussed many of my readings and assignments. During the entire time frame that I was meeting with Sylvain, my father was going through an intensive ten-week rehabilitation for the blind through the Veterans Hospital in West Palm Beach, Florida (my father suffers from macular degeneration and is totally blind). Being without my mother for that length of time as well as suffering the limitations of his disability was a discouraging time for him. We both agreed that our weekly political and social discussions were meaningful as well as delightful. Another strong connection was the fact that when I asked my father who his hero was, he replied that the word "hero" was not in his lexicon. However, he greatly admires Dorothy Day. Having never heard of Dorothy Day, I received quite the education about her when my first text assignment for "social development" was to read Robert Coles' book, *The Call of Service: A Witness to Idealism*. Coles describes his father's and, consequently, his own relationship with Dorothy Day and the concept of social conscience and of good deeds.

As Sylvain and I met and discussed the concept of developing a social conscience, he assigned the next reading, *Common Fire: Lives of Commitment in a Complex World* by Daloz, Keen, Keen and Parks. Through this reading, attending the Northeast Center's teach-in, "Commitment, Compassion and Community," and speaking with both of my parents, I came to realize (or perhaps remember) that the concept of commitment to your community comes to me quite naturally. Listening to Mentor Karen Pass speak at the teach-in on "Developing a Social Conscience: The Need to be Involved," brought to the surface the memories of my parents volunteering at the soup kitchens in downtown Cleveland. Another memory I uncovered was the fact that it was my mother and the Baptist minister who started the food pantry in our hometown. It was a purely volunteer effort that started with my mother, as a representative from the Catholic parish, and the Baptist minister working to collect food and some monetary donations to feed people in need within our community. I was a teenager poised on leaving home when my mother first started this endeavor. Listening to her tell of the efforts and time involved with this commitment made me realize that my social conscience was not taught to me by the schools or by my church, but was nurtured by my parents. Their words and action provided me with a good base for having a strong social conscience. Working with Sylvain was tapping that base and bringing it to the forefront.

The final connection with this study was the timing of the final project, which occurred at the same time as the war in Iraq. Social activism and social conscience were not just words anymore. They were the news on a daily basis. Protests against the war and against the government were becoming very common. The music of my youth was coming full circle. It was all pertinent to today's political situation. I retrieved some old albums from my parents and my siblings, and began listening to all the anti-war and protest songs I had known. I spoke with relatives and friends, taking polls and hearing opinions on anti-war songs, then and now.

The Final Project

It took me months to listen, gather, sort through, and choose the final music for my CD. It was intense and emotional work. The original list of songs for this project numbered 43. They included songs about the Cuban uprising, the Mexican revolution, strife in Australia, and the Cold War. I had enough music for two CDs! I learned that many contemporary artists have been inspired, and indeed, learned their trade from the likes of Pete Seeger and Woody Guthrie. The main topics of these songs, new or old, revolve around politics and human suffering. Political instability and human suffering are old issues that are revisited time and again. The artists are reacting to these issues and using music to speak out. When push came to shove and I had to make my decisions on what songs to include, I used a combination of new and old to reflect my favorites and to communicate the moral energy I thought the artist was trying to convey. To make the cut and be on the CD, I felt the music and the words had to make a connection to me and to my thoughts about social activism and what it means to have a social conscience. I came to realize that the music I listened to as a child was grounded in political and social activism and was pertinent today! The majority of the songs were anti-war/anti-Vietnam songs and some were freedom songs. This was certainly a labor of love because music was and is such a large part of my life.

The Meaning of Music

Music cuts across all generations and lifestyles. It has the ability to reach both children and adults. It has long been a favorite of preschool and primary teachers as a medium for teaching. For a professor of undergraduates to use music may be a novel idea, but it certainly was a learning and remembering experience for me. History has a way of repeating itself. The political events of the past year and half are coming full circle to another grand scale global event. I wanted the listeners of my CD to feel the sorrow, the anger, and perhaps the guilt associated with the past and to try not to let history repeat itself through the actions of our current president and his administration. Will other students feel the same as I did about music and its connection to social conscience? I think the answer is yes. Political songs and social conscience have gone hand in hand for years. African Americans have their roots in songs about freedom from slavery. High profile artists have used their talents for years to get their message out to the common man. Take the Dixie Chicks as a case in point. What Natalie said was disrespectful to the President, but it was what she felt. It wasn't about being from Texas. It was about her stance on the impending war and the reaction from the group's European audiences about America and the coming conflict.

This musical project, along with this whole tutorial, was for me, an awakening to my past and an inspiration to my future. It brought full circle all my previous readings on families and children and how they apply to the broad area of the human services. I intend to use what I have learned and remembered to pass along to my children. Shaping their social conscience and making them aware of the world outside East Nassau and New York is my goal. Sylvain happened to hit a nerve with me with music. I encourage him and all mentors to use this method of teaching. Do I feel exploited or influenced by Sylvain's choice of music and methods of teaching? Absolutely not! I feel all professors, to a degree, use their own favorite methods or mediums of learning in their course work. But the beauty of learning lies in the diversity of the teachings.

Deconstructing the Essay to Beethoven's "Pathetique"

Ninah Beliavsky

What's an essay? What's in an essay? What is a living essay? How do you explain to your students that the form of an essay does not have to be static; that it is a living, breathing creation with feelings, emotions, opinions; that it is not two-dimensional but has a heartbeat. How do you transcend the typical explanation that an essay is built vertically, having a flat representation made out of triangles and rectangles? Can you get away from using these triangles and rectangles? If we appeal to our multiple intelligences (Gardner), if we appeal to artistic and creative experiences, and if we venture into the wealth of the creations that are out there—we will notice numerous similarities among all the arts. We can then draw parallels between the disciplines and broaden our students' views and knowledge. After all, art, music and literature are intertwined at the core of their existence. There is a strong connection between music, art and writing; between a literary composition and classical music; between an essay and a classical sonata. Music is communication from our souls. Music has a miraculous effect on our minds, on our psyche. Music excites, motivates and speaks to us by striking a chord in our hearts and in our intellect.

High Value of Structure

By realizing this interconnection we can help students make associations between one form and another, between patterns, cycles, traditions, movements, expressions—be they political, scientific, mathematical, artistic or musical. It seems that after all we do tend to feel more comfortable with forms and organized patterns and cycles, and the form that is most comforting and pleasing to us is one which has a beginning, middle and end as in a cycle of life or as in a journey. We leave our home, then explore, develop, experience, learn, grow, enjoy; at the end, however, we want to return home again. This journey can be compared to dance choreography, a story, an essay or a melody. If we listen to a melody, or more broadly to a classical musical composition, we can find a similar organization of musical ideas or themes. In the case of a classical sonata we have a similar form. We start in a "home key," travel to other keys, more and more distant, but at the end we return to the home (original) key (Brin). In classical tonality, a key progression follows a specific order—and I believe that this pattern or form gives us a sense of comfort, tranquility, and a feeling of structure which western society so treasures and seeks to accomplish. We don't like chaos. We think in cycles. We cherish traditions. We like organization, structure, order and form. We like to follow logical progressions—those that we consider logical—and classical music provides us with this indisputably logical form. Traditional classical sonatas achieve this logic because they seek to coherently organize the cycle of movements.

Essay and Sonata-Similarity in Form

The sonata usually consists of a number of movements. The first movement of a classical sonata is most often in sonata-allegro form. This musical form or story consists of three sections: exposition, development and recapitulation. During the exposition, two contrasting ideas, melodies or themes are introduced. While the first theme is in the home key (the tonic), the second theme almost always will move to a different key (the dominant). Both themes are often treated as material from which subsequent material emerges and develops. During the development, the themes appear in various keys and new material is introduced. The development contains the climax of the form, and the moment of greatest tension and energy usually occurs just before the end of the development. Usually, the moment the first and second themes are heard again in the home key marks the beginning of the recapitulation or the return. The recapitulation tends not to introduce new ideas and brings the movement to a close (Beliavsky, D.). This gives the listener the feeling of having returned home after a long journey (Brin). So it seems that overall the sonata's form corresponds to an essay's form. The introduction with its thesis statement expresses ideas that will be developed later in the body paragraphs. The body contains the force of an argument with the most interesting and important information at the end of the development. The conclusion may raise ideas or recommendations, but it should not bring up new ideas. And while the conclusion restates some if not all of the introduction, it also strengthens the ideas generated by the body paragraphs and "escorts" the essay to its end.

Reason and Writing

Two hundred years ago in 1799, the German philosopher Freidrich Schlagel wrote that pure instrumental music creates its own text, and that the theme is developed, confirmed, varied and contrasted in the same way as the object of meditation in a philosophical series of ideas (Rosen, 73). Charles Rosen, an American pianist and musicologist, states that Schlagel's observation is directly inspired by late 18th century sonata style. In other words, music has a particular significance and makes sense in some of the same ways as language does. I would certainly agree with Rosen's interpretation of Schlagel's statement that this also makes music "an abstract model for thought, a structure that underlies logic and language, a form of pure reason that precedes language, if such a thing may be said to exist…[We] can see how sonata form came eventually to seem so fundamental a pattern, as if it contained the basic elements of reason…" (Rosen, 73).

In the late 18th century, Samuel Taylor Coolridge, a British poet, compared instrumental music to a historical process, and a few years later the historiographer J.G. Droysen also suggested that the writing of history is "a formal procedure, not a simple setting down of fact or reflection of reality; a history of a Reformation for example, was like a novel by Sir Walter Scott, with a clear beginning, middle and end…" (Rosen, 74). As we can hear the rhythm in poetry, through music one can hear the rhythm of an essay. I believe that this is a unique way to "hear" a piece of literary writing. Music can tell a story with its own form and musical language just like the essay can tell a story with its own appropriate form and language. Therefore, the analogy to music with its contrasting themes, development, climax, and recapitulation can help the writer in the creative process when writing the essay.

Methodology in the Classroom

So what do I do in the classroom? I begin by introducing the structure of an essay. We dissect the essay into its constituents—the introduction with its thesis statement; the body with its topic sentences; and the conclusion. We talk about the structure and the function of each constituent. The students have to identify these different parts in model essays, and then practice writing adhering to the form and editing their own work and the work of their peers. I then ask the students to think of anything at all that might have a similar form or pattern as the essay. I often get various interesting responses from my students. One student compared an essay to an athletic event where the athlete needs to warm up (introduction), then compete (body), and finally cool down (conclusion). Another student thought of a love affair where one meets a person (introduction), develops the relationship in more depth (body), and finally needs to make a decision whether to continue or move on to a different relationship (conclusion). Another student compared an essay to having a dinner beginning with appetizers (introduction), continuing with a main course (body), and finally eating dessert (conclusion). Many of these analogies are very interesting and creative. However, I believe that none of them capture the essence or the rhythm of a creative essay. These comparisons are two-dimensional.

Writing with a Pulse

I want to teach my students that their essay, in addition to having a correct form, needs to make an impact and a lasting impression on their reader—just as music touches the listeners' very soul. I tell my students that their essay needs to be three-dimensional, that it needs to have a pulse. At this time I introduce the notion that we can compare the essay to a piece of music, specifically to a classical sonata. Many sonatas (1st movements) can be brought into the classroom, such as Mozart's *Sonata K. 330* in C Major, Haydn's *Concerto in D Major* and Beethoven's *Symphony No. 5*. We will listen to a sonata I have chosen for class demonstration. Beethoven's *Pathetique* (Sonata No. 8 in C Minor, Opus 13) is a very good example because its first movement is in a clear sonata-allegro form, and it is short enough for class time. Even non-musicians will be able to distinguish between the introduction/exposition, body/development and conclusion/recapitulation. Most importantly students will be able to hear and feel the internal pulse and the story with its mood and climax. I will play the music several times and ask my students what they think are the different parts. I then play it again, pause the CD, and identify the exposition, the development and the recapitulation. I will ask the students how this music makes them feel, what they think is the story behind the music, whether it goes with the title and whether it fits with the life of the composer. We will talk about Beethoven and his tragic life of deafness. Once we analyze the music by discussing its subparts, mood and rhythm, we will make the comparison to an essay. We will read several model essays while listening to the music and focus on the thesis in terms of the musical themes; on the body paragraphs with the most important information at the end as the climax; and the conclusion with its afterthoughts as the recapitulation with its coda (See Appendix A).

Journal Entries

At the end of this unit I will ask my students to write a journal entry summarizing what they learned in class. This is their response to the lesson, in which they can agree, disagree, compare and expand on the ideas brought up in class. The following are excerpts from students' journals:

A. "I think that writing as well as music has the same pattern of life and today's lecture makes me feel what writing is."

B. "Once I was surprised at the fact that most composers do their work through some formal rules not only through inspiration. Similarly, most writers do that. In addition, I think about the power of music and writing that can change people's emotion. Both music and writing make people feel and think something…Sonata composition and writing essay have similar structure and similar influence in people's heart. I think that our life is also like that. Our life has its own theme or thesis and we develop it and reap the fruits of our behavior."

C. "This class makes me more understand both music and essay. This is a wonderful last class of the semester I ever have…"

The students will share their journals in small groups before writing a creative composition comparing the essay to a sonata. The ideas may vary but need to echo our class discussion. The rhetorical focus will depend on the thesis the student chooses; the patterns of organization could include a compare/contrast essay or an argumentative essay. The discussion and analysis of music and its comparison to a written composition lends itself to various other types of creative writing assignments. For example, as the students listen to the music, they are asked to make brief notes for either a fiction or a non-fictional story which they will expand and complete later in class or at home. My students enjoy this assignment because it unleashes their imagination, allows them to experiment with the English language and create their own unique style (See Appendix B for samples of student writing). From this point forward, every time my students write an essay, I will remind them of its creative nature, of its format—its exposition, development, climax and recapitulation, and of the importance of listening to their essay and making sure that it has a rhythm and a pulse.

Notes:

- In the 16th century many terms were used for instrumental pieces, one of which was Sonata, meaning that something was played or sounded as opposed to something sung (cantata).
- A classical sonata is usually a work in several movements, for a soloist or a small ensemble.
- The Sonata form is one of the great accomplishments of western art music. While it has no single starting point, it began in the Baroque era (~1600-1750) and crystallized in the classical era—2nd half of the 18th century—with Mozart, Haydn and later with Beethoven. (Boynick, M.)
- Sonata form, with its great potential for musical expression, has appealed to composers from the time of its birth well into the modern era. Composers of Romantic and Modern eras continued to develop the form and to use it as a vehicle for personal expression (Brin, D. M.)
- Between 1750-1897, Haydn, Mozart and Beethoven composed over 150 symphonies, over 100 piano sonatas, over 50 string quartets, and many concertos—all in sonata form. These works form the core of the classical repertoire. (For a short history of the Sonata, visit www.classicalworks.com)

Appendix A

"Deconstructing the Essay to Beethoven's *Pathetique*" (op 13, C minor)

ESSAY	SONATA
Exposition Introduction	Climax = point of highest tension Recapitulation Conclusion

INTRODUCTION	EXPOSITION
May provide background information to the topic	An opening may contain background information for the exposition – called the introduction.
Introduces the topic and the controlling idea	The introduction is common but not required. It is the setting of the musical material for the rest of the piece
Should indicate how the topic is going to be developed and organized	The exposition contains two contrasting themes 1 & 2; two different melodies
Should progress from general to specific	The two contrasting themes may be "loud or soft," "masculine or feminine," "virtuosic of more romantic."
Like the lens of a camera moving in for a close up picture—each sentence becomes more focused.	The two contrasting themes create *tension* or musical interest that drives the music forward
Includes the *Thesis Statement* (TS) which contains an expression of attitude opinion, or idea about the topic. It clarifies the purpose of the essay.	Both themes are often treated as the material from which subsequent material emerges and develops.
Should be inviting and interesting	These two themes are the building blocks of the sonata and the tension is the argument.

"Deconstructing the Essay to Beethoven's *Pathetique*" (op 13, C minor)

ESSAY DEVELOPMENT	SONATA DEVELOPMENT
The Body paragraphs are the heart of the essay – they have to explain, illustrate, discuss, argue, and prove the Thesis development	The original two themes are manipulated in a number of ways throughout the development in order to biuild to the climax.
Each paragraph should have a main idea or a Topic Sentence.	They may be fragmented, rhythmically and melodically altered, and combined.
Each body paragraph discusses one aspect of the main topic.	In other words, whatever tensions exists between these two themes are worked out to express their inherent drama.
The controlling idea should echo the controlling idea in the Thesis Statement.	In such a way this part is perhaps the most dramatic and carefully detailed section of the sonata.
Develops various aspects of the topic and the central idea.	This part contains the climax of the form.
May discuss causes, effects, reasons, examples, points comparison and contrast, description or narration.	The moment of greatest tension and energy occurs just before the end of the development.
Most interesting and important material is placed in the end.	

"Deconstructing the Essay to Beethoven's *Pathetique*" (op 13, C minor)

ESSAY CONCLUSION	SONATA RECAPITULATION
Brings the development to a logical end.	Marks a return to expository material and brings the movement to a close.
Restates main points.	The tension is resolved.
May restate the Thesis Statement in different words.	Usually does not introduce new ideas or themes.
Should not bring up a new topic.	May contain a *coda* or an afterthough in which introductory material is again restated, this time with enough concluding force to definitely mark the end of the movement. The coda may be separated by silence from everything else for emphasis. (Coda = Italian for close)
May raise ideas, recommendations, and/or questions for further research.	

Appendix B

1. Comparison Contrast

There are similar aspects between the essay and the sonata. They have the same order related to their function. The essay has the introductory paragraph, body paragraphs and the conclusion. Also, the sonata has the exposition, same as introduction, development instead of body, and recapitulation for conclusion.

Another similarity is that they are both imaginary works. The essay is writing about one's opinion, concerned with the certain subject. It is the same as the essay that the sonata is composing about one's feeling connected with some situations.

The final resemblance is that they have special terms. The essay is a type that has a different way to illustrate one's suggesting. In an essay, one can use metaphor, irony, anecdote, fact, fiction, etc. However, the sonata is a genre which has another method to express one's feeling. To compose a sonata a composer uses many techniques, such as forte, andante, allegro and staccato. Using these methods, a composer can make his music various.

In conclusion, the essay and the sonata have several similarities, such as the same system, imagination and having their own vocabulary.

Young Mee, Lee

2. The three parts of the sonata make me think of…

The first part of the music Pathetique is fast and strong enough to recall my teenage life to my mind. At that time I missed someone while I didn't know whom I missed. I wanted to spend all my energy on love and doing something worthy while I didn't know what I really wanted to do. Also I thought that there is somewhere in the world there should be a blue bird or rainbow even though I didn't where the bluebird was. My teenagehood was filled with passion, challenge and frustration. I thought that I could do everything if I decided to do it. There was meaningless sadness when it was raining outside. I wandered in the rain while I did not know where I have to go. I liked sad songs rather than fast dancing music.

However, while I listen to the slow and peaceful second part of the music I can recall a thought which I could get after long and hard journeys. After several times of trials I realized that life is not easy, and life can't be filled with perfect happiness or total sadness. Also, I can control only the present; past and future are not in my hands. Past and future is just a shapeless shadow of my frustration or dream. I can do only small amount of jobs within a day. And very sadly, I realized that it is life.

In contrast, the last part of the steady and peaceful rhythm looks like having similar ideas to my recent thought; still I can do everything if I do small things continuously. My frustration is not heartbreak anymore. It is the best soil to raise my love toward others who are suffering. Now I am learning pharmacy for the purpose of helping patients with all my heart. I get the big picture about the questions that I had in teenage life. Furthermore, my answering to details which are happening to me every day is still an will be going on until I die. I know there will be still affliction for many things but there also will be God's blessing and love, which is enough to overcome the coming suffering, enough to make my mind peaceful, and enough to give my peace to others.

I think that writing as well as music has the same pattern of life, and today's lecture makes me feel what writing is.

Jong Hoon

3. A fictional story influenced by the music

Sadness of Love

Sometimes love can hurt a heart of young people. In case that the young person is an ordinary man and not a rich person, but his lover is a lady from a higher class, the anguish of love will become bigger and worse. There is a sad story about a young man.

They met each other by chance at a dance party in the biggest house in a town. He was a poor musician playing the piano at the party and she was a daughter of the lord of thebig house. She was so beautiful that he fell in love with her and first sight. Later, he could easily meet her at the other parties held in the houses of the rich. One day the brave lad mad his mind to confess his love to the lass.

He ran out to the field and breathed the fresh air and went down into the brook to see his figure in the water. His face reflected from the water and looked nice enough to lure the young lady. On his way home he smiled with imagination of dancing with her at a party. from that day on, his life was filled with vigor and strength. But the day of confession came near, his heart and emotions were fluctuating from anticipations and anxieties. Whenever he thought about a confession, he said to himself "what happens if she refuses to my confession of love? What shall I say or show to her parents or families if they asked me about my future?"

One night, he was invited to a party and met her there when he was playing the piano. But surprisingly, she came in the ballroom with her fiancé to dance with him. Beside them, there parents and families were standing to celebrate their engagement!

At that moment, his heart throbbed violently and he could not breathe. Instantly he became sad. Even though he was playing fast music for celebrating their engagement, he felt grief. Only his music could console him.

Joon Seok Bang

References

Beliavsky, Daniel, April 2002, History of the Sonata, Musical forms, personal conversations.

Boynick, Matt, October 2000, Musical forms, Sonata, w3.rz-berlin.mpg

Brin, David, M., A little history of the sonata, www.classicalworks.com

— Classical musical forms, www.kdfc.com

Gardner, Howard, 1973, *Multiple Intelligences, the Theory in Practice*, Basic Books.

Gardner, Howard, 1983, *Frames of Mind, the Theory*, Basic Books.

Kadesch, M.C., Kolba, E.D., Crowell, S.C., 1991, *Insights into Academic Writing, Strategies for Advanced Students*, Longman

Lane, J., Lange, E., 1999, *Writing Clearly, an Editing Guide, 2nd Edition*, Heinle & Heinle

Macdonald, A., Macdonald, G., 1996, *Mastering Writing Essentials*, Longman

Oshima, A., Hogue, A., 1997, *Introduction to Academic Writing, 2nd Edition*, Longman

Reid, Joy, H., 1988, *The Process of Composition, 2nd Edition*, Prentice Hall

Rosen, Charles, 1995, *Romantic Generations*, Harvard University Press

Smalley, L.R., & Ruetten, K. M., 2000, *Refining Composition Skills, 5th Edition*, Heinle & Heinle

Solomon, Maynard, 1977, *Beethoven*, Schirmer Books, Prentice Hall

Morphic Resonance: An Interview with Rupert Sheldrake

Kevin Gaudette

Editor's Note: *The relation between the imagination and morphic resonance would be, in part, derivative: that is, the imagination would be a manifestation of morphic resonance. Many reactions to this article will be "Waste of time" and "Nonsense". The theory of morphic resonance might well be just that. If, however, it should prove more substantial, present readers will have had a chance to think about its relevance to language learning and to the development of new methodology.*

*All Truth goes through three stages, First it is ridiculed.
Then it is violently opposed. Finally it is accepted as self-evident.*
SCHOPENHAUER

In his pioneering work as a biologist, Dr. Rupert Sheldrake has already experienced all three stages that Shopenhauer points out. A Google Web search on <Rupert Sheldrake ridiculed> will give over 200 URLs, generally by Sheldrake supporters demonstrating the weaknesses in the arguments typically used against unconventional theories such as Sheldrake's. When his book *A New Science of Life*, with its revolutionary theory of morphic resonance, was published in 1981, the editor of *Nature* magazine, John Maddox, ran an editorial calling for the book to be burned—a sure sign that Sheldrake may be onto something important, many think. It is a strange aspect of science in the twentieth century that while physics has had to submit to the indignity of a principle of uncertainty and physicists have become accustomed to such strange entities as matter-waves and virtual particles, many of their colleagues down the corridor in the Biology Department, or in the School of Education, seem not to have noticed the revolution of quantum electrodynamics. As far as many biologists are concerned, matter is made of billiard balls which collide with Newtonian certainty, and these biologists carry on building molecular models made out of colored ping-pong balls.

Dr. Sheldrake's research is based upon a more dynamic hypothesis. Since writing *A New Science of Life* at a Benedictine Catholic ashram in India, his aim has been to try to find a wider paradigm for science—one that is not constricted to an inanimate, mechanistic view of things. As Sheldrake states: "In a way, the bigger picture is the idea of the whole universe as a living organism." Of particular relevance for educators, Sheldrake's research has supported the hypothesis that organisms—including individuals/groups/nations/the planet/the universe—all share a non-material basis for memory, a field of information, unlimited by space or time, called "morphic resonance." Chomsky proposed the LAD–Language Acquisition Device. Bruner proposed the LASS–Language Acquisition Support System. Sheldrake's theory proposes the language acquisition morphic resonance: "In the transmission of ideas or forms…by morphic resonance, there are two things. One is the number of people who do it or the number of times it's being done, and then there must be some variable of intensity"

While many biologists continue to ridicule and violently oppose Sheldrake's concepts of morphic fields and morphic resonance, many quantum physicists are closer to Stage 3 of Schopenhauer: "Finally it is accepted as self-evident" As Theoretical Physicist Amit Goswami, a Fellow at the Institute of Noetic Sciences, states: "I think that Sheldrake's theory of formative causation via morphic fields and morphic resonance will go down in history as a bold departure in the right direction in that he introduced many of the right elements—downward causation, purpose, and non-locality—in his theory. Because of its bold initiative, Sheldrake's theory inspired many scientists (including this author) to investigate similar ideas in other fields." Physicist David Bohm shares Sheldrake's morphic perspective: "…the energies involved in M-fields may be very similar to the energies that allow subatomic particles to communicate nonlocally, regardless of space and time...on some level that is beyond ordinary subjective experience, the human race may really be one organism."

Princeton University's Global Consciousness Project, self-described as "registering coherence and resonance in the world," uses random number generators around the planet to examine subtle correlations that appear to reflect the presence and activity of consciousness in the world. The researchers at Princeton have found that powerful media events such as the death of Princess Diana and the 9/11 terrorism tragedy have produced statistically significant coherence in the random number generators. A strange anomaly is the fact that the random number generators registered significant coherence several hours before the first 9/11 catastrophe. "Significant" in terms of statistics means that a particular phenomenon can not be ascribed to chance.

This Sheldrake article is presented in the hope that more scientists/teachers/artists in the field of education will investigate and experiment with the concepts of the morphic fields and morphic resonance. Relevant are the words of Sir Roger Penrose, specialist in the field of mathematical physics, author of the co-author of Penrose-Hawking singularity theorems and author of the "cosmic censorship hypothesis":

A scientific world-view which does not profoundly come to terms with the problem of conscious minds can have no serious pretensions of completeness. Consciousness is part of our universe, so any physical theory which makes no proper place for it falls fundamentally short of providing a genuine description of the world.

Interview

GAUDETTE: Dr. Sheldrake, you have stated: The key concept of morphic resonance is that similar things influence similar things across both space and time. The amount of influence depends on the degree of similarity. Here in East Asia, the highly cohesive cultures of China, Korea and Japan and have placed great emphasis and resources upon the development of English language skills, often using outmoded and boring methods/materials, based upon mechanistic concepts of behaviorism. In China, Korea and Japan, the results—in terms of conversation and listening skills—continue to be quite poor. Many students—and teachers—are traumatized by the process. Is it possible that the uncomfortable experiences of these hundreds of millions of English students are creating a dysfunctional morphic resonance and a fossilization of errors, which can negatively influence the conversation and listening skills of current and present generations, unless an alternative, more coherent, morphic resonance is developed?

SHELDRAKE: It seems to me quite possible that the uncomfortable experiences of large numbers of English students would be propagated by morphic resonance, including the fossilisation of errors, with a negative effect on the way people learn. If an alternative method could be developed, this would obviously be desirable from every point of view.

GAUDETTE: Could you describe what might be some of the morphic dynamics involved in the development of an English-learning morphic resonance on a mass scale in such highly cohesive societies as China, Korea and Japan?

SHELDRAKE: I have no personal experience of teaching English as a foreign language so can't make any specific practical suggestions. However, the basic principle of morphic resonance is, as the name implies, resonance. If one wants to resonate to people who speak a language, the best way to do that is by listening and by speaking, not by studying grammar in textbooks. That is not how English babies learn English. They just pick it up quite effortlessly by hearing it and by making sounds and gradually learning to speak it. The grammar is also learned implicitly. As people learn to pick up English by morphic resonance, it would facilitate this learning process to others. If I were doing research on developing effective methods, the first thing I would do is compare existing ones. Already the learning by listening and speaking method exists, of course. and was used widely in language laboratories 30 years ago or more. I don't know if there are any formal studies on the effectiveness of that method compared with the standard textbook teaching. There are also intensive immersion methods, including the Suggestopedia method, which claim to be effective in teaching languages such as Spanish. Then of course there is the simple expedient of putting people in circumstances when they have to speak the language, as when English children go on foreign exchanges to France or Germany and live in a family that doesn't speak English. Perhaps you have already compared these kinds of approaches to see which are the most effective. However, it seems to be the case that most language teaching is not based on particular effective methods. My own two sons, who are at secondary school, have learnt French in school for many years and yet cannot speak it and have little interest or motivation to do so. It is taught out of textbooks in a completely artificial way that bears no relation to the way French people learn to speak it themselves. And a standard teacher with modern languages in England seems to be based on these ineffective principles. One result is that the number of people studying modern languages at school and university is dropping dramatically. So here there seems to be a similar experience to the hundreds of millions of Asians who've learned in dysfunctional ways.

GAUDETTE: With the cooperation of BBC TV (see Appendix), you have developed unique international learning experiments, using specially-designed TV programs, which have demonstrated your morphic resonance hypothesis. Could you describe some of the morphic dynamics which might be involved in the use of TV for the cultivation of mass morphic resonance in areas such as creativity scores, as measured by Torrance Test of Creative Thinking? (See Appendix)

SHELDRAKE: I have not experience of the TTCT test so can't comment on it. I think morphic resonance should effect people's performance on any standardised test, and if many people take the same test, it should get easier to do because others have done before them. I think this is the basis of the Flynn effect, whereby IQ scores have been rising over the last few decades. This rise has occurred all over the world. It has not happened because people are getting more intelligent, but simply because they seem to be better at doing standard intelligence tests. I suspect this is because of morphic resonance from all those who have done them before.

Experiments using TV provide a way of bringing about rapid learning in many people which is useful from the point of view of morphic resonance experiments. In my own TV tests, the learning consisted of spotting a hidden picture. Once people had spotted it, they immediately recognise it. It should be possible to set up similar experiments on the internet. My elder son thought of an idea for a morphic resonance test which would in principle be relatively easy to do, although in practice would be hard to organise. When he and his friends were doing the GCSE examinations last year they thought of a way of benefiting from morphic resonance. In the physics and maths papers, for example, they did the last two questions first, and then went to questions 1, 2, 3, etc. This way, it meant that when they did most of the questions, they were about ten or fifteen minutes behind many thousands of other children and could therefore have been boosted by morphic resonance from their answers to the questions. If it were possible to persuade the examination authorities to send out a minority of papers with their questions in a different order, with the last two questions first, it should be possible to see whether, on average, people do better when they are answering questions after others have already answered them.

In learning of physical skills, I think morphic resonance automatically plays a part. For example in learning to play tennis, or ping pong, or to ride a bicycle the only way to learn is by doing it, and by copying others who know how, thus setting up resonance conditions. It would not be possible to learn these skills by sitting in a classroom reading a textbook. So practical learning is already morphic resonance assisted. I wish you luck in developing a better system.

Incidentally, I spoke at a conference in Liverpool last week organised by SEAL, the Society for Effective Affective Learning. Some of the people there were teachers of English as a foreign language and claimed to have developed a much more effective new system. The main person I talked to about this is called Hugh L'Estrange.

References
Sheldrake-Related Websites

http://www.sheldrake.org

Description of the Sheldrake/BBC TV Experiments
http://www.context.org/ICLIB/IC12/Sheldrak.htm

Sheldrake on the Morphic Resonance of the English language
http://www.hootenanny.com/hoot/3/sheldrake.html

Transcript from TV Interview/Discussion
http://www.intuition.org/txt/sheldrak.htm

Discussion with Theologian Matthew Fox
http://www.resurgence.org/resurgence/articles/fox.htm

Dr. Sheldrake and other leading scientists each answer the question: "What do you believe is true even though you cannot prove it?"
http://www.edge.org/q2005/q05_print.html

A Quantum Explanation of Sheldrake's Morphic Resonance—Prof. Amit Goswami
http://www.swcp.com/~hswift/swc/Essays/Sheldrake.html
http://www.findarticles.com/p/articles/mi_m1511/is_8_21/ai_63583788/pg_3
http://fusionanomaly.net/rupertsheldrake.html
http://www.primalspirit.com/pr1_1sheldrake_nature_as_alive.htm
http://www.theosophy-nw.org/theosnw/science/prat-shl.htm

Description of Torrance Test of Creative Thinking
http://www.creativelearning.com/Assess/test72.htm

Glossary of Terms
(from www.sheldrake.org)

Field: A region of physical influence. Fields interrelate and interconnect matter and energy within their realm of influence. Fields are not a form of matter; rather, matter is energy bound within fields. In current physics, several kinds of fundamental field are recognized: the gravitational and electromagnetic fields and the matter fields of quantum physics. The hypothesis of formative causation broadens the concept of physical fields to include morphic fields as well as the known fields of physics.

Formative causation, hypothesis of: The hypothesis that organisms or morphic units (q.v.) at all levels of complexity are organized by morphic fields, which are themselves influenced and stabilized by morphic resonance (q.v.) from all previous similar morphic units.

Materialism: The doctrine that whatever exists is either matter or entirely dependent on matter for its existence.

Matter: That which has traditionally been contrasted with form or with mind. In the philosophy of materialism, matter is the substance and basis of all reality, and is usually conceived of in the spirit of atomism. In Newtonian physics, matter, distinguished by mass and extension, was contrasted with energy. According to relativity theory, mass and energy are mutually transformable, and material systems are now regarded as forms of energy.

Mechanistic theory: The theory that all physical phenomena can be explained mechanically (see mechanics), without reference to goals or purposive designs (cf. teleology). The central metaphor is the machine. In the seventeenth century, the universe was conceived of as a vast machine, designed, made, and set running by God and governed by his eternal laws. By the late nineteenth century, it was commonly regarded as an eternal machine which was slowly running down. In biology, the mechanistic theory states that living organisms are nothing but inanimate machines or mechanical systems: all the phenomena of life can in principle be understood in terms of mechanical models and can ultimately be explained in terms of physics and chemistry.

Meme: A term coined by Richard Dawkins, who defines it as "a unit of cultural inheritance, hypothesized as analogous to the particulate gene and as naturally selected by virtue of its 'phenotypic' consequences on its own survival and replication in the cultural environment."

Memory: The capacity for remembering, recalling, recollecting, or recognizing. From the mechanistic point of view, animal and human memory depend on material memory traces within the nervous system. From the point of view of the hypothesis of formative causation, memory in its various forms, both conscious and unconscious, is due to morphic resonance.

Mind: In Cartesian dualism, the conscious thinking mind is distinct from the material body; the mind is non-material. Materialists derive the mind from the physical activity of the brain. Depth psychologists point out that the conscious mind is associated with a much broader or deeper mental system, the unconscious mind. In the view of Jung, the unconscious mind is not merely individual but collective. On the hypothesis of formative causation, mental activity, conscious and unconscious, takes place within and through mental fields, which like other kinds of morphic fields contain a kind of in-built memory.

Morphic field: A field within and around a morphic unit which organizes its characteristic structure and pattern of activity. Morphic fields underlie the form and behaviour of holons or morphic units at all levels of complexity. The term morphic field includes morphogenetic, behavioural, social, cultural, and mental fields. Morphic fields are shaped and stabilized by morphic resonance from previous similar morphic units, which were under the influence of fields of the same kind. They consequently contain a kind of cumulative memory and tend to become increasingly habitual.

Morphic resonance: The influence of previous structures of activity on subsequent similar structures of activity organized by morphic fields. Through morphic resonance, formative causal influences pass through or across both space and time, and these influences are assumed not to fall off with distance in space or time, but they come only from the past. The greater the degree of similarity, the greater the influence of morphic resonance. In general, morphic units closely resemble themselves in the past and are subject to self-resonance from their own past states.

Morphic unit: A unit of form or organization, such as an atom, molecule, crystal, cell, plant, animal, pattern of instinctive behaviour, social group, element of culture, ecosystem, planet, planetary system, or galaxy. Morphic units are organized in nested hierarchies of units within units: a crystal, for example, contains molecules, which contain atoms, which contain electrons and nuclei, which contain nuclear particles, which contain quarks.

Morphogenesis: The coming into being of form.

Morphogenetic fields: Fields that play a causal role in morphogenesis. This term, first proposed in the 1920s, is now widely used by developmental biologists, but the nature of morphogenetic fields has remained obscure. On the hypothesis of formative causation, they are regarded as morphic fields stabilized by morphic resonance.

Nature: Traditionally personified as Mother Nature. The creative and controlling power operating in the physical world, and the immediate cause of all phenomena within it. Or the inherent and inseparable combination of qualities essentially pertaining to anything and giving it its fundamental character. Or the inherent power or impulse by which the activity of living organisms is directed or controlled. From the conventional point of view of science, nature is made up of matter, fields, and energy and is governed by the laws of nature, usually thought to be eternal.

Organicism: A form of holism according to which the world consists of organisms (or holons or morphic units, q.v.) at all levels of complexity. Organisms are wholes made up of parts, which are themselves organisms, and so on; they are organized in nested hierarchies. The parts of organisms can be understood only in relation to their activities and functions in the ongoing whole. Organisms in this sense include atoms, molecules, crystals, cells, tissues, organs, plants and animals, societies, cultures, ecosystems, planets, planetary systems, and galaxies. In this spirit, the entire cosmos can be regarded as an organism rather than a machine (cf. mechanistic theory).

Paradigm: An example or pattern. in the sense of T. S. Kuhn (1970), scientific paradigms are general ways of seeing the world shared by members of a scientific community, and they provide models of acceptable ways in which problems can be solved.

Teleology: The study of ends or final causes; the explanation of phenomena by reference to goals or purposes.

Teleonomy: The science of adaptation. "in effect, teleonomy is teleology made respectable by Darwin" (Dawkins, 1982). The apparently purposive structures, functions, and behaviour of organisms are regarded as evolutionary adaptations established by natural selection.

Vitalism: The doctrine that living organisms are truly vital or alive, as opposed to the mechanistic theory that they are inanimate and mechanical. Living organization depends on purposive vital factors, such as entelechy (q.v.), which are not reducible to the ordinary laws of physics and chemistry. Vitalism is a less far-reaching form of holism than organicism (q.v.), in so far as it accepts the mechanistic assumption that the systems studied by physicists and chemists are inanimate and essentially mechanical.

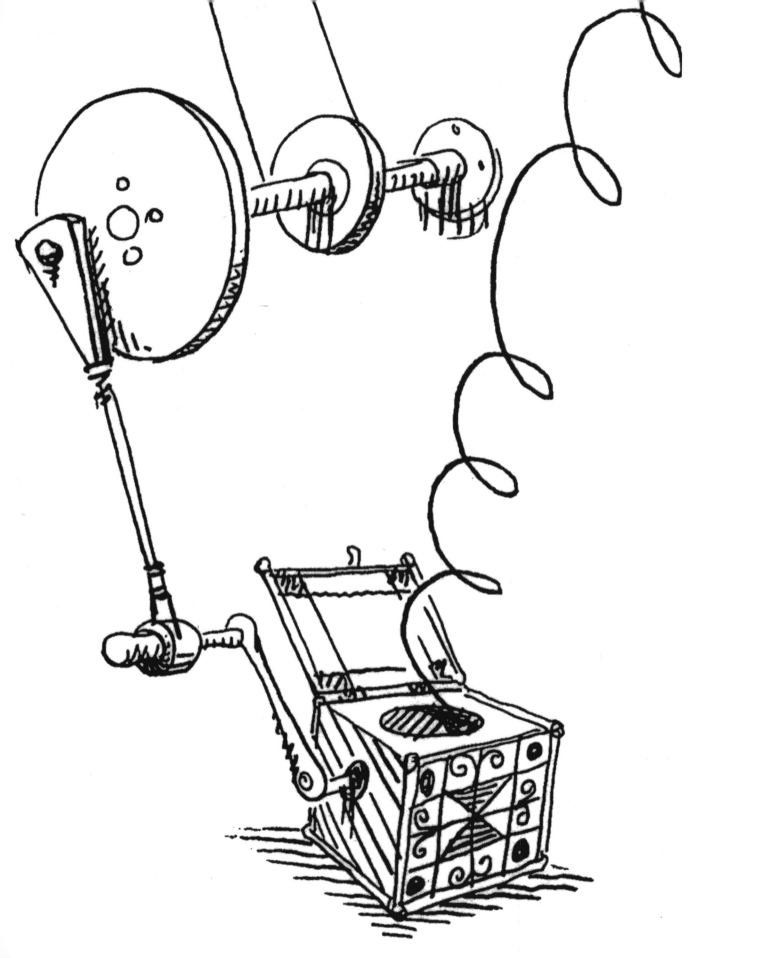

Transforming Literature: Writing across Cultures

John Joseph Courtney

Editor's Note: *Although this writer makes rather extensive reference to the pages and paragraphs of a particular edition of Frankenstein, these references should be viewed as examples in his approach to writing instruction. Different editions and other works of literature could certainly be used in this manner with equal success.*

Non-native language learners must not only respond to a given text on an experiential level, they must become a part of the text's creation. That is, they must be involved in imaginative, critical, emotional—and ultimately—cross-cultural experiences. The texts need to become living texts, and the L2 learners' interactions with them need to be dynamic, exploratory and ongoing creative processes. Collie and Slater (1987) highlight this radical view of involvement as does Kramsch (1998) who discusses how all readers need to reconstruct for themselves their own understanding of the context, and thereby define their place vis-á-vis that context (60). Cross culturally, this interactive process with literature opens up investigations of the "similarities and differences between self and others" (Maley, 2001, 185) and leads to an awareness of and insights into "the other" (Kramsch, 1993).

Tomlinson (2001a) notes that the following processes might occur in a native speaker's response(s) to a poem:

- Visualize
- Read the poem "aloud" in your mind
- Talk to yourself
- Connect the poem to your own experience
- Connect the poem to other works of art
- Fill in the gaps left by the writer
- Evaluate the poem
- Interpret the poem
- Feel emotion (104)

Masuhara (2000) adds "experience images, heat, thirst, smell and possibly even a sense of movement" and describes such reactions to and reflections of texts as ways listeners and readers "create multi-dimensional mental representations in actual experience" (106). Listeners and readers form and work with interpretations and transform their ideas and, ultimately, their experiences. Considering the varying (and limitless) individual and cultural responses to a text: "text could be understood as different forms of discourse in diverse communities, including acts of speech or pictures" (Courtney 2002, 257).

Creating Texts in Relation to Texts

How could we engender these views toward literary texts with L2 learners? Learners need to be given ample opportunity, with appropriate guidance, to create texts in relation and response to texts. Provide activities and implement learning processes that focus the learners in transforming texts. Students are thereby involved in developing their critical abilities, emotional experiences, imaginative insights and cross-cultural awareness. Specifically, in guiding a learner in the transformation of a literary text, the following personal and educational developments are built upon:

GUIDING READERS

- Creatively backgrounding or expanding a story
- Building-up background on characters, families and relationships
- Empathetically taking on a role of a literary character, image or object
- Transforming key elements of a text, such as character, narration and genre
- Hypothesizing diverse scenarios

- Responding cross-culturally to literature
- Identifying, critiquing and exploring thematic issues
- Writing companion stories

Reading to Frankenstein

Kramsch (1998, 2001), Parkinson and Thomas (2000), Maley (1997), Goh (1994), Lazar (1993), Duff and Maley (1990) and Carter and Long (1987) describe some of these experiences with literature. Here twelve writing activities based on a graded reader of *Frankenstein* by Mary Shelley (retold by Patrick Nobes, Oxford Bookworms 3, 1989) are offered. They will be discussed in relation to the learners' personal and educational developments listed above. *Frankenstein* is a story of a benevolent and obsessed scientist by this name who creates a nameless monster. Horrified by his creation, he rejects it, thus initiating cycles of isolation, despair, violence, death and trauma in relation to a potentially kind-hearted monster.

Writing Task #1

The first three pages of the story are given to the students. After reading them either aloud in small groups or as a whole class, the students are instructed to write the beginning of the Frankenstein story (one page). Frankenstein's story begins at its end with Frankenstein being at the pinnacle of exhaustion and psychological and moral degradation. The story of Dr. Frankenstein having been tracking "a huge figure" across the ice, and now on death's bed, Frankenstein's story offers myriad possibilities. Each student could either pretend that they are him or be a third-person observer (narrator). After they have finished their writing, different accounts will be discussed and compared in groups and as a whole class.

Writing Task #2

The students read page 4 and then focus on paragraph 2 (beginning at "My mother hoped…"). The paragraph relates how Dr. Frankenstein's mother adopted a little girl, Elizabeth from a poor family and that Dr. Frankenstein's love for her would deepen. After reading, they will be instructed to look carefully at the picture on page 5, which shows a lonely-looking Elizabeth in the foreground of Dr. Frankenstein's family in a darkened landscape. The students will then write an original and creative account (at least two or three paragraphs) of what life was like in Dr. Frankenstein's family and how it changed after Elizabeth was adopted when Dr. Frankenstein was five years old. They will be told to use their imagination and be as detailed as possible.

Writing Task #3

The students read and study the first two paragraphs on page 6. The story here relates how Dr. Frankenstein was intrigued with questions of creating life during his schooling and had a shocking experience of the mysterious and "terrible power" of lightning. After reading, they will be asked to think back in their own lives to an event that greatly changed their lives. If they cannot think of one, then they can consider an event that changed a friend or relative's life. (Alternatively, they can make up an event.) Then they will be instructed to write one or two pages describing the experience.

Writing Task #4

Assuming that the students have only read the first two chapters of the book, they are given the third and fourth paragraph from page 53, Chapter 15, the last chapter of Frankenstein (beginning at "We laid his body…"). Here the story returns to the book's beginning, Frankenstein's end in devastating death. The monster asks the dead Frankenstein for forgiveness. The students are asked to write one or two pages in response to the following questions:

Who (or what) do you think this monster was?

Do you think Frankenstein did something wrong?

What could have happened?

Writing Task #5

After the students have read Chapter 3 (pages 6-9), they are asked to focus on paragraph 3 on page 7 (beginning "After the professor's talk…"). The professor entreats his students to use science and their God-given intelligence for the benefit of mankind, an endeavor Frankenstein undertakes with a commitment that becomes obsessive. After discussion brings out the idea that Frankenstein thought that the "secrets of life" entailed discovering how life began and creating it anew from the dead, the students are instructed to write one or two pages about what they believe the "secrets of life" might be and whether such secrets could be destructive. They are told to be creative and to use their imagination.

Writing Task #6

After the students have read Chapter 4 (pages 10-13), they are asked to first write two creative and original paragraphs describing Frankenstein's sudden change of emotion. Frankenstein succeeds in creating his monster and then is repulsed by its extreme ugliness and abnormality. He escapes but has recurring, horrid and traumatizing nightmares and visions. The students are also instructed to write at least two paragraphs describing a sudden change in emotion that they or someone they know have had. Later the different accounts will be discussed in small groups.

Writing Task #7

The students are instructed to read Chapter 5 and the first page of Chapter 6. In the story Frankenstein returned home to his family after receiving his father's letter relating the murder of his brother, William, the scientist understood that the monster did this horrible crime. The students are told to pretend that Frankenstein decides that he cannot return home. Instead, he replies to his father's letter with his own letter. The students are instructed to pretend that they are Frankenstein and write the letter to their father.

Writing Task #8

It will be assumed that the students have read the first eight chapters. The students (in groups of three) are told to go back to Chapters 7 and 8 and summarize briefly in writing ten of the events or developments that affected the monster's feelings or understanding. These two chapters relate the monster's experiences from his point of view. Wandering into the countryside, he is humiliated as people are horrified of him. By chance, he happens upon a family whom he observes unawares; over time he becomes educated, understanding about humanity, only to be traumatized. After the students have finished their summaries, they will be told to put the events/developments into a different order and exchange them with another group to reorder.

Writing Task #9

For this activity it is assumed that the students have had previous work on prepositional phrases. After having read Chapter 9, pairs of students will be instructed to find and list as many prepositional phrases as they can from pages 30-31. These pages recount the monster's further humiliating encounters, and the murder of Frankenstein's brother, William, in the monster's words. After about ten minutes, they will be told to create a new, written story (about two or three paragraphs) that makes use of eight to ten of the prepositional phrases, which they have found. When the students have done this, stories will be read and discussed.

Writing Task #10

After the students have finished Chapters 10 and 11, they are told to look at page 36. In these chapters, Frankenstein agrees to create a female monster through sympathy for his monster; however, realizing the horror of this endeavor, he destroys it, immediately traumatizing his monster. Through discussion it is brought out that we do not know anything about Frankenstein's state of mind when he was creating the female monster. (Chapter 11 begins "One evening two months later…" (p. 36).) The students are instructed to write a three or four page account of these two months from Frankenstein's perspective. A follow-up task could be for the students to write a two or three page account of these two months from their own perspective.

Writing Task #11

After students have finished Chapter 13 (or even the book), they are told to narrate Elizabeth's experience of her wedding day from her point of view (in at least two pages). In this chapter, Frankenstein's monster avenges the destruction of the female monster by murdering Elizabeth, the scientist's wife, on her wedding night. Alternatively, the events could be narrated from the monster's or the student's point of view.

Writing Task #12

Upon completion of *Frankenstein*, the following topics could be given to the student-writers:

• Write a letter from Frankenstein to the ghost of Frankenstein's mother, or from Frankenstein's monster to the mother that he never had, or from your mother or father (or relative or close friend) to Frankenstein or Frankenstein's monster.

• Write a sequel to *Frankenstein* in which Frankenstein possibly continues to live.

• Transform *Frankenstein* into a drama.

• Create a series of news articles, advertisements, diary entries, songs, letters, poems, epithets, epitaphs, and obituaries connected to *Frankenstein*.

• Write a companion story to *Frankenstein*, which includes related themes, characters, settings or events or a combination of these.

Backgrounding and Expanding Stories

Writing Task #1 is unique in that in creating Frankenstein's story, student-writers are attempting to go back into his past, providing background for his current predicament. But so little context is given, just "a huge figure" that Frankenstein has been tracking across the ice, the writers must create a new story. They are hypothesizing and inventing simultaneously. In Writing Task #2, backgrounding becomes specifically focused as a single event and description of a family is expanded in much detail. This is a particularly useful undertaking as it will allow both the writer and readers to imagine and reflect on how Frankenstein's boyhood environment might have been a factor in Frankenstein's drive to create a monster. In tasks #10 and 11, students are adding to the story at crucial points in its development. They are attempting to get into the mind of a key character and imagine what that character was thinking, experiencing and performing, while keeping in mind the contexts in which their expansions need to fit into.

Characters, Relationships and Empathy

Dr. Frankenstein's emotions as he created a female monster he hated for a male monster he abhorred, yet pitied, and Elizabeth's emotions as they move from bliss to horror on her wedding night—these events and states of mind offer students tremendous opportunity to confront the emotive impact of literature firsthand in intriguingly personal and critical ways. Those characters' emotions were intense, but the story only makes reference to them on the surface, and there are certain accounts and perspectives completely missing (e.g., tasks #10 and #11). As the student-writers think about what was going through these characters' minds, they are drawn to reflect on their personal experiences and schematic awareness, such as cultural understandings. For example, students might lead themselves to such questions as "From my experience, what circumstances would be as dreadful as being compelled to create a monster for someone I judged to be a murderous heathen?", "And how would I feel partaking in such an ordeal?", "What would I do?", "How would I behave?", and""Would I agonize over the consequences?"

In effect, the students are engaging in a process as Kern (2000) describes of "situated practice", involving the learners making connections between texts and thoughts, feelings and experiences, to""critical framing", where the learners are initiating and responding to cognitive and social challenges, inquiries and reflection. Furthermore, as student-writers feel and see the experiences and emotions of literary characters, they develop their sensitivities and awareness of their own emotional experiences and tendencies. And through empathy the learners change. Masuhara (2000) notes," of all the reactions in responding to a literary text, emotion seems to be the most pervasive of all of adding values, interest and meaning to the text and in giving readers motivation to read on" (106). And in adding values, interest and meaning to learners!

Transformation and Hypothesizing in Relation to 'Text'

There are other writing tasks in which students are attempting to build-up background on characters and relationships and are responding empathetically, Dr. Frankenstein could be represented in two ways: First, as a determined and resolute pursuer of solutions to the conflicts he faces, or, second as a man who can no longer cope, shunning responsibility, denying reality, or a well-intentioned, enterprising young man suffering from insanity.

In all of these tasks, the time frames vary—from one day (task #11) to an unspecified and potentially long period. The learners will be free to experiment with genre, characters, events, places, developments and build-up and incorporate the content that they see as important, stimulating and vital for the story's unfolding and attraction. As the learners are encouraged to look deeply into Dr. Frankenstein's mind (in task #10), they can detail the process, the labor and, possibly, criminal activity that he went through to obtain the female body parts, the indifferent and calculated construction of the essential machines juxtaposed with Dr. Frankenstein's inward strife and, perhaps, employ different narrated "voices" of Frankenstein. A writer could even lead up to the point where she delves into the souls of Dr. Frankenstein, Dr. Frankenstein's monster and the female monster at the moment of obliteration (of the female monster). In the summary writing of task #8, a different sort of transformation occurs, but potentially just as imaginative. How would you describe a series of events or developments that affected the monster's feelings and understanding?

Responding Cross-culturally to Literature

Kern (2000) highlights transformation and recreation of "texts" as the most comprehensive and vital skill to develop in learners' literary and language education. It involves complex processes through which learners are working with and on texts, where "text" is spoken, written or sensory language/content that forms a coherent whole. So a student's created letter of task #7 is a text, which could be part of any number of other texts, depending on how the learner is focusing his attention and activating imaginative and creative processes. Likewise, a single event, set of circumstances, theme or image touched upon in the letter could become a text for the learners to think about and work with.

What the students are doing, in effect, as they notice, confront and respond to variegated content and themes, is looking at literature cross-culturally. In the transformations discussed above, they are looking at how they might respond to these fictionalized situations by drawing on their own experiences, knowledge, attitudes, cultures and emerging awareness of other cultures. As student-writers engage in these processes more thoroughly, they are encouraged and guided in giving a freer rein to their imaginations and "taught" to employ their personal convictions in their writing. Real and meaningful issues, experiences, content and language will be explored.

The literary transformations actually draw a multitude of critical, experiential, emotional and imaginative thoughts and understandings together simultaneously. Student-writers are empathetically seeing characters, and re-seeing them, imagining places, constructing events, discovering feelings, describing pictures, picturing experiences, and re-imaging, reconstructing, rediscovering, re-describing and re-picturing them, as they create, and recreate, their stories. When a learner probes more and more in detail, she will need to reflect on, for example, what experiences or ideas in her culture(s) would be related to being manipulated into constructing a potentially terrifying, maleficent and pernicious female monster. "What kind of person or entity would I be in these circumstances?" Furthermore, "what kind of creature, person or entity could the monster be?"

Cross-cultural Themes

Probing cross-cultural themes actually occurs—to different degrees—as the student-writers address all of the topics outlined above. Every time a learner is given an opportunity to look critically and imaginatively at a literary text, she is implicitly put into a frame of finding and creating those personal and cultural experiences and thoughts that are meaningful to the story at hand. Both ideas and pictures are brought to mind. Masuhara (2000) refers to these experiential processes of interacting with literature as being—"multi-dimensional in the sense that is sensory, cognitive and emotive at the same time" (106). Tomlinson (2001a) describes the activation of an "inner voice" through which literature is "experienced" both cognitively and affectively, linguistically and non-linguistically, sensuously and reflectively. This "inner voice," and the habit to listening to it, is formed in learners if they are encouraged "to talk to themselves in private, egocentric speech" with plenty of time to think (Tomlinson 2001b, 28), to reflect on their thoughts, generate images and create. The writing tasks advocated here are set with the understanding that the learners will need time and space for careful deliberation, personal connection and "multi-dimensional" and "inner voice" experiences.

Training, Integration and Other Stories

Some of the writing tasks offered here might not be initially open to some students to meaningfully respond to. Of course there might be linguistic constraints but, for students coming from backgrounds of learning by rote memorization, there might be accompanying cognitive and cultural constraints. Lazar (1993) notes that some learners might "lack the confidence to reach interpretations on their own, possibly because their previous learning experience has relied little on taking personal responsibility" (191). She recommends a gradual approach of guiding learners "to become more self-reliant in producing their own interpretations" (191). A beginning could be made with mini-tasks, activities and questions, which from the very early stages of a learner's linguistic abilities, cognitive development and cross-cultural awareness could meaningfully focus learners to work with "texts." McRae (1997) uses a text with the single word, wall written horizontally and vertically a number of times to form a square with an empty inside (also see Vethamani, 1996, 210-212). "What does it mean?" "What do you think?" "How do you feel?" Then put *me* into the square, and what changes?

And the questions and guidance could become more specifically orientated to meet the pedagogical needs of the individual or group. In relation, starter-activities could involve the learners in any of the following: replacing the adjectives in the letter(s) of Writing Task #7, writing one or two sentences for Frankenstein's story (Writing Task #1) individually or in a pair and then passing it to another to add to, talking about and making a list of characteristics of Frankenstein's poor family (see Writing Task #2) or a poor family in their culture, predicting the story from any point in it with as short of a text as a sentence, phrase or word, and so on. The learners' interpretative experience with the text might even begin with them drawing a picture of Frankenstein, the monster(s), Elizabeth, and any of *Frankenstein's* 24 pictures on its 55 pages could provide fodder for cross-cultural explorations.

In these early stages of forming their real, and creative interpretations, the students are beginning "to explore their own, as well as foreign, culture, discover cultural attitudes and assumptions that they have, and confront, challenge, assimilate and build upon diverse cultural perspectives and systems" (Courtney 2002, 257). As learners become more confident, practiced and open in approaching and responding to literary texts through imaginative and critical processes of transforming those texts, the experiences and developments discussed above will become richer, deeper and more integrated for them. This will become particularly apparent as the student-writers respond with increasingly developed, heart-felt commitment, renewed understanding(s), vivid pictures and cross-cultural insight(s) with their other stories in relation to such writing tasks as #3, 6, 9, 11 and 12. How would you write a companion story to Frankenstein? Write a letter from Frankenstein's monster to the mother that he never had. Transform your experience(s), feelings and pictures cross-culturally.

Appendix

The following students' writing on and transformations of *Frankenstein* has been unedited. The first piece is an extract of a letter from Frankenstein's monster to the mother that he never had.

Dear Mom,

First of all, I want to tell you that I'm fine and I hope you are fine too. I want to see you as soon as possible. I have many problems. Nobody love me, care of me even my creator, Mr. Frankenstein. I want to escape from all terrible problems. Now I know nobody love and care me as you. The time pass very slow when I face the problems but the time pass very fast when I take a rest and think of you. I want all problems that happened with me become only a nightmare it will disappear when I wake up. Every night I see you in my dream. I think of your love, warm and acting. I can not stand with the problems anymore. I need your shoulder to cry on, your lip to give me some advices, your eyes to look after me with love and care. Day after day, I wait the time to see you. Ocean apart I will sail, mountain apart I will climb. Nothing can obstruct me from you. Mom, In my imagine you are the most beautiful and kind woman. I want you to know that when the last time of my life has come, if tomorrow never comes. Mom, you are the person who I think of before I die. My life start from you and it will end with you.

I know I'm ungrateful son. I never serve you. I want to be your lovely son. Be with you take care of you. When you get old. I have just want you to know how much you are to me. Take care of yourself.

God bless you
Arnon Maythasupasan, Thai student-writer

The follow extract is a narration of Elizabeth's experience and feelings on her wedding day. (Dr. Frankenstein's first name is Victor.)

After the wedding, I go to honeymoon with my husband, Victor. We traveled by boat together and go to the hotel that stand on the other side of the lake. We planned to spend the time at our room. The place that I go to honeymoon was a beautiful place. It is the mountains and the lake that calm and beauty. But suddenly, "the wind became stronger and soon a great storm broke above us" (47) Noise was fright us and I saw Victor was worry about it. He told me he saw the monster. The monster, what monster I don't know that. He asked me to go to our room but he didn't go with me, He wanted to search for the monster. And he told me he will come back when he was sure the monster was not in or around the hotel. I went to our room, I taken a shower and I ate Ma-Ma cup noodle when I waited Victor. I lay on bed and watched television. I waited for a long time until I heard a noise from the door, somebody knocked the door. I think that is Victor I opened the door. Suddenly I frightened he was not Victor, I don't know him. He was a horrible face, he was a huge figure and I think he is the monster that Victor mentioned. The monster stared me, I was fright and I became to cry. I wanted Victor came to help me from the monster. Suddenly the monster told me he was hungry and he wanted some drank. I made Ma-Ma cup noodle and Cola-Cola with him. He ate greedily I believed he was hungry. When he ate I asked him about his name and why him came to my room. He answered me, "My name is Frankenstein's monster. I am creature that Frankenstein created. I came to see you Elizabeth I wanted to see your face the face of Victor' lover. You are so beautiful no wonder that Victor love you because you are a good woman and a kind woman. I thank you for this foods it's very nice. Nobody do a good think for me like you. But you are Victor's lover I want to say sorry, I'm so sorry. I must kill you."

Pattraporn Preechawipat, Thai student-writer

The following extract is from a letter from Dr. Frankenstein to the ghost of his mother.

I am fascinated by my work. I want to know the meaning of the life very much! I attempt to create the life! My diligent work. I have one's own laboratories. However. I have neglected family members. I regret very much! My work very successful. I reached the hope at last. I created it! A person. No. should say that a bizarre entity! I let it come back to life with the strength of the tunder and lightning. But I am very afraid, because though I have made it. I can't control it, It is so strong. Too dangerous. Not knowing why, it hates me. Hates me very much.

Xing Xiao Ye (Leon), Chinese student-writer

References

Carter, R. and Long, M.N. 1987. *The Web of Words: Exploring Literature through Language.* Cambridge: Cambridge University Press.

Collie, M. and Slater, M. 1987. *Literature in the Language Classroom.* Oxford: Oxford University Press.

Courtney, J. 2002. "Cultural Isolation and Cultural Integration: A Communicative Language Activity." *The English Teacher,* 5, 256-264.

Duff, A. and Maley, A. 1990. *Literature.* Oxford: Oxford University Press.

Goh, C.C.M. 1994. "Language Learning Tasks for Literary Texts." *Guidelines,* **16**(2), 91-103.

Kern, R. 2000. *Literacy and Language Teaching.* Oxford: Oxford University Press.

Kramsch, C. 1993. *Context and Culture in Language Teaching.* Oxford: Oxford University Press.

—. 1998. *Language and Culture.* Oxford: Oxford University Press.

Lazar, G. 1993. *Literature and Language Teaching: A Guide for Teachers and Trainers.* Cambridge: Cambridge University Press.

Maley, A. 1997. "Creativity with a Small 'c'." *The Journal of the Imagination in Language Learning and Teaching,* 4, 8-12.

—. 2001. "Literature in the Language Classroom." In R. Carter and D. Nunan (Eds.), *The Cambridge Guide to Speakers of Other Languages* (180-185). Cambridge: Cambridge University Press.

McRae, J. 1997, March. "'It's just my cup of tea': Representational Language in Language and Literature Teaching." Paper presented at the Second Annual ELC/Thai TESOL SIG Conference: Literature Pathways to Language Teaching Revisited, Bangkok, Thailand.

Masuhara, H. 2000. "Experiencing Literature through Language." In C.S. Heng, M.A. Quayum and R. Talif (Eds.), *Diverse Voices: Readings in Languages, Literatures and Cultures* (pp. 104-111). Serdang: Universiti Putra Malaysia Press.

Parkinson, B. and Thomas, H.R. 2000. *Teaching Literature in a Second Language.* Edinburgh: Edinburgh University Press.

Shelley M. 1989. *Frankenstein.* Oxford: Oxford Bookworms, Oxford University Press.

Tomlinson, B. 2001a. "Connecting the Mind: A Multi-dimensional Approach to Teaching Language through Literature." *The English Teacher,* 4, 104-115.

—. 2001b. "The Inner Voice: A Critical factor in L2 Learning." The Journal of the Imagination in language Learning and Teaching, 6, 26-33.

Vethamani, M.E. 1996. "Common Ground: Incorporating New Literature in English in Language and Literature Teaching." In R. Carter and J. McRae (Eds.), *Language, Literature and The Learner: Creative Classroom Practice* (204-216). London: Longman.

Imagination:
The Bridge to Meaning

Katherine L. Granelli

Seeing all possibilities, seeing all that can be done
and how it can be done marks the power of the imagination.
Robert Collier

It is ironic that current attempts to help children become literate seriously neglect the imagination which many researchers consider central to the process of learning (Harris, 2000; Donaldson, 1978). Theoreticians in this general orientation emphasize the merging that occurs between interaction, objects and ideas in unique ways to recreate what exists, to recognize what never was, and to enhance cognitive development (Bartsch, 1939; Warnock, 1994; Heal, 2003). Others stress that imaginative engagement makes it possible to connect objects, symbols and ideas where no connection existed previously (Bronowski, 1978; Barrow, 1988). What all of these notions have in common is that they position the imagination at the core of literacy learning. Perhaps this is why imagination is regarded by some as the highest level of thinking (Egan and Nadaner, 1988). In this paper, no new data is presented. Instead, various works that deal with the imagination and the development of literacy are presented in a fashion that constitutes a coherent and consistent theory.

Suppression of the Imagination

Meek (1991) proposes that "When [children] leave school, their level of [literacy] attainment will attest to their fitness to belong to, or to be excluded from, the group of powerful literates who dominate...others" (p. 238). In her book, *Releasing the Imagination*, Maxine Greene (1995) refers to "Social Imagination as the capacity to invent visions of what should be and what might be in our deficient society" (p. 5). It is vital for teachers to practice social imagination in order to invent visions of how to better recognize and foster each child's mode of literacy expression. Yet, the authentic ways that children represent the world are often ignored in the presently mandated educational content and delivery of curriculum (Schuster, 2003). Many voices are not heard in today's classrooms due to political agendas that do not match what seems to be natural student literacy development. Meek suggests that "Literacy is determined by the literate...especially where [it] is related to power" (1991, 234). It appears that children remain oppressed simply because the literacy expressions they use to convey their ideas and intelligence go unnoticed, unrecognized and, of most importance," *unrealized* due to the suppression of imagination.

It is only imagination that affords students the freedom to receive, interpret and express information and ideas through a variety of literacy expressions. In the classroom, imagination is a medium of human innovation that offers alternative ways to construct meaning rather than being a 'frill' that is unrelated to literacy learning (Strecker & Wells, 2001; Traub, 2002). Yet, current political policy mandates the use of practices that strip the learning experience of much of its potential for creativity, enjoyment, authenticity and imagination (Yardley, 2000; Ohanian, 1999). As a result, there is no support of an atmosphere of effective learning that coincides with the inherent modes of cognitive processing. Instead, teachers are being mandated to both present and receive crucial literacy information through use of a narrow, 'en masse' reading curricula and standardized assessments at the exclusion of other avenues of literacy learning and assessment (U.S. Department of Education, 2001; NCTE, 2002).

The Vital Role of Imagination

When only viewed through the lens of standardized assessments and related practices, the literacy abilities of children are represented in restricted and misleading ways. Actually, literacy expression comes dressed in a variety of fashions that range from oral language to visual arts to written words: imagination plays a vital role in each of these areas. Yet often learners' multiple and alternative ways of communicating are often left unrecognized due to the exclusion of the imagination (Duckworth, 1996). As Drummond (1994) suggests, in order for assessment to work for children, it must be seen as a means of gaining and increasing understanding about individual students and not as an occasion to compare individuals against some notional standard.

In order for individual literacy abilities to be recognized and valued, society needs to expand its idea of what constitutes intelligence. As Howard Gardner (1983) proposes, "Only if we expand and reformulate our view of what counts as human intellect, will we be able to devise more appropriate ways of assessing it and more effective ways of educating it" (p. 4). Presently, many children seem to possess a deficient literacy profile (Coles, 2003). The incorporation of imagination into the educational forum is desperately needed in order to broaden the idea of what actually constitutes intelligence (Ohanian, 2002; Schudel, 2001), as well as to accommodate the modes of communication used by all children. This paper will attempt to address the many ways that imagination influences literacy development.

The world cannot be perceived without its being given some significance;
and it is the function of the imagination to create the meanings that are in the world.
Warnock, 1994, p. 63

More Than Manipulation of Sound in Words

Though literacy and imagination are both present throughout life (Barton, 1994; Brann, 1991), without the imagination, it is difficult (if not, impossible) to engage in many literacy events and transactions. Literacy is more than the simple assignment and manipulation of sound in words (U. S. Department of Education, 2001). As Phillips (1997) proposes, "Literacy, more than just the act of decoding, is the act of thinking, reinventing, revising, weaving patterns of understanding through cooperation and collaboration to create meaning in our lives" (p. 3).

Imagination enables the creation of meaning during literacy events because, as Greene (1995) proposes, imagination is the "backdrop of…remembered things and the funded meanings to which they give rise, that we grasp to understand what is now going on around us"(p. 20).

Serving as a backdrop for what is remembered and perceived, the imagination brings perception and thought together and triggers alternative thinking (Sutton-Smith, 1988; Brann, 1991). At the point of alternative thinking, there is an inclination to conceive of the unusual (Barrow, 1988). Upon the conception of the usual, elements that seemed to be unrelated become connected. Once connected by the imagination, there is an intermingling of perception and thought that leads to meaning (Warnock, 1994). In this way, imagination can be viewed as a quality of unusual and effective conception that directly contributes to understanding and critical thought (Barrow, 1988). This is evidenced during literacy events when a new cognitive conception is created by linking prior experience with newly presented experience (Rosenblatt, 1995). When imagination links past and present experience, it gives intelligible form to literacy transactions (Bartlett, 1932; Bartsch, 1939).

First comes thought, then organization of that thought into ideas and plans; then transformation of those plans into reality.
The beginning, as you will observe, is in your imagination.
Napoleon Hill

Language Interactions, Children and Imagination

Every literacy event stems from our desire to use language in our negotiations with the world (Cambourne, 1988). During these negotiations, oral language is one of the earliest sign systems used to communicate. Yet in *infancy*, children are unable to understand oral language. In its initial phases of exposure, oral language has no meaning to an infant. I propose that through imaginative transaction, children are eventually able to make the connection between the abstract spoken language they hear and the concrete meaning behind it. Initially, the language interaction can be shared in a variety of ways such as telling or reading stories, talking, touching, showing, or singing. These language interactions—full of emotion, words, sights and sounds— become appealing to the child on an aesthetic level first (Rosenblatt, 1994; Meek, 1991), before any knowledge of the literal message contained in the event is realized. At this stage, the literacy experience is a matter of perceiving sensory stimulation that eventually leads to meaning. Imagination is needed during such interactions because, as Coleridge (1804) proposes, the primary imagination is the living power and prime agent of all human perception.

Bartsch (1939) proposes that imagination is especially triggered by linguistic input. On a basic level, the infant experiences the sound of a spoken word through the sense of hearing. Since imaginative engagement triggers alternative thinking (Sutton-Smith, 1988;

Brann, 1991), the imagination then begins to create possibilities for making connections between the word heard and something or someone in the infant's environment. As suggested by Warnock (1994), "we need...imagination as a bridge between what we see or hear and what we may claim to be a true interpretation of that seeing or hearing" (p. 71). Using the imagination as a bridge, the infant begins to regard the spoken words he hears as a person, object or feeling. In connecting these seemingly unrelated entities, he begins to create meaning. His perceptual response to the exposure of language, received through the senses, begins his literacy journey. Early literacy transactions occur through any of the senses of touch, taste, sight, sound or smell in the same way. At this stage, the imagination serves to connect the sensory elements that are readily accessible to the infant in a concrete form in a meaningful way (Bartlett, 1932).

Imagination and Representation of Oral Language

As the child leaves infancy, he shifts direction from an experience where he merely perceives sensory events. He begins to inwardly categorize while continuing to conceptualize, which helps to prepare for future success in school (Donaldson, 1978). At this time, literacy development exists in the acquisition of the linguistic skills that eventually lead to school-based reading and writing (Roskos & Christie, 2000). The specific linguistic skills that lead to reading and writing are those that begin with the representation of language and are followed by those skills that eventually lead to the conceptualization of language. In relation to this stage, Donaldson (1978) claims that the child's

> ...conceptual system must expand in the direction of increasing ability to represent itself. He must become capable of manipulating symbols. Now the principle symbolic system to which the child has access is oral language. So the first step is the step of conceptualizing language (p. 90).

In the process of conceptualizing oral language, the child uses his imagination to make meaning of what is perceived through the creation of images. The way that meaning is made of what is perceived at this stage relates to what I refer to as the "associative components of the imagination." This leads to the next stage of literacy development that takes place in **toddlerhood**. At this stage, the child begins to associate mental pictures with the sensory experiences in his environment through use of his imagination. As suggested by Brann (1991), imagination is the ability to connect internal visual presentations to external perceptions.

The associative function of the imagination takes an object, word or idea, attaches a picture to it and holds it in the mind for future recall (Sutton-Smith, 1988; Brann, 1991). Then, when the word is perceived in future interactions, the child is able to remember the mental picture, as well as to associate the picture with his previous responses to the word. In infancy, children perceive oral language through use of the imagination by connecting seemingly unrelated entities in a meaningful way. Then, in toddlerhood, they associate oral language to people, objects and feelings making basic connections between these elements through image. Bronowski (1978) proposes that visual memory, integration and speech take place fairly close together in the temporal lobe which can possibly explain the influence of the imagination at this stage of literacy development.

In the next phase of literacy development, which happens sometime in the **preschool** years, children begin to represent people, objects and feelings as oral language through use of the imagination. For infants, toddlers and then preschoolers, literacy development consists of imaginative experiences which invoke language exploration and conceptualization. As proposed by Johnson (1987), imagination is indispensable for our ability to make sense of our experience and find it meaningful. However, children first need to conceptualize oral language in order to manipulate the symbols of written language. From this perspective, literacy is viewed as language based (Kress, 1997; Goodman, K. 1996). At this stage of literacy development, imagination is needed to further refine the child's previous understanding of oral language.

Language—An Act of the Imagination

Sutton-Smith (1988) proposes that imagination is the power that *represents*. Signifying the continuing role of the imagination in literacy development, language is understood through representation (Oukanian, 1999) regardless of the sign system used. Pugh, Hicks and Davis (1997) suggest that language itself is an act of the imagination. Their idea makes sense when language is viewed as an invented and symbolic social entity used as a semiotic system that allows symbols to represent experiences and ideas (Goodman, K., 1996; Barton, 1994). Based on this premise, it can be assumed that in order to negotiate language in both oral and written form, children need first to become symbolic thinkers and users. As they begin to grasp the concept that both words and graphics can represent meaning as well as mediate the reading or recall of a specific message (Dyson, 1989), children also begin to need to use the imagination to interpret and make signs that stand for meaning (Berghoff, Borgmann & Parr, 2003).

> Reading...is not a passive exercise. The child, particularly one who reads a book...has nothing before it but the hieroglyphics of the printed page. Imagination must do the rest; and imagination is called upon to do it.
> GEORGE F. KENNAN, 1904

Imagination—The Highest Level of Preschool Development

Imaginative engagement during play provides a way for the child to attain moments of spontaneous insight (Rugg, 1963) in a natural way. The integral components of literacy development found in the authentic, social setting of play reflect natural development, and not training from without. "The best method [of literacy learning] is one in which children do not learn to read and write but in which both these skills are found in play situations" (Vygotsky, 1917, p. 118). Action and the creation of voluntary intentions are also incorporated in the imaginative sphere of play as well which led Vygotsky (1917) to claim that imagination is the highest level of preschool development. Full of emotion, language, and socialization, typical play experiences possess the essential ingredients of early literacy development. Because play requires active engagement and is pleasurable, it is an intrinsically motivating experience that allows children to become deeply absorbed in exploring, experimenting and creating a forum for learning that focuses on process rather than on the attainment of a particular goal or outcome (Wolfberg, 1999). As related to literacy development, the processes that children focus on during play are the social aspects of literacy development as well as refinement of the representational components of language conceptualization through use of the imagination. Since the imagination is historically construed and situated and cannot float free of its social contexts (Sutton-Smith, 1988), imaginative engagement during play provides a place for the child to execute the social components of literacy development (Goodman, Y., Altwerger & Marek, 1989). The preschool child brings the literacy events he witnesses in his social world to share with his play partners (Barton, 1994; Goodman, Y., 1997). These early literacy activities are first carried out in their imaginative games, inventions and experiences during play.

Smith, Meredith and Goodman (1987) suggest that "Youngsters can be observed in the natural state of play exploring their language" (195). During imaginative dramatizations, children propose complex ideas, situations and tasks all in an attempt to imitate the literacy practices of those people who are most important to them as well as to explore the parameters of language and, eventually, symbolize language in writing. Literacy development evolves within and is shaped by children's interactions with other symbolic media *as well as other people* (Dyson, 1989). Therefore, play connects the necessary social and semiotic conditions for literacy learning to occur through use of the imagination. Play experiences provide a natural, safe place for children to test the waters of conceptual thought. Since play experiences "form a common thread connecting people, ideas, materials and phrases" (Paley, 1986, xv), they are the fertile grounds in which imaginative ideas, realized as symbolic thought, root themselves for future use in the conceptual practices of literacy.

Creating Imaginary Situations

Eventually, children move away from the socially based, concrete imitation stage of literacy development and into a more abstract exploration stage which is, again, realized through imaginative engagement. As the child progresses in his linguistic abilities toward becoming a conceptual thinker, imaginative engagement enables him to move from a current, imitated, social experience to a symbolic representation of his linguistic abilities that leads to abstract thought. With regard to this stage of literacy development, Vygotsky (1917) maintains that "Superficially, play bears little resemblance to the complex, mediated form of thought and volition it leads to. From the point of view of development, creating an imaginary situation can be regarded as a means of developing abstract thought" (103-4).

The creation of imaginary situations enables the child to develop abstract thought by affording him the opportunity to reflect on his mental representations through action (Lillard, 1993; Siegler, 1991). At this stage in literacy development, the child becomes an abstract thinker who explores the semiotic possibilities of substituting one object for another (Libby, S., Powell, S., Messer, D. & Jordan, R., 1998) leading to the eventual substitution of a symbol for an object. During this stage Vygotsky (1917) also suggests that, "Literacy is a particular system of symbols and signs…that is a second-order symbolism, which gradually becomes direct symbolism. This means that written language consists of a system of signs that designate the sounds and words of spoken language, which, in turn, are signs for oral entities and relations. Gradually, this intermediate link, spoken language, disappears, and written language is converted into a system of signs that directly symbolize the entities and relations between them." (106)

Using Imagination to Represent, Mediate and Recall Language

Since the imagination enables people to see things differently than they are—i.e. to conceptualize (Barrow, 1988; Devon, 1988), it is through engagement in imaginative experiences that children are able to create the images and inventions that represent, mediate and recall language concepts. Language, in any form, is a symbolic system for thought (Vygotsky, 1934) making the representational attributes of the imagination integral in the process of semiotics. In infancy, children are first oral language receivers and perceivers. During toddlerhood, they begin to conceptualize oral language through images using the imagination. Later, preschoolers continue to refine oral language usage while beginning to use written language. However, before making the leap from oral to written language, the development of actions and gestures continue to be refined and imagination plays an important role in this process.

The progression from oral to written language through the acquisition of symbolic thought is first experienced through the senses (Rosenblatt, 1995), provoked by social engagement (Barton, 1994) and, then, explored physically (Maude, 2001) before it can be transformed into a conceptual framework. For the preschool child, *actions* and *perceptually available phenomena* have a great influence on mental representations (Lillard, 1993; Bartsch, 1939). Therefore, in order to eventually use and assign meaning to the symbols of letters in written words, it is necessary to first explore the representational capacity of the imagination through physical involvement.

Your imagination stand as your own personal laboratory. Here, you can rehearse the possibilities,
map out plans, and visualize…Imagination turns possibilities into reality.
ROBERT COLLIER

Play—The Imagination in Action

Vygotsky (1917) proposes that "Imagination…originally arises from action" (129) and claims that, for preschool children, *play is the imagination in action.* Cognitive growth begins with the concrete, natural, and simple moving in the direction of the abstract, distant and complex (Dewey, 1897; Donaldson, 1978). For the preschool child, it can be said that literacy learning in terms of concrete, natural and simple experience is realized through imaginative engagement during play events. As Meek (1991) proposes: "The great virtues of children's play [is] in introducing the young to a wide range of symbolic systems…[and] the beginnings of the power of literacy" (88). Play is the symbolic language of the imagination with a vocabulary of emotions that is part of the natural language of childhood (Lennon & Barbato, 2001).

Imaginative Gestures to Substitute Language

The incorporation of movement, which is so typical in imaginative play, influences literacy development. According to the work of Wallon (1938), movement enhances cognitive memory. The physical motion involved in imaginative play assists the child in triggering memories that have been stored by the imagination while also creating memories that are sparked by imaginative engagement. It is through the creation of such memories that the child is able to make and store visual perceptions. In the same way, the child can later recall stored visual perceptions and attach them to the *current* visual perception of a written word through imaginative engagement. As Maude (2001) proposes, "Play is seen as a means of enabling children to…use physical engagement to enhance the development of language, social and cognitive development" (p. 27). As the child engages in imaginative play in a physical way, he begins to use his body to act out imaginative scenarios. At this time, there is a subtle shift from spoken language usage to gestural language usage which actually begins the process of written and other alternative visual representations of speech. Where earlier in his literacy development the child substituted words for entities, he now substitutes actions for language through imaginative play.

As Bateson (1999) proposes, "this 'play' looks something like this: 'These actions in which we now engage do not denote what those actions for which they stand would denote'" (180). Using gestures and physical action, he may imagine he is cooking a meal as he moves through the steps that are typically involved in the cooking process. Among his play partners, his gestures communicate his intentions in an imaginative way. Using gestures and actions to portray his experience, he is using an *alternatively visual representation for language.* He begins to use both his mind and his body through imaginative engagement as a means of communication. Vygotsky (1917) explains the symbolic function of children's play in the following way:

"The child's self-motion, his own gestures, are what assign the function of sign to the object and give it meaning. All symbolic representational activity is full of such indicatory gestures…From this point of view, children's symbolic play can be understood as a very complex system of 'speech' through gestures that communicate and indicate the meaning of playthings." (108)

Using imaginative gestures, language begins to become decontextualized and represented in symbolic ways. As Vygotsky (1917) proposes, "Symbolic representation in play is essentially a particular form of speech at an earlier stage, one which leads directly to written language." (111)

Imaginative Dramatization: A Study of Complex Thought

Paley (1990) proposes that, during imagination dramatizations, children are free to change rules and experiment with new combinations of behavior and ideas which leads to the study of complex thought in a natural way. At this stage of literacy development, the earlier foundations of language exploration and conceptualization continues and ranges freely across modes of interpretation, representation and expression. During imaginative dramatizations, the substitutions and uses for language shift and change as often as the combinations of play partners and play situations do. Language exploration develops and evolves in a natural way as the preschool child experiments with uses and substitutions for language with his peers.

As proposed by Cambourne (1988), it is necessary to first explore language orally as a precursor for using language in the form of reading and writing. The initial desire of the child to explore the oral language they hear during play through movement, sets the stage for further use of the imagination to shift from real representations of language to the creation of lingual semiotic systems.

Since exercise of the imagination during play experiences allows children to assign new meanings to ideas, situations and objects in an experimental manner, imaginative engagement is a central form of representational cognition that allows them to begin to experiment with substitutions. Exploring the idea of substitution is possible in play activities because this is where the child first learns to pretend (Lillard, 1993). In pretend situations, the imagination is used to connect unrelated entities in a meaningful way. Through play activities, the child uses his imagination to become a conceptual thinker making meaning between objects, people or ideas and written words by first using his imagination to substitute one concrete object for another and then progresses to symbolic representation. Next, the representational function of the imagination begins to create internal visualizations to represent external entities (Brann, 1991).

Beginning with the substitution of one concrete object for another, the child uses an object during pretend play in a way that is different from the object's originally intended function or purpose. When pretending to use the telephone during a play experience, there may not be a telephone available for use. At this time, the child substitutes a block or other play object for a telephone using his imagination to pretend that the block is a telephone (Bateson, 1999). As a child engages in imaginative play, he may also imagine that a cardboard box is a bed substituting and using one object to represent another. *This type of imaginative representation is a precursor for eventually using combinations of letters to represent actual objects, ideas or feelings in the form of written words. Imaginative engagement in pretense is necessary in both the situations of substituting one object for another as well as substituting combinations of letters for objects.* Because "pretense scenarios invite children to free their own mental representations from their usual referents" (Lillard, 1993, 383), pretense scenarios are necessary to make the semiotic link between two seemingly unrelated entities like written words and concrete objects.

The Imaginative Function of Visualization

Progressing from substituting one concrete object for another to one in which the abstract symbols of letters are used to represent an object, the next stage of literacy development is realized through the imaginative function of visualization. With regard to this progression in imaginative processing, Brann (1991) proposes:

> *Perception is an activity that takes place in the presence of its object; in it sign and signified object are one. Then, imitation begins as an internal motor reproduction of an object or action subsequently remanifested; here a distance is beginning to be put between sign and object. Then, images represent objects in their absence by resembling symbols; on this, the semiotic middle level, sign and signified object are well and driven apart and figurative symbolic representation is in full force. (298-9)*

Brann continues to propose that, in the process of visualization, imagination acts as the mediator between the senses and the reason by representing perceptual elements in their physical absence in image form. During an imaginative dramatization, a child may use a mental visualization to imagine that there is a door to his make-believe house in a certain area of his play situation. Connecting this stage of imaginative engagement to literacy development, when a child looks at a written word, it means nothing at first. From the perspective of visual perception alone, written words are just lines and squiggles on a piece of paper with no meaning. It takes imaginative engagement to assign meaning to the lines and squiggles and to use them to represent something or someone. Since words act as signs that represent something which need not be perceptually present at the moment, the function of the imagination that enables the child to visualize a mental picture when looking at a specific combination of letters also enables him to read written words in a meaningful way. Vygotsky (1917) proposes: "It is here [in play] that the child learns to act in a cognitive, rather than an externally visual, realm by relying on internal tendencies and motives and not on incentives supplied by external things" (96). By connecting unrelated entities in a meaningful way,"imagination assigns meaning to the written word.

Imagination: Mastery of the Language Code

The conceptualization of language in its written alphabetic form is a complex process since the acrophonic system used in writing has absolutely no immediately recognizable interpretation of the actual object being represented (Robinson, 2001; Ferreiro & Teberosky, 1996; Olson, 1992). As Duckworth (1996) suggests, "words do not create the sense or intention or feeling; the words accompany it, or seek to express it, or refer to it" (21). The vital role of imagination in this movement from spoken language, to gestural language, to substitutions for language, to written language is to provide mastery of the semiotic code embedded within each stage of literacy development (Barthes, 1977). As proposed by Kress (1997), "Imagination is an aspect of the processes of sign-making" (108). In the processes of sign making, imagination is needed in order to both create and interpret signs to represent meaning. Johnson (1987) claims that the imagination is central to human meaning and rationality when making significant connections, drawing inferences and solving problems. Imagination makes the connection between a word and an object, person or idea by inferring meaning between the two entities. The imagination connects elements to structure seemingly unrelated, abstract domains into coherent patterned, unified representations. As signs, words indicate something which need not be perceptually present at the moment. Imagination enables children to deal with situations and objects from a distance (Bartlett, 1932).

When a child sees a written word, the word remains an unrelated, separate entity until the imagination is used to connect the word to an object, person or idea which creates meaning. Imagination stores perceptual experiences and elements as memories (Bartsch, 1939). These memories are then connected to present experiences through the "gateway of the imagination" (Dewey, 1934) to form new conceptualizations. In the process of conceptualizing both graphic and written forms of language, the new conceptualization is the assignation of a symbol (picture or word) to an object, person or feeling that is perceived, invented or actually seen. As Brann (1991) proposes, "the specific representations of the imagination are discrete symbols, and the source of its materials are perceptual memories" (17). In this way, imagination is needed to engage in the semiotics of written language.

Linking the Rules of Imaginative Play to Language-Based Literacy

During the preschool years of literacy development, the child first tests the possibilities for language usage as well as alternative means of expression and then sets up socially accepted rules that revolve around the uses of words through imaginative engagement. Through his imaginings, the child is initially able to experiment with both the rules of language usage as well as different speech styles (Meek, 1991). Though this free stage of language experimentation begins in solitary play situations, it eventually shifts direction to move toward language usage that reflects group conformance. Harris (2000) proposes that, later in his literacy development, the child begins to realize that his language usage must fit into a larger social scheme in order to remain a member of the playgroup. Harris also suggests that the exploration, creation and practice of the possibilities for language use is experienced only within the confines of the newly created belief systems of the group during a given, specific play event. Every imaginative play situation has rules (Paley, 1990; Mado-Jones & Egan, 2001). The rules of language usage are explored through joint, group games which create socially conventional uses of language. It is through use of the imagination during play experience that language usage is employed, explored and expanded upon in socially acceptable ways.

The Symbol Construction of Written Language

In the same way that imagination affects literacy development by connecting concrete entities to abstract symbols, imagination assigns the rules of symbol-construction to written language. Harris (2000) suggests that involvement in imaginative experiences are both a correlate and an advance predictor of later success of belief tasks since the process of simulation carries over from pretend play to belief understanding. In literacy learning, this belief understanding enables a child to easily adopt the notion that various combinations of signs (in this case letters) are socially accepted substitutions for actual objects or thoughts. As children begin to create and comply with the imaginative substitutions they make during play situations, they simultaneously compose mental reminders that encode the information implied by their play partners for future use (Harris, 2000). The tendency of the group to remember the substitutions as well as to use them in the same way again sets the stage for the child to adopt the belief that combinations of letters represent actual objects, people or thoughts. Examination of the magical, make-believe components of the imagination explains this idea further.

Turning Rules into Desires

Vygotsky (1917) proposes that there is an attribute of play that turns rules into internal desires. He suggests that carrying out rules is a source of pleasure derived of strong impulse which dictates and directs the child while creating a new form of desires. The presence and use of imaginative substitutions during play seems to create and later foster a desire in children to believe in the magical properties and conceptualizations found in being able to read the written word. In the same pleasurable way, imaginative engagement may also create an urge and desire in children, driving them to want to learn to read the written word. To the child, the imaginative substitutions commonly made during pretend situations are part of the social world of make-believe.

Imagination will often carry us to worlds that never were. Without it, we go nowhere.
CARL SAGAN

The School-Age Years

As children enter their early school years, the necessary imaginative foundation for literacy learning has been laid. At this stage, the once externally expressed, physical imagination realized during play shifts. When children are finally able to read written words, the literacy experience becomes an internal manifestation of the previously explored and accepted conceptualizations of language. The literacy experience is now dictated by imaginative reflection that comes from deep within. "The old adage that child's play is imagination in action can be reversed: we can say that imagination in adolescents and schoolchildren is play *without action*" (Vygotsky, 1917, 129). The imaginative experience is no longer acted upon outwardly, but inwardly, in the mind. There exists a reliance on the imaginative memory of the previously acquired conceptualizations in order to both literally read written words as well as *to build upon them*. Delving into the memory of stored language conceptualizations, the child relies on the imagination to make sense of the printed words on the page (Rosenblatt, 1994).

At this stage of literacy development, the imagination has the power to reproduce language conceptualizations stored in the memory under the suggestion of the associated image of written words. Hubbard and Ernst (1996) propose that by recalling the stored visualizations of language, the imagination enables children to provide literal interpretations of written words. Rosenblatt (1995) refers to this component of the reading experience as an "efferent" one. The interaction of previous and present experiences facilitates a literal interpretation of what is read. Without the imaginative foundation of linguistic conceptualizations in the form of internal visualizations, children would merely be interpreting the oral code of a symbol system during the reading process without any regard for what the signs mean.

Entering a Place of Alternative Experience

Beyond the literal or efferent interpretation of written text, there exists the opportunity to transcend current life and enter into a place of alternative experience (Brann, 1991; Rosenblatt, 1995). Rosenblatt (1995) refers to this as the "aesthetic" reading experience. She proposes that readers bring their own personal experiences to the interpretation of written texts. This stage of literacy development is initially realized through the imaginative foundation of role play. Engagement in role play appears to be a prerequisite for reading comprehension since both the reader and the player need to mentally locate themselves in an imaginary place (Harris, 2000).

For school-aged children, imaginative engagements create a space where literature can be viewed "as a means of enlarging their knowledge of the world, because through literature they acquire not so much additional "information as additional experience. Literature provides a *living through*, not simply *knowledge about...*" (Rosenblatt, 1995, p. 38). After the imagination recalls stored language conceptualizations during the act of reading, the imagination then recombines these former experiences to create new mental images and form new ideas. Through the vehicle of imagination, children are magically transported to new places and experiences making the reading event a lively and creative experience. As proposed by Harris (2000), imagination is a sophisticated mode of thought dominated by free association and inventive thinking that provides the ability to conceive of alternatives to reality.

Through use of the imagination during literacy transactions with text, the variant possibilities of interpretations for written words can be realized (Matthews, 1988). The imagination works to equip the child with the capability to move beyond the literal interpretation of written text toward the awakening, inventing and adopting of new perspectives. It creates the possibility for viewing commonplace ideas in new ways. As proposed by Brann (1991), "Imaginative memory not only stores for us the passing moments of perception; it also transfigures, distances, vivifies, defangs—and reshapes formed impressions, turns oppressive immediacies into wide vistas" (p. 797). Imagination is the component of literacy development that creates a way for children to explore their ideas in new environments by living through the experiences provided in a text. Greene (1995) proposes that the child is able to contemplate the viewpoints and understand the emotions of others that were never before realized by using his imagination as he reads. The imagination challenges the child to reach beyond what exists on the page as written word toward a possibility of what might exist out in the world.

Conclusion

Though literacy is typically defined as interaction with text, consideration of the broader spectrum of literacy as a way of making meaning to serve as an individual mode of expression is essential in order to recognize the many ways in which imagination influences literacy development. If attention is given to the idea that literacy is a part of thinking, as Barton (1994) suggests, and that this part of thinking results in communication, then effective pedagogic literacy practice would deem necessary an acknowledgment of the many forms of literacy expression that exist in schools. By using imaginative vision, people can create alternative explanations and perspectives that differ from their own which fosters a respect for the many diverse forms of literacy expression. As Warnock (1994) proposes, there is importance in "believing that there is more in [one's] experience of the world than can possibly meet the unreflecting eye, [and that this] experience is significant…and worth the attempt to understand it" (22). Understanding the unique expressions individual children use in their representation of the world is important in order for every child to be understood, accepted, and recognized by society in a way that eventually results in their identification as a respected member of society.

The many modes of communication used by children in today's classrooms are worth the attempt to understand. Therefore, the vital role of literacy pedagogy should not only be that of meaning-making within a specific social and cultural environment. Of most importance, the role of literacy pedagogy should be focused on an attempt to understand the unique expressions individual children use in their representation of the world (Kress, 1997). Eleanor Duckworth (1996) writes about the importance of valuing the unique expressions of individual children. She proposes that people who view things one way often have trouble envisioning other ways of making sense. She points out that, just because a child may not process in the same way as is dictated in today's classrooms, it does not mean that the child is hopeless or unintelligent. It only means that the child is thinking differently—differently, but still *adequately*. This different but adequate thinking enlists the creative components of the imagination which results in multiple and alternative perspectives.

Recognition of the importance of imaginative activities such as art programs and play experiences, as well as the many other experiences that allow for diverse thinking, is needed in today's classrooms in order to get back to teaching and learning from a perspective that best matches the authentic, natural instincts of the child. Toward this end, consideration of the re-inclusion of the most essential tool in literacy development, the imagination, is necessary. Imagination, more than the integral ingredient it is in becoming a literate individual, is a platform toward equality that creates the possibility of recognizing and valuing the individual, variant modes of literacy expression in existence. *Imagination is a medium to freedom* (Greene, 1978; Petrosimone, 1993).

References

Barrow, R. (1988). Some observations on the concept of imagination. In K. Egan & D. Nadaner, *Imagination and Education* (pp. xiv, 79-90). New York: Teacher's College Press.

Barthes, R. (1977). *Image, Music, Text.* (S. Heath, Trans.). New York: Hill and Wang.

Barton, D. (1994). *Literacy: An Introduction to the Ecology of Written Language.* Cambridge, MA: Blackwell Publishers Ltd.

Bartlett, F. C. (1932). *Remembering: A Study in Experimental and Social Psychology.* NY: Cambridge University Press.

Bartsch, R. (1939). *Consciousness Emerging: The Dynamics of Perception, Imagination, Action, Memory, Thought, and Language.* Philadelphia: John Benjamins Publishing Company.

Bateson, G. (1999). *Steps to an Ecology of Mind.* Chicago: University of Chicago Press.

Berghoff, B., Borgmann, C. & Parr, C. (2003). *Cycles of Inquiry with the Arts.* Language Arts, **80**, 353-362.

Brann, E. (1991). *The World of the Imagination: Sum and Substance.* Lanham, MD: Rowman & Littlefield Publishers, Inc.

Bronowski, J. (1978). *The Origins of Knowledge and Imagination.* New Haven, CT: Yale University Press.

Cambourne, B. (1988). *The Whole Story: Natural Learning and the Acquisition of Literacy in the Classroom.* Auckland, New Zealand: Ashton Scholastic.

Coleridge, S. (n.d.) Wisdom quotes on imagination. Retrieved September 10, 2003, from www.wisdomquotes.com/cat_imagination.html

Coles, G. (2003). The federal hickory stick for teaching reading. Retrieved February 26,2003, from http://www.educationnews.org/federal_hickory_stick_for_teachi.htm

Collier, R. (n.d.). *Imagination Quotes.* Retrieved September 10, 2003, from http://www. Greaterhorizons.com/imagination.html

Devon, T. (1988). *Myth and Education.* In K. Egan & D. Nadaner, Imagination and Education (pp. 30-44). New York: Teacher's College Press.

Dewey, J. (1897). My pedagogic creed. *The School Journal,* **54,** 77-80. Retrieved (2003, January 27), from http://www.infed.org/archives/e-texts/e-dew-pc.htm John. Dewey—My Pedagogic Creed@the informal education archives.

Dewey, J. (1934). Art as experience. New York: Perigee Books.

Donaldson, M. (1978). Children's minds. New York: W.W. Norton & Company.

Drummond, M. (1994). Learning to see: Assessment through observation. Markham,Ontario: Pembroke Publishers.

Duckworth, E. (1996). "The having of wonderful ideas" and other essays on teachingand learning (2nd ed.). New York: Teachers College Press.

Dyson, A. (1989). *Multiple Worlds of Child Writers: Friends Learning to Write.* New York: Teachers College Press.

Egan, K. & Nadaner, D. (1988). *Imagination and Education.* New York, NY: Teachers College Press.

Ferreiro, E. & Teberosky, A. (1996). *Literacy before Schooling.* Portsmouth, NH: Heinemann.

Gardner, H. (1983). *Frames of Mind: The Theory of Multiple Intelligences.* New York: Basic Books.

Goodman, K. (1996). *On Reading: A Common-sense Look at the Nature of Language and the Science of Reading.* Portsmouth, NH: Heinemann.

Goodman, K., Smith, E.B., Meredith, R. & Goodman, Y. (1987). *Language and Thinking in School: A Whole Language Curriculum* (3rd ed.). New York: Richard Owen Publishers, Inc.

Goodman, Y., Altwerger, B., & Marek, A. (1989). *Print awareness in preschool children: The development of literacy in preschool children.* (Occasional Paper No. 4). Tucson, AZ: Division of Language, Reading and Culture. University of Arizona.

Goodman, Y. (1997). Multiple roads to literacy. In D. Taylor (Ed.), *Many Families, Many Literacies: An International Declaration of Principles* (pp. 56-61). Portsmouth, NH: Heinemann.

Greene, M. (1978). *Landscapes of Learning.* New York: Teachers College press.

—, (1995). *Releasing the Imagination: Essays on Education, the Arts, and Social Change.* San Francisco: Jossey-Bass.

Harris, P. L. (2000). *The Work of the Imagination.* Cambridge, MA: Blackwell Publishers Ltd.

Heal, J. (2003). *Mind, Reason and Imagination: Selected Essays in Philosophy of Mind and Language.* NY: Cambridge University Press.

Hill, Napoleon (n.d.). *Imagination Quotes.* Retrieved on September 10, 2003, from http://www.greaterhorizons.com/imagination.html

Hubbard, R.S., & Ernst, K. (Eds.). (1996). *New Entries: Learning by Writing and Drawing.* Portsmouth, NH: Heinemann.

Johnson, M. (1987). *The Body in the Mind: The Bodily Basis of Meaning, Imagination, and Reason.* Chicago: University of Chicago Press.

Kennan, G. (1904). *The Columbia World of Quotations.* (1996). Retrieved September 9, 2003, from http://www.bartleby.com/66/66/32366.html

Kress, G. (1997). B*efore Writing: Rethinking the Paths to Literacy.* New York: Routledge. Lennon, J. & Barbato, P. (2001).

—, The Emotions: A Vocabulary Before Language. *Journal of the Imagination in Language Learning and Teaching,* **6.**

Libby, S., Powell, S., Messer, D., & Jordan, R. (1998). Spontaneous play in children with autism: A reappraisal. *Journal of Autism and Developmental Disorders,* **28,** 487- 98.

Lillard, A. (1993). Young children's conceptualization of pretense: Action or mental representational state? *Child Development,* **64,** 372-386.

Madoc-Jones, G., & Egan, K. (2001). On the educational uses of fantasy. *Journal of the Imagination in Language Learning and Teaching,* **6.**

Matthews, G. (1988). The philosophical imagination in children's literature. In K. Egan & D. Nadaner, *Imagination and Education* (pp.186-197). New York: Teacher's College Press.

Maude, P. (2001). *Physical Children, Active Literacy: Investigating Physical Literacy.* Philadelphia: Open University Press.

Meek, M. (1991). *On Being Literate.* Portsmouth, NH: Heinemann.

Modell, A. (2003). *Imagination and the Meaningful Brain.* Cambridge, MA: MIT Press.

NCTE Resolutions. (2002). *On the reading first initiative.* Presented at the NCTE Annual Business Meeting, Atlanta, GA. Retrieved January 28, 2003, from http://www.ncte.org/resolutions/readingfirst2002.shtml

Ohanian, S. (1999). *One Size Fits Few: The Folly of Educational Standards.* Portsmouth, NH: Heinemann.

— (2002). *What Happened to Recess and Why Are Our Children Struggling in Kindergarten?* New York: McGraw-Hill.

Olson, J. L. (1992). *Envisioning Writing: Toward an Integration of Drawing and Writing.* Portsmouth, NH: Heinemann.

Ouaknin, M. (1999). *Mysteries of the Alphabet.* New York: Abbeville Press Publishers.

Paley, V. (1986). *Mollie Is Three: Growing Up in School.* Chicago: University of Chicago Press.

— (1990). *The Boy Who Would Be a Helicopter: The Uses of Storytelling in the Classroom.* Cambridge: Harvard University Press.

Petrosimone, D. (1993). Imagination really means freedom. *Journal of the Imagination in Language Learning and Teaching*, 1.

Phillips, D. (1997). Following the imagination: Defining literacy. *Voices in the Middle*, 4, p. 2-5.

Pugh, S., Davis, M., Hicks, J. & Hicks J. (1997). *Metaphorical Ways of Knowing: The Imaginative Nature of Thought and Expression.* Urbana, IL: NCTE.

Robinson, A. (2001). *The Story of Writing: Alphabets, Hieroglyphs & Pictograms.* New York: Thames & Hudson.

Rosenblatt, L. (1994). *The Reader, the Text, the Poem: The Transactional Theory of the Literary Work.* Carbondale, IL: Southern Illinois University Press.

— (1995). *Literature as Exploration* (5th ed.). New York: The Modern Language Association of America.

Roskos, K. & Christie, J. (Eds.). (2000). *Play and Literacy in Early Childhood: Research from Multiple Perspectives.* Mahwah, NJ: Lawrence Erlbaum Associates, Publishers.

Rugg, H. (1963). *Imagination.* New York: Harper & Row.

Sagan, C. (n.d.). *Imagination Quotes.* Retrieved September 9, 2003, from http://www. wisdomquotes.com/cat_imagination.html

Santiago, R. (1997). Imagination in the teaching of reading. *Journal of the Imagination in Language Learning and Teaching*, 4.

Schudel, M. (2001, November 9). No-fun zones: Schools take a recess timeout. *CityTalk*, Winter. Retrieved January 13, 2003, from http://www.findarticles.com/m0HKV/4_10/82880556/p1/article.jhtml

Schuster, K. (2003, February 23). School put to the test. *Newsday.* pp. A8, A37.

Siegler, R.S. (1991). *Children's Thinking.* Englewood Cliffs, NJ: Prentice-Hall.

Strecker, S. & Wells, J. (2001). The arts meet the language arts in kindergarten: A photo essay. *Language Arts*, 78, 543-547.

Sutton-Smith, B. (1988). In search of the imagination. In K. Egan & D. Nadaner, *Imagination and Education* (pp. 3-29). New York: Teacher's College Press.

Traub, J. (2002, November 10). No child left behind: Does it work? *New York Times.* pp.24-27, 30-31.

United States Department of Education. (2001). *No Child Left Behind Act.* Retrieved January 13, 2003, from http://www.whitehouse.gov/news/reports/no-child-left-behind.html

Vygotsky, L. (1917). *Mind in Society: The Development of Higher Psychological Processes.* (M. Cole, V. John-Steiner, S. Scribner, & E. Souberman, Trans. & Eds.).(1978). Cambridge, MA: Harvard University Press.

Vygotsky, L. (1934). *Thought and Language* (A. Kozulin, Trans. & Ed.). (1999). Cambridge, MA: MIT Press.

Wallon, H. (1938). *The World of Henri Wallon.* (G. Voyat, Trans. & Ed.). (1984). New York: Jason Aronson.

Warnock, M. (1994). *Imagination and Time.* Cambridge, MA: Blackwell Publishers Ltd.

Wolfberg, P. (1999). *Play & Imagination in Children with Autism.* New York: Teachers College Press.

Yardley, J. (2000, April 9). A test is born. *New York Times.* p. 32-36.

Poetry Writing: A Neglected Method in ESL Pedagogy

Claudia Gellert Schulte

Having English as a Second Language (ESL) students write poetry can be highly effective in promoting a wide range of goals. These include motivation, personal growth, conceptual development, fluency, creativity and imagination, use of concrete language, appreciation for the nuances of word meaning, and sensitivity to word usage. I will describes a series of activities that were developed for high school classes but are equally applicable to adults. These activities are suitable for students who have written little or no poetry previously, and often have misconceptions about it. Once they had been given a few tools, these same students invariably had a great deal to say and were only too ready to say it. The strategies I developed were intended to open the wellsprings of expression and provide channels for their extraordinary energy and need to tell their stories.

First, students are introduced to the practice of speaking in poetic form. They are then taught the importance of sensory detail and encouraged to describe scenes from their part of the world. Awareness of the senses and the importance of concrete detail is heightened by keeping "sense lists" from the present and the past. Students practice recognizing and creating metaphors, and learn to choose words carefully through haiku. They write poems describing people, and sometimes give new names to themselves and others. Issues such as grading and publishing student work are discussed. The last section of this paper presents an overview of how poetry writing can develop conceptual and other skills needed for successfully coping with the increasingly complexities of the modern world. In my many years of teaching, nothing has ever come close to the joy I've experienced when a student first realizes that she knows English well enough to create a poem. By this I mean not just something that looks like a poem on the page, but carefully crafted lines which, when spoken, convey something to listening classmates which she never could have told them any other way. Despite a limited grasp of grammar, the miracle of poetry has enabled a few well-chosen words to excavate something real and powerful from a deep but seldom-seen place inside her. Though her storehouse of English words was limited, the ones she found were cast in a whole new setting, like a gemstone encased in just the right ring, allowing their beauty and expressive power to shine forth.

A Mission Statement

Our mission is to prepare our students for the future, and in today's dizzying, high-tech, information-glutted world, this is a lot harder than it used to be. The constant influx of new data and concepts requires a whole new array of processing tools for those who would hope to keep up; and the gap keeps widening between those who are equipped for this task and those who will be left behind. Not many people, educators or others, would consider poetry to be one of the requisite tools for dealing with the stringent demands of the information age. Yet, it is clear to me that it has a unique potential for building higher-order concepts, for fostering synthetic thinking based on patterns and networks, and for stimulating creativity, originality, and imagination—the very kinds of skills that are most needed and sought-after today by employers and universities.

Since language and thought are inextricably interwoven, developing good, creative

100

thinking is part and parcel of developing skillful, conceptually rich linguistic ability. Another crucial aspect of this is flexibility: learning to respond to subtle inner impulses, and follow their thought processes into unusual places, rather than always following set forms, Henry Widdowson has argued for recognizing poetry's ability to break the linguistic and conceptual status quo: "Poetry is always in some sense a denial of authority and a celebration of divergence. As such it encourages the kind of scepticism, recognition of relative validity, and critical scrutiny of established modes of thought and expression which, I have argued, it should be the purpose of education to develop." (Widdowson, 1992, 82)

What we are really talking about here is the ability of poetry to promote fluency, which I see as the ability to use language to respond to whatever new demands life presents: whether in the area of work, academic study, interpersonal communication, personal writing, or even inner dialogue. Fluency entails becoming flexible enough on a variety of levels to become one's own person, to listen to one's own voice and learn to speak with it, to perceive the world freshly rather than through stale concepts. It is the ability to be real in one's thinking, feeling, writing, and being. It is an invaluable tool for any time, any place, but particularly for today's complex, rich, ever-changing, brave new world.

Unfortunate Attitudes

For the past twelve years I have taught poetry writing to intermediate and advanced ESL students at two Philadelphia inner-city high schools. Virtually none of them had written much poetry in English, though a handful had done so in their native language. Most of them were afraid of poetry, and had the usual range of misconceptions: that poems were written in old-fashioned language unconnected to anything they knew; that poems contained fancy, difficult words; that poems usually rhymed; and that writing them was something advanced native speakers did—certainly not learners still struggling with the basic rudiments of the language. Another initial assumption by some was that when we were writing poems, we were wasting valuable time that should have been used for the really important things. Unfortunately, many of these attitudes also appear to be common among second language educators. Apart from misconceptions about what poems are and how to write them, there is a widespread assumption that poetry is a "frill," to be assigned much lower priority than the "basics" of reading, grammar, and vocabulary. The following section will discuss why poetry is as valuable as any of these, and deserves more attention in a balanced curriculum aimed at optimal linguistic, cognitive, and personal development.

There are many simple forms that were developed for children but are suitable for all beginning poetry writers, especially those with limited English. A classic guide is Kenneth Koch's *Wishes, Lies, and Dreams* (1970) which allows the novice to get a feel for writing poetry by completing such lines as "I used to be____, but now I'm_____." I have always known about these techniques, have intended to use them for years, and still intend to some day! Nevertheless, I find that my own preference is to start off with a minimum of structure. Instead, I use methods that will enable them to directly express in their own natural style and rhythm what is closest to them and what they most want to say. They start off listening to themselves, finding out what that sounds like, and building from there. Anything that engages the students' curiousity and builds their confidence will work since there is so much they are already waiting to say. The main thing is to share our enthusiasm for the wonders of poetry, read lots of it aloud, and above all, find time for it in a crowded curriculum. In the section to follow, I will present some of the reasons why it is so very important and infinitely rewarding to do so.

Benefits of Poetry Writing in L1 and L2

There are many reasons why poetry writing is basic to any good language program, including second language education. Here is an outline of some of the factors I consider most important:

1. **Motivation**
   A. It can give voice to a student's deepest feelings and concerns, many of which are "off limits" in other types of writing.
   B. Students at all levels can get a feeling of accomplishment from creating a piece of writing which has beauty and expressiveness, even if they lack sophisticated technical knowledge of the language and have difficulty with longer pieces. Such success often dramatically affects the images they have of themselves as learners.
   C. Reading poetry aloud helps students appreciate the beauty and expressive possibilities of the language they are learning.
   D. Creating something beautiful from the student's cultural heritage or personal experience validates both the student and the culture. It can be very gratifying to watch students gather around a bulletin board containing work from a variety of cultures, as they enjoy both the richness of their collective experience and their own pride in having contributed to it.

2. **Personal Growth**
   A. It allows students to communicate with each other through voicing their deepest feelings and most meaningful personal experiences.
   B. It promotes their understanding of other cultures on an emotional and experiential level.
   C. It helps make them keen, active observers of both their inner and outer worlds.
   D. Like all artistic expression, it enables them to "let off steam" in a creative, positive way. It often happens that adolescents with the worst behavior problems become the most articulate and energetic poets. For those who are trying to work things out, be heard, and be appreciated, it is both a useful tool and a supportive companion.

3. Overall Educational Benefits

A. It promotes authentic and concise writing vs. empty and over-used abstractions.

B. Both reading and writing poetry introduce the student to a wide variety of genres, literary devices, voices, and styles.

C. Poetry encourages metaphorical thinking, which aids all aspects of learning. According to Williams (1983), metaphors "organize and connect information," and involve "recognizing and understanding patterns and general principles which give meaning to specific facts" (59). In the process of "making the strange familiar," we "break preconceived connections and generate new and unusual ones (72)."

D. It develops creativity and imagination in general. The great Russian psychologist and thinker Lev Vygotsky—a conoisseur of poetry who took time to read it to his children despite the pressures of time and failing health—was passionate about the value of extending the boundaries of the mind through imagination. He wrote:

> Each step in the child's achievement of a more profound penetration of reality is linked with his continued liberation from earlier, more primitive forms of cognition. A more profound penetration of reality demands that consciousness attain a freer relationship to the elements of that reality, that consciousness depart from the external and apparent aspect of reality that is given directly in perception. The result is that the processes through which the cognition of reality is achieved become more complex and richer.
> (1987, 349)

E. Poetry encourages visual thinking, a key factor in effective reading which is often underdeveloped in children who turn on the television more often than they open a book. It has been found that learners who are trained to generate mental images as they read can substantially improve reading comprehension (Williams 1983). Vygotsky (1994) believed that extended visual thinking in childhood is crucial for the development of intellect.

F. Poetry promotes thinking in terms of networks and patterns, yet another higher-order cognitive skill. Vygotsky claimed that in the development of thinking, "one must turn from a study of concepts as isolated entities to a study of the 'fabric' made of concepts" (1986, 204). Poems are uniquely suited to this type of thought process since, as Roger notes, "the precise contextual value of every word, phrase, clause and sentence of a poem can be inferred only from its interaction with all the others in the text" (1983, 41).

4. Second-Language Acquisition

A. It can help increase awareness of the sounds and rhythms of the language.

B. It acquaints the learner with a variety of registers, dialects, etc.

C. Compared to other writing genres, it may promote fuller vocabulary acquisition by presenting new words in meaningful contexts, rich with sensory and emotional impact. In addition, I have found that it is often the choice of a specific word, rather than a syntactical structure, which focuses a poem's power and impact, or creates confusion if the sense is slightly off. As a result, learners seem more likely to explore the expressive power of individual words, as well as subtle nuances of word meaning, than in other forms of writing.

D. Poetry promotes verbal fluency by allowing for the use of smaller syntactical units, which encourage experimentation and expressive flexibility.

E. Through use of metaphor, poetry is likely to enhance what Danesi (1992) calls "conceptual fluency"— i.e., familiarity with how the world is mapped metaphorically in the target language. L2 learners tend to be deficient in this skill, despite the fact that many or even most linguistic concepts are metaphorical in structure. As a result, they generally tend to relate new concepts back to L1 structures, resulting in conceptual discrepancies.

According to Danesi, the typical L2 curriculum provides "little or no opportunity to access the metaphorically structured conceptual domains inherent in SL discourse (p. 491)."

F. The need to express a deeply felt meaning or perception can lead to increased awareness, and hopefully increased retention, of the syntactical and grammatical points needed to achieve successful expression.

The point has been made that poetry offers a goldmine of possibilities for the cognitive, imaginative, creative, personal, and linguistic development of learners at all levels. The next section will give a limited overview of some resources available to those who wish to tap this vast potential for learning.

A Word about Resources

The approach I will describe here is a particular sequence of activities I have developed over the years which, with variations, has worked for me and feels comfortable—but there is also an abundance of other material which could prove at least equally valuable, whether in place of or in conjunction with the methods offered here. A sampling of these is listed in the bibliography. Many of their ideas overlap in some ways with mine, and probably have influenced me indirectly; this is unavoidable, since while all of the activities included here are original and not taken from printed resources, certain themes are universal to good poetry teaching, such as exploring sensory language, accessing memories, and practice with creating images. Having said that, I do wish to acknowledge a classic work on poetry in the classroom which provided much of my original inspiration and guidance: *The Inward Ear*, by Maley and Duff (1989). It is a treasure trove of suggestions for exploiting the vast potential which both reading and writing poetry hold for L2 learners from the secondary level on. It contains numerous activities for both individuals and groups, covering such topics as using sensory words, understanding what makes a poem, working with pictures, accessing memories, visualizing, and playing with meanings.

In the "hands-on" department, both the fun and the creativity of poetry writing can be greatly enhanced by the use of magnetic poetry sets, available in bookstores. Consisting of individual magnetic words that are moved around on a metal surface, these allow the students to set their imagination free by making unlikely word associations. The results are often quite surprising. Other than teaching materials, one of the most important resources you can own is a collection of poetry you can get truly excited about reading aloud. While it shouldn't be so complex that the students will get nothing from it, it should be challenging enough to be interesting and to invite speculation which can help construct meaning. New words can generally wait until after a first reading to be explained, allowing for a gradual unfolding of meaning. Other poems you collect will serve as models for specific activities such as the ones described here. In addition, it is essential to provide a library of poetry books the students can browse through once they have gotten past the beginning stages. Though it may feel as if they are "not doing anything," it is often very helpful to devote some time to letting them find their own inspiration and points of departure from the poems they most relate to—and this will very widely. Just make sure they are clear about when credit is due to the author.

One of the most valuable resources of all is the students' own experience—the stories and memories that have shaped their lives and their eagerness to tell them, to be seen and understood. In the words of storyteller Rex Ellis, "It's really hard to hate someone whose story you know." Sometimes, too, poetry gives voice to feelings that are too deep or painful to express any other way. Many refugees from war hold memories of traumas that are beyond the confines of ordinary words; in such cases, poetry is uniquely suited to step in, to catch the unspeakable as it overflows from a mind that has seen too much (see Section 8).

Another helpful resource is the motivation engendered by students' being able to tell their stories. While it is not easy to write poetry in a language one hasn't grown up with, as long as their writing is valued and encouraged they will work hard to meet the challenge—and will soon discover that finding just the right word or structure to express a deep feeling, a distant memory, or a subtle perception can be a powerful educational experience as well as an emotional and aesthetic one. Finally, you may find the best resource of all to be the energy that is engendered when poems are shared and displayed. Few things can match the excitement of a student who, though struggling to read and write at the most basic level, sees her own simple but expressive piece of writing posted on the bulletin board along with her more accomplished—and recognized—peers. While the teacher may have helped with technical polishing or offered a fitting word, there was nothing rudimentary about her ideas and insights—and she takes great pride having that known. The excitement is contagious: others who may have been slow to produce pick up momentum, as they realize that many of those whose work are on display are no better students than they are.

Steps Toward Writing Poetry

1. Finding a Voice

This is Just to Say

I have eaten
the plums
that were in
the icebox

and which
you were probably
saving
for breakfast

Forgive me
they were delicious
so sweet
and so cold.

I have seen William Carlos Williams' "This is Just to Say" used in several ways to elicit ideas. Part of what drew me to it is that it is so far from anything most of the students have ever thought of as poetry, and thus is a great springboard for discussing what is and is not poetry. After I distribute the poem I read it out loud, then ask, "Is this a poem?" Opinions vary, and often they assume that it's a poem because of the way the lines are arranged—in which case my next question is, "If you took a note your mother left you asking you to buy a loaf of bread and arranged it like this, would that be a poem?" Eventually I get them to realize that there is something going on here that doesn't meet the eye—the writer is apologizing, but is secretly glad he ate the plums. I point out how—though some would have considered it a poem in any case—in many poems we have to read between the lines and bring something of ourselves to the reading in order to perceive the subtleties. We discuss how the concept of what a poem is has changed in modern times.

Next, I ask them to imagine that they have just found this poem on their kitchen table, and reply to it using the same form—just a few words on each line, divided into stanzas. I tell them it can be any type of response. They can give a direct, straightforward answer, or play with it and be imaginative. Answers run the gamut—and range from forgiving sweetness to angry profanity:

First of all

First of all I want to know/why you ate my stupid plums?
You just don't know how long/I've been wanting to eat those plums
I feel like you took my heart/out of my chest, girl
And don't even think about making it up to me/because there's nothing
you can do or say to make me feel better./That was my breakfast.

(Female, Haiti)

I think

I think you/Were hungry
That is why you/Ate the plums
It's fine/I understand
I will buy more plums from/the supermarket/for breakfast
I forgive you/because it's just some plums
No big deal about this/It's OK.

(Female, Liberia)

Now that the students have a feel for speaking naturally with a new sound and rhythm, I ask them to write to someone else using the same form. It can be someone real or imagined, living or dead: their mother, me, Mickey Mouse, Napoleon, or Michael Jackson, just so they really want to say it. It often becomes a small revelation when something that may have been bothering them, or that aroused feelings of anger or guilt, can be made into something beautiful and considered a work of art—even if a minor one:

For the Child of My Dreams

Someday, somehow/I will hold you with all my
heart./Someday, somehow/I will be there when you need/
that warmest hug./Somewhere, somehow I will be
the air you need and/the food you're fed with.
Oh, child of my dreams,/I will make the air cool
and I will change this world/for you.
Someday, somehow/I will make you the richest kid
in the world.

(Female, Ethiopia)

2. Memories

From learning to speak our minds in a new voice we go right to memories—and begin to learn to access the things we really want to speak about. Often I have started with Nikki Giovanni's "Knoxville, Tennessee:"

I Always Like Summer

I always like summer/best
you can eat fresh corn/from daddy's garden
and okra/and greens/and cabbage/and lots of
barbecue/and buttermilk/and homemade ice-cream
at the church picnic/and listen to/gospel music
outside/at the church homecoming
and go to the mountains with/your grandmother
and go barefooted/and be warm/all the time
not only when you go to bed/and sleep

The point here, of course, is sensory detail. Would this have been as interesting if the first part of the poem had read, "I always liked summer because there were lots of good things to eat" and left it at that? Everyone sees the point. This is the first mention I make of the importance of sensory detail, but by no means the last; I keep up a steady barrage of reminders from this point on. You need to make the point early, and keep hammering it in relentlessly, that probably the single most important key to writing good poetry is to make it concrete, make it real, by using a wealth of tangible details from all of the senses. This is what binds reader to writer, engaging his whole being from the ground up and placing him experientially in the midst of another person's world.

At this point I hand them a sheet containing several poems about childhood memories, mainly of parents and grandparents. We observe how the mention of just a few simple objects brings us right in, engages our attention, makes us feel as if we are there. Periodically, I will paraphrase the poem without those details so the point keeps getting driven home. "Mother's Biscuits" (excerpted) brings in the element of touch to an unusual degree, along with smell and other senses:

> In a big bowl she'd fluff in flour,/Make a fist-dent
> For buttermilk and lard which she squeezed/Between her fingers
> The way a child goes at a mud puddle,
> Raking dry flour/From the sides until it mixed right...
> I'd take some/When leaving late to the schoolbus
> And up the road/I'd run, puffing through biscuit crumbs
> My haloed breath/Into the skin-sharp morning air.
>
> Freda Quenneville

3. Making a Sense List

After reading a variety of simple memory poems and identifying the senses they evoke, it is now time for the students to focus on what they are receiving through their own senses. First I ask them to make a "sense list" of impressions they are experiencing in the present moment in a particular place with a lot going on. Likely choices are the school cafeteria, their own kitchen, a restaurant, or a party. Holding a sheet of paper sideways, they make six columns for each of the five senses plus feeling (emotion), which is optional. They are to take this paper with them to the chosen location and jot down sense impressions in each of the columns, in as much detail as possible. It's not enough to say "a lot of people"—get right down to the nitty-gritty of "a girl in a yellow dress with pink flowers making bubbles with her gum." They won't get it right away; usually it takes several generations, with a lot of my refusing to be satisfied and pushing for more and more detail. It can even be an ongoing assignment: check it the first day, then send them back out to add to it. For those who really get into it, it can be great fun.

Next, I assign a sense list from memory. They choose a place in their native country where they spent a lot of time as a child, and make a list using the same categories. As with anything requiring this kind of concentration, I usually let them start it in class—just closing their eyes and relaxing into it—in case some might have trouble finding a quiet enough spot at home. (I also want to make sure they actually do it, since there are always those who are allergic to all new and strange assignments!) Again, the trick is to not necessarily accept what comes at first, but to insist on ever greater detail.

See: My grandmother sits on the bed. She eats the soup with no teeth.
Hear: She gasps for breath. She always mumbles about how she will die soon.
Taste: My grandmother eats salty soup and a sweet apple.
Touch: The bowl of soup on the table is very hot. My hands press her body.
Smell: When she coughs there is a bad smell. Her skin smells a little bit too.
Feel: The sound of her cough makes me cry and love her too much.

Once they have really done this, they are ready to take some of their sense impressions and turn them into a poem in which they remember the past. Although they have the choice of either using material from their list, or finding new ones for the poems, it is always interesting to see the sense list items incorporated into the final result:

My Grandmother

My grandmother is sitting/on the bed
With white hair/No teeth/Mumbling/She will die soon.
She looks thin/Gaunt/She's nothing but skin and bones.
What a pity!/When I see her/I am sad/Crying
I always/Want to take care of her
Press her back/Legs/Arms
My hands/Make her smile
Comfortable/Happy.

(Female, Vietnam)

4. People

At this point the students have gotten a feel for the power of rich sensory detail in evoking a scene from the past. Other people often figure strongly in the scenes they have depicted, as well as in their sense lists—mostly through watching and listening in increasingly unique ways. Next we take a look at some poems which are actual portraits of particular people—and notice the kinds of images that bring the person right into our presence: Then, with silence and focusing, the students take time to remember those who were closest to them—who inspire the most powerful memories—and invoke their presence using what they have learned about concrete imagery:

The Man Who Walks around All Day and Night

The man who walks around / all day and night is innocent
like a newborn baby. / His eyes' colors are like a rainbow.
He likes to play like a little child. / Every day he walks around
the houses looking for a child to play with.
On Sunday morning he takes a walk on the beach;
and he sits on the rock looking at the sea going up and down.
He looks at the birds fly away.
And he looks at the African sunset.

(Female, Liberia)

5. Metaphor

One thing we have noticed along the way is that many of the most powerful sensory images are not descriptions of "reality" as we know it, but are lies of a sort, fantasies, ways of talking about things as if they were something else. We discuss how this kind of language can make the reader see something in a whole new way, and find examples, a particularly good one being Langston Hughes' well-known "Dream Deferred." They practice finding their own original comparisonss (avoiding the cliches everyone has heard before), worded as similes to start with: e.g., "As mad as…," "school is like…" For many, however, this does not come easily, and it takes much practice and encouragement. I tell them how metaphorical thinking, and visual imagery in general, will help them to become better thinkers. They get my little speech about how reading involves visual thinking and imagination, and how children who grow up watching TV, movies and video games are often limited in imagination, which is related to intelligence in general. Ears perk up, brains shift into a higher gear, and the results are often impressive. This first example finds its inspiration in Langston Hughes:

Broken Love

What happens to a broken love?/Does it make your life miserable
like an old car, or make you dry/like a river without water?
Or does it break like a pencil,/or like a glass that drops on the floor?
Maybe it's just a feeling that comes and goes—
or does it kill?

(Female, Liberia)

Here is another example of metaphor's ability to express the subtleties of intense emotion:

You

My life is a song/Unfinished…
You come/Change its tune

My life is a tree in the winter/Stripped of its leaves…
You come/Carry the warmth of the Spring

My life is a quiet river/Water flows and ebbs every day
You come/Waves and wind

I am a white mare/Running…without target
You are a carpet of green/A blue and pure stream
Make me look back and halt

(Female, Vietnam)

6. Parents

Many years ago I came across a poem in which the poet describes the early lives of her parents, and thought it would serve as an interesting springboard for getting into the topic of family background. Little did I know what treasures that topic would unearth.

I wonder about the first time/my mom met my dad.
She was walking the forest,/taking water from
the lake, had long hair,/long dress. As she passed
she overwhelmed him with her long hair,/nd he called to her.
She started to walk fast; he called her/one more time, then she
looked at him. He said,/"Come, let's walk in the forest together."
Then I imagine/her feeling his face./He tried to take
the grass from her/hair; it felt like/he was picking
roses.

(Female, Liberia)

Parents' stories allow us to share in the intimate personal experiences of those who grew up—and, unlike their children, continued to grow up—in the native country. In addition to being touching stories in their own right, imbued with heartfelt feelings and perceptions that can only arise from the perspective of love, they are a window into the cultural and family traditions that shaped their children's lives.

7. Haiku

There were years when I never got around to haiku. Those years I was more concerned with calling up memories, expressing feelings, developing a command of rich sensory imagery, and exploring identity. But when I did start fitting it in, I realized right away that it contributed some absolutely indispensable elements to the process of learning to write good poetry; i.e., a sense of how important each word was, how much could be conveyed with a very few words, and the heightened impact the rest of the words had when unnecessary words were taken away. I found a nice way to introduce haiku in *Adventures in Literature* (Bronze). Students are asked to remember a scene in nature they had experienced, then write about it in a paragraph. After reading three sample haiku and coming to understand the basics of the form, they distill their paragraph down to an essential image. The goal is to stay within the traditional seventeen syllables, but we are flexible:

I like the tree
I like when a bird sits on it
And the wind is flowing around
With love songs

The pink butterfly
Flies toward me
I feel like I am a flower

(Female, Cambodia)

8. Name Poems

A couple of years ago we were reading *Morning Girl* by Michael Dorris, the beautiful story of a Native American girl and her brother, Star Boy. We discussed how in many cultures people are given names which fit their unique personalities, talents and abilities, or experiences that have affected them deeply. Names can even be given temporarily for healing purposes, to help a person through a crisis by enabling him to perceive himself differently. This area is something many of the students pick up on fairly readily, relating it to their own experiences with nicknames. The book *The Wishing Bone Cycle* contains many intriguing examples of poems by the Swampy Cree Indians describing how different individuals came to receive their names. After reading examples from the book, I ask the students to write two name poems, one about themselves and the other about someone they know; they can start with either one. As with family history poems, these can take us deep into personal memories which often provide us with beautiful windows into the native culture:

My name is River Water
I love the river because when the/Sun is hot the river water is cold…
My name is River Water
I remember my grandmother/looking at me and laughing
And laughing, because I love water/And I am afraid of water…
I love drinking river water early/In the morning like my grandmother
My name is River Water
Now here I am far away from the river.

(Male, Liberia)

While some of the name poems involve the unfolding of personal stories and memories, others can be a way of describing a friend from a new perspective or of conveying a personal insight metaphorically in a concise, haiku-inspired vignette:

I am a Sunflower/I spread incense through/the garden
I am a yellow egg/Around me are green leaves
I have fun/When I bloom in Summer

Showing people / I am a gift of God
I swing in the wind / I am a sunflower

(Female, Bangladesh)

9. War

Once the students are off and running, you will find a wide variety of poetic forms to explore, and an endless series of topics will present themselves. Of the various possibilities, the subject of war deserves special mention because the poems it inspires have particular impact and poignancy. At least within the population I teach, it is an unfortunate fact that many of the students' clearest and most intense memories have to do with wars they have experienced, either first-hand or through the impact on their families. Most of my African students are refugees from the constant turmoil that kept them on the move, separated their families, and disrupted their education. Many of them were witnesses to violence and death, sometimes involving immediate family members. Cambodians and Vietnamese, while too young to have witnessed these horrors first-hand are strongly affected by their families' stories. A number of years ago I used as a model a poem about the war in Bosnia which resonated with the experience of quite a few students. As happened often—but particularly dramatically in this case—they were able to utilize a catalyst in this way to unlock vast stores of powerful, emotionally charged memory:

The young boys, hardly become men,/fighting and shooting guns
during the war. They were shooting/because their brothers and sisters
and mothers were dying./Shooting and fighting with guns they'd never
seen before in their lives./Brother, my brother, was one of the fighters
His fingers touched what he wasn't supposed to touch. He got hit
by a bullet at the front. No one there to try to stanch the blood.
He tried and tried/to press his wounded leg. But no one was there
to help him.

(Female, Liberia)

Conclusion

Once the students have practiced these methods or similar ones, they will have a solid basis for continuing on to explore new frontiers in poetry writing—if they have been continually prodded into using sharp, detailed, original images, and have gotten used to considering the impact of each word. It also helps to point out how poets use words in unusual ways, and often play with sounds through alliteration and repetition of lines. Rhyme, while generally too constricting for beginning poets, is yet another element they can experiment with, and throw into the mix on occasion. Beyond that, as long as you continue reading and sharing poetry that strikes a chord with you, you will have an endless wellspring of further ideas for modeling and inspiration; poems students discover during free reading times can contribute ideas as well. It is very important to stay tuned in to what they are responding to, which sometimes means being ready to abandon your own plans, beliefs, and sometimes even tastes, to "go with the flow."

Quite often the students will have things on their minds that are burdensome or painful, whether experiences from the present, or traumatic events from the past, such as war. Putting such feelings into a poem can not only provide relief and fulfillment for the moment, but can also be a deeply healing process for the long term. Generally, there is an openness to sharing very private thoughts and feelings with classmates that would be difficult to achieve with other forms of writing or other classroom activities. It is also possible to combine poetry with journal writing by allowing a poem to be submitted as an alternative to a regular journal entry, thereby encouraging the use of poetry as a tool for deep personal reflection. There is a whole field called Poetry Therapy which deals with some of the ramifications of using it for healing and growth (Fox, 1997). You may wonder at times just how much "help" you can offer while still ensuring that the poem is basically the student's, and not a joint venture. My own feeling is that in addition to correcting mechanics, it is entirely appropriate to help a student find clear wording for a thought or feeling that he would otherwise be unable to express. This can, in fact, be an extremely powerful way for students to internalize points of grammar and usage and become aware of subtle nuances of word meaning. We need to always be on the lookout for such learning opportunities. If a point isn't clear, or if a word seems not quite right, dig—find out what the student is really trying to say. The payoff can be enormous.

Grading Poems

A word needs to be said about the issue of grading poetry. Obviously, it would be counter-productive to reserve the highest grades for poems that could be published in a literary journal. Effort must pay off if motivation is to be maintained, and those with minimal literacy skills who nevertheless try their best need to be rewarded. For the most part, I award credit through other means than number of letter grades. The main criterion is whether they have tried to do what they were asked to do; i.e., how much effort and imagination they put into doing what the assignment called for. I am rather fussy about this since I feel it is essential to master specific skills at particular times in order to get the full benefit of the process. If they came up with something good but that is not what I assigned, I praise it and give them credit for an "extra" poem, while still requiring them to do the one assigned. I allow for some exceptions, such as for a student who really enjoys working within a particular style, or another who has a hard time grasping figurative language, but continues to write in other ways. To keep track of who has done what, I find it helpful to number the assignments rather than have to figure out which is which. In order to keep the process going and derive the maximum benefit from it in terms of motivation and continued progress, it is essential to either publish student work or display it on bulletin boards or around the classroom. This validates their efforts, helps them see themselves as both competent writers and creative artists, and brings others out of the woodwork in an attempt to see if they can do something worth sharing as well.

References

Danesi, M. 1992. "Metaphorical Competence in Second Language Acquisition and Second Language Teaching: The Neglected Dimension." In J.E. Alatis (ed). *Georgetown University Round Table on Languages and Linguistics*. 1992.

Fox, J. 1997. *Poetic Medicine: The Healing Art of Poem-Making*. New York,. Tarcher/Putnam.Giovanni, N. 1994. Knoxville, Tennessee. New York: Scholastic.

Koch, K. 1970. *Wishes, Lies, and Dreams: Teaching Children to Write Poetry*. New York. Vintage Books.

Maley, A. and Duff, A. 1989. *The Inward Ear: Poetry in the Language Classroom*. Cambridge University Press

McClosky, M.L. and Stack, L. 1996. *Adventures in Literature*. New York. Heinle & Heinle.

Norman, H.A. (ed). *The Wishing Bone Cycle: Narrative Poems From the Swampy Cree Indians*. New York. Stonehill Publishing Co.

Quenneville, F. 1966. "Mother's Biscuits," in S. Dunning et al., *Reflections on a Gift of Watermelon Pickle and Other Modern Verse*. New York: Scholastic Book Services.

Rodger, A. 1983. "Language for Literature." In C. Brumfit (ed). *Teaching Literataure Overseas: Language-Based Approaches*. ELT Documents 115, Pergamon Press.

Vygotsky, L.S. 1986. *Thought and Language*. A. Kozulin (ed). Cambridge, MA. MIT Press. (Original work published 1934.)

— 1987. Imagination and Its Development in Childhood. In W. Rieber and A. Carton (eds). *The Collected Works of L.S. Vygotsky*, Vol. 1. New York. Plenum Press.

— 1994. "Imagination and Creativity of the Adolescent." In R. Van der Veer and J. Valsiner (eds). *The Vygotsky Reader*. Oxford. Blackwell.

Widdowson, H.G. 1992. *Practical Stylistics*. Oxford University Press.

Williams, L.V. 1983. *Teaching for the Two-Sided Mind: A Guide to Right Brain/Left Brain Education*. New York. Touchstone Books.

Learning English through DVD Feature Films

Jane King

A Global Preview

1) Technology will doubtless have a great impact on student learning in the present century. English teaching and learning have already swiftly moved into a new era. Teachers can develop a vast array of meaningful project-based learning activities for students to use technology in learning English.

2) Students have the tendency to become infatuated with showy multimedia, graphics, animation, and sound effects to showcase their final presentation, yet remain incapable of transforming information creatively and critically. In addition, their dearth of practice in English public speaking and presentation is often painfully obvious.

3) Adopting a film project approach promotes real language use and familiarizes students with a diversity of learning styles and multiple intelligences in a rich constructive learning environment.

4) DVD films provide numerous pedagogical options and are a rich resource of intrinsically motivating and authentic materials. Undertaking a film project is an activity that allows students to explore a film in a project-based scenario and exhibit their understanding and critical reviews of it through technological tools and then present their views to a real audience.

5) Positive outcomes of DVD film project learning include increased motivation, active participation, improved student/teacher interaction and collaboration, better-developed research, task and time management skills.

Introduction

In the traditional language lab classroom, students used to sit in their isolated booths passively listening to monotonous audiotapes, more often than not being lulled by them into a mindless nap. Now vibrant and exciting multimedia-driven computer-assisted learning seldom fail to attract their attention. They are compelled to leave their cozy booths and learn to use PowerPoint and other computer applications for their presentations. In coming to grips with this E-generation, teachers should leave behind former expectations and go beyond information recall, oral recitation, worksheets, and rule/vocabulary grammatical explanations in the English classroom and provide highly engaging learning activities that are both motivating and challenging. Teachers must adapt to learners who are living in an age of visual technology and massive information, in a world where rapid changes take place every day.

A "film project" as we are using the term, is an activity that allows students to implement PowerPoint and DVD clips in an oral presentation. Students are designated a DVD feature film to explore and review and to exhibit their understanding and critical review of it through a multimedia presentation. This project offers multiple ways for students to apply prior language skills and demonstrate their English proficiency in a highly creative way. When DVD feature films, which here refer to public viewing version films and internet films, are exploited as texts in project-based learning, many features are added to this form of project learning: authentic and real-life situations; challenging, fun-filled and intrinsically motivating activities; the immense range of subject, culture, communication, and inspiration that films entail can be used as stimuli for research and discussion, rich sources of slang, idiomatic and colloquial English as well as a combination of stunning visual effects and stirring music, all of which are capable of powerfully riveting students' attention.

Theoretical Basis of Project-Based Learning

The basic features of project-based learning are quite different from familiar and established language learning in many aspects. In the traditional classroom, the teacher explains new vocabulary and grammatical rules, and students work out exercises on worksheets and take endless quizzes and tests that require no more than the reproduction of information, a form of cognitive learning that is usually ranked at the lowest level. In project-based learning, on the other hand, students are encouraged to engage in inquiry and higher order thinking skills, and are allowed to work autonomously to enhance their own knowledge and demonstrate their learning in oral reports. Projects that have depth, duration, and complexity will challenge students and help them to develop a variety of social skills relating to group work and negotiation through cooperative learning. Such projects are flexible enough to suit students' individual learning styles and strategies. Project-based learning requires team work and group process skills such as leadership, delegating and assigning roles, intensive collaboration, negotiation, organization, planning, and technical expertise.

The use of project-based learning with language learners impacts upon content materials, teaching roles, and the focus of assessments in the classroom. Content materials are not limited to printed materials and lectures: non-print materials such as films, interviews, and TV videos can be effectively used for instruction. In regard to the function of teaching, not only does the teacher work as an adviser, but she/he also serves as a resource provider and guide to facilitate student learning. Additionally, projects can shift the focus of assessment from textbook-oriented testing to authentic and performance-based evaluation. The learning process itself together with the tangible accomplishments of students becomes more highly valued than test scores.

Style and Intelligence Diversity

Learning styles theory offers teachers insights into the use of student learning styles in language learning and the impact of teacher teaching styles on student learning. Classroom activities designed by teachers should address all learning styles; the utilization of one particular style might frustrate students with other learning styles. Teachers need to become more aware of their students' strengths and weaknesses to improve the curriculum and methods of instruction. Project-based learning is an effective way of adapting to individual differences and of actively involving the entire gamut of students, from kindergartners to adult English learners possessing varying levels of English proficiency (Katz, L 1999; Moss and Van Duzer, 1998).

In order to accommodate intelligence diversity, many teachers have successfully implemented Gardner's theory of multiple intelligences (1983) into their classrooms and developed activities that benefit all learners. Armstrong (1994) later added several key points to the multiple intelligences theory, viz., each person possesses all seven intelligences; most people can develop each intelligence to an adequate level of competency; intelligences usually work together in complex ways and there are many ways to display intelligence within each category. Project learning multiplies the ways that individual students can contribute to their project work because they allow learners to apply and accommodate various kinds of intelligence in completing a project in ways they can be proud of. The following table classifies the different kinds of intelligence and identifies a corresponding assignment appropriate to that intelligence in the development of a film project.

TABLE 1: ROLES OF MULTIPLE INTELLIGENCES IN CREATING FILM PROJECTS
Linguistic: Read movie reviews, actor/actress background, behind the scenes, collect information and research (internet, newspaper and library).
Logical-Math: Conduct survey, analyze data, write outline, indicate logical development and organization, design a flowchart.
Spatial: create visual media, create graph or pie, design graphics and layout, animation.
Bodily-Kinesthetic: Participate in skits and role playing, prepare props, equipment, and films, do the film editing.
Musical: Prepare background music and sound effects.
Interpersonal: Coordinate, delegate, assign roles, negotiate, promote team spirit, give and conduct interviews, resolve conflicts.
Intrapersonal: Provide journals ideas and film reviews, consider alternatives, reflect on and assess the project, report progress

Constructivist Learning

In recent years, Piagetian and constructivist learning principles increasingly exerted an influence on language learning. The fundamental principles (Duffy & Jonassen, 1991, 1992; Piaget, 1955, 1972; Vygotsky & Vygotsky, 1978) in relation to language learning include the following principles: 1) Learning is an active and collaborative process; 2) Learning must be situated in authentic and real life settings; 3) Learning is knowledge constructed from previous knowledge and experience; 4) Teachers act as facilitators. Constructivism embodies a much more learner-centered paradigm than other communicative approaches. It favors problem-based and process-oriented learning within a rich and facilitative learning environment. As to the closely tied relationship between technology and project-based learning, technology increases "the versatility and value of project-based learning as a curriculum tool. Technology can help create a rich environment for individuals and teams to carry out in-depth projects that draw on multimedia and information resources form throughout the world" (Moursund, 1997). English learners are no longer passive recipients of teacher-imparted English knowledge; instead, they actively and collaboratively engage in authentic tasks in a meaningful and real-world context and should not be subjected to abstract instruction out of context.

Cognitive Learning Activities

Internet-loaded computers provide students access to abundant information resources. The mass of language data available to students is overwhelming. Many information collection activities are quite popular among students and teachers who have Internet access. However, some scholars warn that giving students information is not identical to giving them knowledge (Fox 1991; Taylor & Swartz, 1991). Knowledge is the result of the process of knowing, which can only occur as the learner actively constructs what s/he knows. Using information is an intrinsic feature in this process. Thus it is extremely important for students to "perceive of themselves not only as collectors of information that has been requested by their teacher, but as generators, organizers, and analyzers of that information" (Harris, 1994). Harris also adds that information that is actively sought and interpersonally shared in a context of mutual interest can make school come alive for students. The most motivating and successful activity structures are those that encourage students to collect and share information…and then use it to actively create high-order ideas (Harris, 1995). The teacher takes the role as a facilitator in promoting students' critical thinking skills, reflecting on the language data and requiring them to integrate, synthesize, and critically evaluate information.

Students who are accustomed to memorizing texts or being "spoon-fed" English often have trouble synthesizing ideas, organizing concepts and applying principles to real situations in English academic studies. Kabilan (2000) believes that learners can only become proficient language users if they not only use the language and know meanings, but can also display creative and critical thinking by means of the target language. Creative and critical thinking skills should not be taught separately; rather they ought to be embedded in meaningful, purposeful and task-based learning. Casanave & Freeman (1995) purposely involved their Japanese students in a film presentation project that required complex thinking, organizational and presentation skills, and language skills. They chose to give higher priority to students' "educational growth—the development of curiosity, critical and analytical thinking abilities, and skill in problem posing and exploration" (Casanave & Freeman, 1995) than with students' linguistic proficiency. Though at times they may have been disappointed with those students' final presentation projects characterized by a lack of insightful, analytical thinking, they, nevertheless, praised their students for their ability to put together a coordinated show, a task that may not have been either deeply intellectual or English-language oriented, but one that did require intensive collaboration, negotiation, organization, planning, and technical expertise.

Bloom's Cognitive Taxonomy

Film Studies as a discipline presently requires the viewer to read a film critically: how a film conveys its meaning and how the audience can best discern all that a film is attempting to communicate. From my own teaching experience, I have observed that even if students have not learned critical skills in viewing a film as a printed text, they certainly tend to be infatuated with showy multimedia, graphics, sound effects and background music and work hard to impress their peer audience. In order to enhance the quality of students' presentations, I employed Bloom's (1956) cognitive taxonomy and developed some possible film activities and topics for students to differentiate levels of thinking and formulate higher order questions for their projects. I challenged them to move from lower cognitive levels of knowledge and comprehension to higher levels, where they engage in analysis, synthesis, and evaluation.

Taxonomy and Activities

1. **Knowledge**
   Work on worksheets or study questions.
   Define new words or phrases.
   Answer when, who and where questions.
   Remember facts and terms.
   Identify examples or details of the movie.

2. Comprehension

Paraphrase new words or expressions.
Outline the storyline.
Read movie reviews.
Summarize the plot in writing.
Retell the story orally.
Describe the most impressive scene.

3. Application

Role-play one scene in the movie.
Present the plot in new forms.
Solve a problem or prove a point.
Interview producers or characters.
Produce promotional commercials/ads for the movie.
Predict what would happen if…

4. Analysis

Undertake a character analysis.
Compare the differences and similarities.
Compare or differentiate the same movies in different versions.
Analyze the causes and effects of some events in the movie.
Contrast the personalities of two characters.
Generate criteria for movie presentations or movie reviews.
Identify conflicts or problems that make up particular situations.
Analyze the use and effectiveness of film techniques (foreshadowing or flashbacks). Describe the interrelationships among characters.

5. Synthesis

Create a new ending.
Come up with an unusual title and justify it.
Analyze "what if" possible situations in the movie.
Make a new version of the movie.
Define the conflicts in the movies.
Identify the major theme.

6. Evaluation

Evaluate the movie with given criteria.
Provide feedback for peers.
Conduct a self-evaluation.
Defend your movie review.

DVD Feature Films

DVD provides more pedagogical options and benefits as the current movie medium of choice, replacing VHS tapes over the last few years. Besides its durability, compactness, availability, and high audio/visual quality, there are a number of special features offered on DVD, including interactive menus, theatrical trailer, behind the scenes commentary, language options and subtitles. DVD offers as many as eight languages and thirty-two sets of closed captions, selectable without the aid of a caption decoder. It also provides program-mable censoring, and nine special interactive features, such as slow motion, freeze, random-access viewing, multiple camera angles and multiple movie endings (Chun, 1996). Immediate scene access is a feature that helps tremendously in teaching with movies because it becomes much easier to find an exact scene in seconds and avoid the constant rewinding required when using VHS tapes. It is also timesaving and efficient for students to show their chosen scenes during presentations. The music function in DVD players allows students to play a theme song, or background music during a presentation. Among other features, theatrical trailer and behind the scenes are excellent supplementary materials that can be used in a film project.

Feature films are more intrinsically motivating than videos made for EFL/ESL teaching because they embody the notion that "a film is a story that wants to be told rather than a lesson that needs to be taught" (Ward & Lepeintre, 1996). Moreover, the realism of movies provides a wealth of contextualized linguistic, paralinguistic and authentic cross-cultural information, classroom listening comprehension and fluency practice (Braddock, 1996; Mejia, 1994; Stempleski, 2000, Wood, 1995). Films are such valuable and rich resources for teaching in that they present colloquial English in real life contexts rather than artificial situations, and seemingly endless opportunities for exposure to different native speakers, slang, reduced speech, stress, accents, and dialects.

Student-Created PowerPoint Presentation

Oral presentations serve as a purposeful activity in that such an assignment entails searching for information, organizing that information, interpreting it and shaping it into a document and finally sharing results with others. Computer applications make the whole process of oral presentation more interesting for presenters and the created product more appealing for audiences. A series of eye-catching PowerPoint slides cannot fail to attract an audience's attention, since content can be presented realistically with pictures. PowerPoint is a presentation program that provides numerous predefined templates for novices who are developing their first electronic slideshow. The beginners may just select a background template, create screens with text and graphics, and then sequence the presentation. Advanced computer users will add media elements for fun or a professional look since the distinctive feature of PowerPoint is that it includes a wide array of fonts, backgrounds, text colors, clip art and multimedia elements that can be incorporated into a presentation. PowerPoint greatly helps inexperienced presenters in delivering a speech. At first, constructing PowerPoint requires the active processing of information and an outline of main ideas on the screen, with a limited amount of text on the screen. Presenters learn to condense and organize information. Additionally, PowerPoint is effective at cueing the memory, that is, functioning as a set of electronic index cards; it helps retrieve information and provides back-up notes a presenter can fall back on in case s/he suffers a mental lapse. Presenters' speech anxiety is tremendously reduced because the audience's attention is divided and the focus is not always on them. A wide number of divergent results both in process and product between PowerPoint presentations and strictly oral presentations has been observed (Schcolnik,1999): students personalize their presentations by choosing background colors, graphics, fonts and even sound and video for each slide; students are more involved and committed to the quality of their work and take great pride in and have an increased sense of ownership of (Fogarty, 1997) their products.

Procedure

About 300 college students with different majors participate in the film project. Four or five students are placed in small groups of their choice to avoid time conflict problem. The scheduled 20-30 minutes of presentation time are evenly distributed among all members, which means every member of each group has to report parts of the content orally. The teacher allots available weeks for students to schedule their presentation dates in the course of one semester, usually every other week, for students to choose from. All presentation dates are scheduled at the beginning of the semester.

In order to deepen their viewing experience and think creatively in terms of the film medium, the first step is to inform students that they should go beyond simple information recall and give personal responses and interpretations of a given film, which are to serve as a basis for discussion. Two types of projects are offered as options to students. The first is an information-based presentation that simply provides a synopsis, key words, actor/actress background, memorable quotes/scenes, behind the scenes, and the use of up to five minutes of selected scenes on DVD to reinforce or elaborate their oral report on PowerPoint. The other option is a student-initiated, problem-based presentation that is much preferred and graded highly for it promotes high order thinking skills and focuses on inquiry and analysis. This kind of presentation encourages students to engage in brainstorming and formulating a discussion question collaboratively. They must be creative in their production of ideas, and support them with logical explanations, details and examples.

Suggestions

Learning English through film viewing represents a novel approach that involves students who tend not to be overly enthusiastic in learning English in traditional ways. Even the sullen and withdrawn begin to participate and gain confidence in the process by working collaboratively in a group. Most traditional teaching materials lack a realistic and meaningful context and fail to deal with contemporary issues that are relevant to their lives. For the most part, students' past English learning experiences have been primarily textbook-oriented and test-driven in nature, with the focus on analyzing numerous details of language rather than absorbing the general gist of communicative discourse. Film projects provide a refreshing learning experience for students who need to take a break from rote learning of endless English vocabulary and drill practices, and replace such abstracted tedium with authentic materials from the real world. Students are quick to adapt to technology, are eager to work together and end up with a strong sense of achievement. For most students, a film project represents their initial experience in attempting to communicate ideas and organize their presentations in an efficient and attractive way. They take pride in designing layout, graphics, animation and other visual effects for the project and in presenting their final creative product in front of their classmates. Though a competitive climate among students may emerge in the process, this may not prove to be altogether unwanted; rather, such an environment is likely to serve as a positive motivational force in striving for excellence. Most students are willing to invest the time and effort into a film project upon realizing that their presentations are not only appreciated by their classmates, but also serve them as a source of inspiration.

Another finding indicates that when students are given autonomy and their own choice of topic, they invest their work with enthusiasm and become active in their pursuit of learning. Students are allowed to choose projects that fit their own interests and abilities. They become more responsible for their own learning because they hold themselves accountable for choosing how to demonstrate their English proficiency. Students are challenged because they have to work purposively, with a clear goal in mind. Students exhibit growth in problem-solving, and social skills, and also task and time management skills through the realization of this assignment.

Completing this Project

In the process of completing a film project, students learn to use a variety of tools and resources in creative fashion to arrive at an end product. As a rule students put on very impressive technology shows, having made use of the Internet, word processing, a digital video camera and editing equipment to wow their audience. Yet, they oftentimes lack the ability to go beyond factual memorization and superficial understanding of the content, even in the final presentation. Though they have practiced English in endless decontextualized exercises and tests, they still remain in the dark when it comes to using English to communicate ideas and opinions. They are petrified of making grammatical errors and taking risks and this prevents them from confidently reconstructing a deep understanding reproduced in their own words from the materials and information they have collected. Reading texts copied from Internet resources are an all too typical approach. The most frequently used question skill is making comparisons between movies. They limit themselves to contrasting the most obvious differences and similarities between two movies.

Exploration of Film Topic

Thus, a major challenge for students and teachers is to go beyond superficialities and arrive at in-depth investigations and explorations of film-related topics. In other words, posing driving questions pertaining to a film, and then developing logical reasoning, and analytical and critical thinking skills are some problems for teachers to ponder after student-created PowerPoint presentation. Other topics for consideration related to film project learning include the following:

1. Teacher Expectations:

Clearly state teacher expectations, provide grading criteria and end of project self-assessment. Using technological tools should not be the central focus of the film project. They are incorporated into the classroom to supplement the film project that emphasizes the application of speaking, reading, and listening skills. The emphasis of project learning is placed squarely on the learning process of researching, organizing, and negotiating that lead up to the final presentations. It is important to evaluate the intangibles of the project such as teamwork issues and unsuccessful experiences. A student-teacher conference, held both before and after the presentation, is a good way for students to learn how to overcome their problems and how they prepare the final version of their product. Students tend to read movie reviews in Chinese instead of using English search engines. It is probably advisable to have students turn in research materials as parts of a portfolio assessment and performance-based assessment to ensure they read English texts.

2. Public Speaking:

Provide more opportunities for practicing effective public speaking skills. As a rule, activities should be repeated twice a year to gauge progress. Generally, EFL university-level students have some academic research skills, but they lack training and experience in public speaking. Encourage students to review some basic presentation skills:

A. Establish rapport and maintain eye contact with the audience.

B. Use communicative or oral English and explain unfamiliar terms, if necessary.

C. Refer to written cue cards or notes and avoid reading word by word.

D. Begin the presentation with a thesis statement and maintain a leisurely pace of speech with a clear introduction; avoid rushing through it nervously.

E. Outline main ideas and expand on them.

F. Have a logical development and supportive details in the body and a strong conclusion that summarizes the main points or closes with a memorable statement.

G. Time the presentation in advance.

3. Presentation Checklist:

In order to start students on the road to presentational success, the instructor should distribute an oral presentation checklist (Buck, 1999) or rubric at the beginning of the project that clearly defines teacher expectations, helps construction monitoring and serves as grading criteria.

4. Advantages of Multimedia:

Students often encounter the same problems, such as using PowerPoint and DVD clips, failing to explain the text on the PowerPoint screen or why they are showing the DVD clips and how they relate to their presentation. PowerPoint and DVD create a powerful effect, help keep students' attention, and illustrate main ideas clearly. However, it is important to explain the purpose of multimedia tools because they are to be used to supplement or support film projects, and they should not take the place of the students' own oral presentation. Several tips are suggested in preparing students to deliver their speeches:

A. Avoid excessive dependence on visual aids, which may only serve to distract the audience's attention. A maximum 5-minute showing of DVD clips in a 20-minute presentation should be emphasized in advance to prevent the dominance of visual aids in the presentation or making them the central focus of the presentation.

B. The speech should be relevant to the text or pictures displayed on PowerPoint. Notes should be used sparingly and the screen referred to only on occasion; PowerPoint is primarily intended to enhance the speech and reinforce the main ideas.

C. Allow time for the audience to read a longer text; otherwise, they may not be able to grasp the main points.

D. Condense information and limit the text on the screen.

    1. Texts should be easily viewed and read by the entire audience.

    2. Edit texts on PowerPoint, looking out for misspellings or grammatical errors.

    3. Use English-captioned films instead of Chinese-captioned counterparts.

    4. A microphone should be prepared for learners in advance to ensure optimal voice quality. The instructor should not need to ask shy presenters to project their voice in a big classroom. If possible, control the lighting when using visual aids and always leave a light on in the back of the room, so the audience can still maintain eye contact with the presenter.

5. Oral Report:

Presenting an oral report in a classroom situation is a complex task and requires good teamwork and the ability to work within time limitations. Thus, it is essential for students to know in advance how to handle all necessary equipment. A discussion about the equal importance of both rehearsal and performance will prevent students from encountering unexpected technical problems and experiencing panic on the day of the presentation. The instructor should make available her/his office hours or a scheduled conference with students should take place in the hall where the presentation will be given. The teacher can provide appropriate suggestions, if any, for possible revision and students can rehearse their presentations and gain adequate familiarity with equipment.

Conclusion

The incorporation of PowerPoint and DVD into film projects has been deemed to be positive and worthwhile by the students themselves in their end of semester evaluations. This technology-oriented project provides an excellent vehicle not only for helping students to engage in authentic English tasks in which they immerse themselves organizing, synthesizing, and evaluating information, but it also serves to expand students' capacity in articulating, displaying, manipulating and communicating information. Project-based learning offers students the opportunity to actively engage their multiple intelligences, high-order thinking skills and it also helps students develop group process skills, task and time management skills such as problem-solving, collaboration, and negotiation. Information technology brings new opportunities and challenges to project-based learning that is going to be an important component of college English learning in the near future. Thus, the primary concern for teachers in project-based learning is not just to teach English usage, but to help students use English, make sense of the vast amount of information available to them and develop higher-order cognitive skills.

References

Abdullah, M. H. (1998). *Problem-based learning in language instruction: A constructivist model.* (ERIC Document Reproduction Service No. ED 423550).

Armstrong, T (1994). *Multiple Intelligences in the Classroom.* Alexandria, VA: Association for Supervision and Curriculum Development.

Bloom, B.S. (1956). *Taxonomy of Educational Objectives: The Classification of Educational Goals: Handbook I, Cognitive Domain.* New York;Toronto: Longmans, Green.

Buck Institute Education (1999). Project-based learning: Oral presentation checklist. Retrieved From http://www.4teacher.org/projectbased/912pre.shtml.

Braddock, B. (1996). *Using Films in the English Class.* Hemel Hempstead: Phoenix ELT.

Chun, Vernon (1996). DVD: A new medium for language classrooms? Retrieved from http://www.langue.hyper.chubu.ac.jp/jalt/pub/tlt/96/sept/dvd.html.

Casanave, C.P. & D. Freeman (1995). Learning by collaboration and teaching: A film presentation project. *Pedagogical Perspective on Using Films in Foreign Language Classes.* Keio University SFC Monograph #4.

Duffy, T., & Jonassen, D.H. (1991). Constructivism: New implications for instructional technology? *Educational Technology,* 31 (5), 7-12.

— (1992). *Constructivism and the Technology of Instruction: A Conversation.* Hillsdale, NJ: Erlbaum.

Fogarty, R. (1997). *Problem-based Learning: And Other Curriculum Models for the Multiple Intelligences Classroom.* Skylight Pub.

Harris, J. (1995). Educational telecomputing projects: Information collections. *The Computing Teacher,* 22(7).

Katz, L.G. (1989). *Engaging Children's Minds: The Project Approach.* Norwood, NJ:Ablex.

— (1999). Coping with EFL Students' Oral Presentation Problems. Proceedings of the 14th conference on English teaching and learning in R.O.C., 199-213.

King, J (2001,March). Enhancing English teachers' facilitating skills. *Soochow Foreign Languages and Literatures,* **16.**

Moursund, D; Bielefeldt, T & Underwood, S (1997). *Foundations for the Road Ahead: Project-based Learning and Information Technologies.* The International Society for Technology in Education (ISTE).

Mejia, E., Xiao, M.K. & Kenney, J. (1994). *102 Very Teachable Films.* Englewood Cliffs, NJ: Prentice Hall Regents.

Moss, D. & Van Duzer, C. (1998). *Project-based learning for adult English language learners.* (ERIC Document Reproduction Service No. ED 427556).

Piaget, J. (1955). *The Language and Thought of the Child.* Cleveland: The World Publishing Company.

—— (1970). *The Psychology of the Child*. New York: Orion.

Schcolnik, M. & Kol, S (1999, March). Using presentation software to enhance language learning. *The Internet TESL Journal*, 5(3).

Stempleski, S. (2000, March/April). Video in the ESL classroom: Making the most of the movies. *ESL Magazine*, 10-12.

Taylor, W.D. & Swartz, J.D. (1991). Whose knowledge? In D. Hylnka & J.C. Belland (Eds.), *Paradigms Regained: The Uses of Illuminative, Semiotic and Post-modern Criticism as Modes of Inquiry in Educational Technology*, (pp.51-62). Englewood Cliffs, NJ: Educational Technology Publications.

Vygotsky, L. & Vygotsky, S. (1978). *Mind in Society: The Development of Higher Psychological Processes*. Cambridge: Harvard University Press.

Ward, J. & Lepeintre (1996). The creative connection in movies and TV: What "Degrassi High" teaches teachers. *The Journal of the Imagination in Language Leaning and Teaching*, **3**.

Wood, D. (1995). Film communication in TEFL. Video Rising: *Newsletter of the Japan Assoc. for Language Teaching*, 7(1).

Literature in the History of English Language Teaching

Andrzej Cirocki

The reading of all good books is like conversation with the finest persons of past centuries.
RENE DESCARTES

One hand limp by his side, the other to his brow, the young Aristotle languidly reads a scroll unfurled on his lap, sitting on a cushioned chair with his feet comfortably crossed. Holding a pair of clip glasses over his bony nose, a turbaned and bearded Virgil turns the pages of a rubricated volume in a portrait pointed fifteen centuries after the poet's death. Resting on a wide step, his right hand gently holding his chin, Saint Dominic is absorbed in the book he hold unclasped on his knees, deaf to the world. Pointing to the right-hand page of a book open on his lap, the Child Jesus Christ explains his reading to the elders in the Temple while they, astonished and unconvinced , vainly turn the pages of their respective tomes in search of a refutation.

Stark naked, a well-coiffed Mary Magdalen, apparently unrepentant, lies on a cloth strewn over a rock in the wilderness, reading a large illustrated volume. Drawing on his acting talents, Charles Dickens, holds up a copy of one of his own novels, from which he is going to read to an adoring public. Learning on a stone parapet overlooking the Seine, a young man loses himself in a book held open in front of him. Impatient or merely bored, a mother holds up a book for her red-haired son as he tries to follow the words with his right hand on the page. The blind Jorge Luis Borges screws up his eyes the better to hear the words of an unseen reader. In a dappled forest, sitting on a mossy trunk, a boy holds in both hands a small book from which he's reading in soft quiet, master of time and of space.

All these are readers, and their gestures, their craft, the pleasure, responsibility and power they derive from reading, are common with mine.

I am not alone.

MANGUEL, 1997:3-5

Teaching foreign languages has long and cherished traditions. Following Winniczuk (1983), boys in ancient Greece were educated by three teachers namely, a grammaticus, a kitharistes and a paidotribes (a physical education teacher). A grammaticus was supposed to help his students to acquire grammar rules as well as to teach them to write, read, and of course, count. When the students had learnt to write and read, their teachers used to bring textbooks of Homer's eposes and Aesop's tales. The more the students read, the more ambitious the list of readings was. Apart from Homer and Aesop, the students studied the works of Hesiod, Salon and Theognis. Also, the students learnt various hymns which were sung during religious celebrations. At this level, the students started to work with the second teacher, a kitharistes who taught all the boys to play the lyre. Accompanied by the lyre, the boys sang, solo or in choirs, religious or patriotic songs or hymns.

As Winniczuk (1983) notes, an important part of the ancient curriculum was devoted to reading/studying literary works. Apart from reading famous poets' works, the students read and delivered maxims or dicta written by the author of Doctrinae Chilonis. What were the reasons for studying these works? Well, the teachers' aims were not only to enable their students to learn a certain number of texts to be able to deliver them in religious or other ceremonies: They wanted their students to receive larger benefits namely, moral education, and consequently, to point the right way of conduct to their students. Thus, ancient teachers and educationists not only appreciated countless literary values of the texts but they also treated the topics as an educational factor, leading their students to the perfection of the body and spirit and, even more importantly, to loyal service to their motherland.

Latin in the Middle Ages

In the Middle Ages teachers used to work with written texts during Latin lessons. For instance, St. Augustine suggested that students beginning their study of a second language learning should master practical skills instead of grammar rules. In order to achieve this, he advised them to use simple texts, thanks to which students were supposed to discover the language and its basic rules (Ronowicz, 1982:18). St. Augustine's ways of teaching were applied while teaching Latin, which was an important, living language. According to Kelly (1968), the first contacts of students with the foreign language were grounded on reading and reciting simple texts, singing songs and dialogue-based role playing, which was a perfect training of pronunciation and intonation.

As Manguel (1997) notes, Ambrose, Augustine's friend, was an extraordinary reader. "When he read," said Augustine,"his eyes scanned the page and his heart sought out the meaning, but his voice was silent and his tongue was still" (42). To Augustine, however, such reading manners seemed strange. The implication was that this method of reading, this silent perusing of the page, was in his time something out of the ordinary, and that normal reading was performed out loud. Augustine argued that silent reading was good for private learning whereas reading texts out loud was good for sharing the revelation of a text with some companions. Augustine, a scholar who loved Latin, was in the habit of reading anything he found for sheer delight in the sounds. Following the teachings of Aristotle, he knew that letters "invented so that we might be able to converse with the absent" (45), were "signs of sounds" (45) and these in turn were "signs of things we think" (45). The written text was a conversation, put on paper so that the absent partners would be able to pronounce the words intended for them.

Following Mackey (1965) and Titone (1968), language teaching in Europe first crystalised round Latin as it was the principal medium of instruction, scholarship and communication. Latin was taught "to enable clerics to speak, read and write in their second language" (Mackey, 1965:141). Christian schools of various kinds increased in number in the West during the centuries following the administrative disintegration of imperial Rome. The reigning conquerors had little interest in literature or philosophy, but educated Romans, including numbers of Christians, clung to schools of classical culture into the sixth century. Municipal schools in Gaul ceased to exist earlier, therefore, the record was silent after A.D. 474. With a shade of sarcasm one could say the last days of the empire gave rise to textbooks that were supposed to serve for centuries, namely, Donatus'"Grammar (5th c.), Priscian's Grammar (6TH c.), Martianus Capella's Marriage of Philology and Mercury (5th c.).

Christian catechetical schools, which arose in the second century were followed in the fifth and sixth centuries by cathedral schools, that is, schools controlled by bishops. Rome invested mainly in secondary education, but Christians were encouraged to advance their narratives and doctrines at all levels, not overlooking the elementary. To reach illiterates, Christians turned to visual means to reinforce their lessons so that their churches might be used for educational purposes. Although Parish schools may have arisen early in the fifth century, the historical record was inaccurate until 529. Monasticism came to the West in the fourth century, but it was St. Benedict who formulated the rule that specified two hours of daily reading, a prerequisite of successful education. Monasteries became the principal seats of learning, continuing so for centuries. By the tenth century some monasteries had included schooling for two sets of students: those preparing for a monastic vocation (oblate) and those whose aims were secular (externi).

Chivalry, Cicero, Quintilian

The later Middle Ages witnessed the rise of the great cathedral schools followed by the ascendancy of the universities and complexities of scholasticism. Another system of education chivalry for the secular aristocracy may be traced to late ninth century beginnings. It came slowly to thrive in the baronial halls and knightly hostels of the twelfth century, members of which were little interested in academic disciplines or speculative branches of knowledge. Chivalry represented a different configuration of St. Benedict's manuscript. Namely, it highlighted the world of political and military action, a related code of honour, a curriculum strong on physical education, hunting, horseback riding, weaponry; and in the more refined courts, practice in courteous conduct, dance, song, poetry (recitation), heroic tales (providing models of communication skills, written and oral) and stage performances. The interest in graceful conduct led to the development of a form of didactic literature especially pertinent to the training of court pages. The first and most noteworthy of such works on courtesy was The Doctrina Magistri Joannis Faceti, which appeared in the 12th century.

The Renaissance connoted the new life (la vita nuova) that commenced to flower in fourteenth century Italy. Dante Alighieri (1265-1321) and Giotto di Bondone (ca. 1267-1337) impressed Giovanni Boccaccio (1313-75) respectively as reviving literature and painting. Other writers of the time also saw a renewal in the visual arts and literature. Theirs, they affirmed, was as an age of reawakening. The term La Rinascita (rebirth) was coined by Giorgio Vasari (1511-74) to describe developments in the visual arts in Italy that brought art closer to nature. As in the visual arts, so in literature, a burning interest in nature was evident. Also evident was an enhanced interest in human emotion. However, most dramatic in the Italian Renaissance was the powerful interest in the culture of Greece and Rome. Convinced that the age before theirs had corrupted the classical heritage and eager to revive it, some writers began to concentrate on the rhetoric of Cicero and Quintilian.

Humanism in fifteenth century Italian educational thought emphasized the sculpture, architecture, and especially the literature of ancient Rome and Greece. Humanism in its narrowest form in schools focused attention on the letter of the texts, losing the spirit at the same time. Moreover, aristocracy preferred good Latin in their documents, as well. Therefore, vocational opportunities were presented to boys competent in writing and editing Latin texts. The great books identified by renaissance theorists and teachers were called good literature, which included works both in prose and poetry. Such literature was considered good for two reasons. First, it turned attention from quotidian vicissitudes to knowledge of telling cases of human history and of deeper values. Also, it stimulated imagination, freeing mind from the tyranny. Literature was believed to enable a viewing of conditions and issues from more than one perspective. Secondly, it provided models useful in the cultivation of written and oral communication skills. For renaissance educational theorists, the substantive and the stylistic had to be integral. Substance without style could neither move imagination nor inspire. Likewise, style without substance was trivial. It was likely to amuse, but it was useless in the formation of leaders, for leaders had to be imbued with moral principles.

A Perfect Training in Rhetoric

Literature was widely made use of during foreign language lessons in the sixteenth century. For instance, English grammar school teachers used to apply poetic as well as prosaic text recitations and stage performances of specially designed texts for foreign language learners. In Poland, however, Latin and Greek dramas were staged in almost all Jesuit colleges. These dramas added splendour to school, religious and political ceremonies. Staging these plays was not only to entertain people but also to master Latin, which was extremely popular with the nobility. As far as the students were concerned, reciting long parts was a perfect rhetoric training and a thorough preparation for future service (Oko D., 1970). From the sixteenth century, however, vernacular languages began also to be studied as foreign languages. At first they were learnt informally and in a practical way by those who needed them for social purposes. Meanwhile the teaching of the Latin language, which over the following centuries gradually lost its unique position as the language of scholarship, became stultified in narrow formalism. Since the modern languages in turn became school subjects, the formalism of Latin teaching was transferred also to them. Thus, language teaching method first swung from the active oral use of Latin in Ancient and Medieval times to the learning by rule of the Renaissance grammars, back to oral activity with Comenius, back to grammar rules with Ploetz, and back again to the primacy of speech in the direct method (Mackey, 1965:151).

Grammar Translation

There is evidence that the teaching of grammar and translation has occurred in language instruction through the ages (Kelly, 1969), but the regular combination of grammar rules with translation into the target language as the principal practice technique became popular only in the late eighteenth century. In the nineteenth century, grammar-translation was seen as a mental discipline, the goal of which might be to read literature in its original form or simply to be a form of intellectual development. The basic approach was to analyze and study the grammatical rules of the language, usually in an order roughly matching the traditional order of the grammar of Latin, and then to practice manipulating grammatical structures through the means of translation both into and from the mother tongue. The method was very much based on the written word and, therefore, texts were widely in evidence. The teachers used to present the rules of a particular item of grammar, illustrating its use by including the item several times in a text and eventually writing sentences and translating it into the mother tongue. The text was often accompanied by a vocabulary list consisting of new lexical items used in the text together with the mother tongue translation. Accurate use of language items was central to this approach. Grammar-translation laid little or no emphasis on the speaking of the second language or listening to second language speech. It was mainly a book-oriented method of working out and learning the grammatical system of the language (Stern, 2001). Language learning was implicitly perceived as an intellectual activity incorporating rule learning, the memorisation of rules and facts related to first language meanings by means of massive translation practice. Grounding itself on psychology, this method for learning modern languages was justified, like Latin and Greek had been, as a mental training.

The Direct Method

There was a great revival and burning interest in literature in the second half of the nineteenth century. It resulted from the direct method, which referred to the eighteenth-century natural method, advocating teaching foreign languages in the ways resembling an L1 acquisition of a child. The language teaching reforms from 1850 to 1900, particularly in Europe, attempted to make language teaching more effective by a dramatic change from grammar-translation. Numerous methods were developed during this period, but the most persistent term to describe the various features of new approaches in language teaching was the term "direct method". This method was characterised by the use of the target language as a means of instruction and communication in the language classroom and by the avoidance of the use of the first language and of translation as a technique. Therefore, the standard procedure involved the classroom presentation of a text by the teacher. The text was usually a short, specifically constructed foreign language narrative in the textbook.

Difficult expressions were explained in the target language with the help of phrases, synonyms, demonstration or context. To elucidate further the meaning of the text, the teacher asked questions about it, and the students read the text aloud for practice. Much time was spent on questions and answers or general talk about the text. Since the direct method class involved much use of the spoken language, stress was also laid on the acquisition of a good pronunciation. At the beginning of the 1920s, the reading method came into existence. West (1926) argued that learning to read fluently was more vital for Indians learning English than speaking. West was in favour of giving priority to reading not only because he regarded it as the most useful skill to acquire in a foreign language, but also because it was the easiest skill with the greatest surrender value for the student in the early stages of language. As in the grammar-translation method, the application of the first language was not disallowed in language instruction. The introduction of the second language was oral—as in the direct method—because facility in pronunciation and inner speech was regarded as an important aid in reading comprehension. What is more, vocabulary control in reading texts was considered very important, and so was the distinction between intensive reading for detailed study and extensive rapid reading of graded readers.

The reading method introduced into language teaching some essential elements namely, the possibility of devising techniques of language learning geared to specific purposes—in this case, reading; the application of vocabulary control to second language texts as a means of better grading of texts; and thanks to vocabulary control, the introduction of techniques of rapid reading to the foreign language classroom. The significance of literature in teaching was a major motive for a literature-based syllabus, as well as the design and publication of graded readers which are deeply rooted in humanistic and constructivist theories. Both of them present a cultural, linguistic and personal growth model of teaching literature in the classroom. The cultural model viewed literary texts as a source of information about the target culture (Lazar, 1999). In this respect, graded readers provided students with the social and historical background as well as literary movements. Simply, put, literature could provide learners with access to the culture of the people whose language they were studying.

Rejection of Literature

While the principal methods of the first half of the twentieth century (the grammar-translation method and the direct methods) had developed mainly in Europe, audio-lingualism was created in America (Stern, 2001). The dominant emphasis in audio-lingualism was placed on listening and speaking. While reading and writing were not neglected, listening and speaking were given priority and in the teaching sequence preceded reading and writing. Despite the fact that audio-lingualists did not mind cultural aspects of second language instruction, language learning in the first instance was perceived as the acquisition of communicative skills. As far as the role of literature was concerned, it was strongly rejected. Audio-lingualists thought that every new experience left some traces in the learner's memory store. Therefore, audio-lingual teachers feared that learners could learn strange or even inappropriate patterns from literary works (colloquial expressions, slang, sentences whose structure was incongruent with grammar rules.) and would never be able to dispose of them. Thus, audio-lingualism did not see any potential values of literature. What is more, teachers were often afraid of negative influences of literary works. For instance, Robert Lado (1964) believed that the aim of teaching was achieving desired results and not entertaining students.

As an alternative to the audio-lingual method, the cognitive theory developed from the mid-sixties in response to the criticism levelled against the audio-lingual method (Stern, 2001). Broadly speaking, the aim of cognitive teaching was the same as the one suggested by audio-lingual theorists but certain differences in objectives were apparent. Cognitive theory was less concerned with the primacy of the audio-lingual skills. Instead, it emphasized the control of the language in all its manifestations as a meaningful system, a kind of consciously acquired competence which the learner could then put to use in real-life situations. The cognitive approach did not reject the conscious teaching of grammar. Neither did it avoid the presentation of reading and writing in association with listening and speaking. Instead of expecting automatic command of the language and habit-formation from drills, it sought the intellectual understanding by the learner of the language as a system. Therefore, literature could not play a significant role in the foreign language classroom. However, teachers happened to apply literary texts, specially designed for foreign language teaching, to relax their students after exhausting and language-focused exercises. Simplified versions of these texts appeared highly valuable for developing reading skills.

Communicative Language Teaching

Cirocki (2004) following Short and Candlin (1984:91) notes the difficulty and the inaccessibility of literary texts in a non-native English speaking environment. That and the lack of a suitable methodology for the teaching of English through literature contributed to the fact that teaching through literature was neglected and deemphasised in the foreign language classroom. However, during the 80s, teaching English through literature enjoyed a renaissance. It has come together with the Communicative Language Teaching (CLT), which also, following Brown (2000), offers distinct characteristics. First, classroom objectives are not restricted to linguistic or grammatical competence but focus on all the components of communicative competence. Second, language techniques are designed to involve learners in the pragmatic, authentic, functional use of language for meaningful purposes. Third, fluency and accuracy are seen as complementary principles underlying communicative techniques. In the communicative classroom, students are encouraged to use the target language productively and receptively in unrehearsed contexts.

According to CLT, literature provides an appropriate way of stimulating second language acquisition as it provides meaningful and memorable contexts for processing and interpreting new language (Duff and Maley, 1990; Lazar, 1993). Moreover, the application of literary texts as well as graded readers in the foreign language classroom is often a successful way of promoting authentic activities where students need to share their feelings and opinions, such as discussions and group work. This is because literature is very rich in multiple levels of meaning. Focussing on a task which demands that students express their own personal responses to these multiple levels of meaning can only serve "to quicken the students' acquisition of language" (Lai, 1993a:33).

Conclusion

Teaching foreign languages as well as making use of literary texts in the process of second language acquisition has been with us since the dawn of time. However, these texts were applied for different purposes in different periods. Consequently, it led to the fact that in some periods teaching languages without literary texts was hardly conceivable. Conversely, there were periods in which literature was neglected. Nowadays, Communicative Language Teaching (CLT) is at its prime and, therefore, laborious research is being carried out. Thanks to this research, English language teachers would ascertain what role literature plays in the Communicative Approach (CA). Furthermore, analysing the results of the detailed research, foreign language teachers would be able to work out a revolutionary new model of English language teaching through literature.

Reference

Brown, H. D. 2000. *Principles of Language Learning and Teaching*. New York: Longman. pp. 206-207

Brumfit, C.J. and Carter, R.A. 2000. *Literature and Language Teaching*. Oxford: Oxford University Press.

Cirocki, A. 2004. "The place of graded readers in the English language classroom." *The Teacher* **8/9**: 46-49

Duff, A. and Maley, A. 1990. *Literature*. Oxford University Press.

Kelly, L.G. 1969. *25 Centuries of Language Teaching*. Rowley, Mass., Newbury House Publishers.

Lado, R. 1964. *Language Teaching: A Scientific Approach*. New York, McGrew-Hill.

Lai, F.K. 1993. "Effect of Extensive Reading on English Learning in Hong Kong." *CUHK Educational Journal*, **21**(1), 23-36.

Lazar, G. 1993. *Literature and Language Teaching*. Cambridge. Cambridge University Press. pp. 62-67

Litak, S. 2004. *Historia Wychowania*, t.1: do Wielkiej rewolucji francuskiej. Kraków: Wydawnictwo WAM.

Manguel, A. 1997. *A History of Reading*. New York: Penguin Putnam Inc.

Mackey, W.F. 1965. *Language Teaching Analysis*. London: Longmans, Green & Ltd.

OkoD, J. 1970. Dramat I teatr szkolny. Sceny jezuickie w XVII wieku. Studia staropolskie, tom XXVI, Wroclaw-Warszawa-Kraków, Ossolineum, PAN.

Ronowicz, E. 1982. Kierunki w metodyce nauczania języków obcych. Warszawa: WSiP.

Short, M and Candlin, C. 1989. "Teaching Study Skills for English Literature." In M. Short (ed.). *Reading, Analysing and Teaching Literature*. London: Longman.

Stern, H.H. 2001. *Fundamental Concepts of Language Teaching*. Oxford: Oxford University Press.

Titone, R. 1968. *Teaching Foreign Languages. A Historical Sketch*. Washington DC: Georgetown University Press.

West, M. 1926a. *Learning to Read a Foreign Language: An Experimental Study*. New York: Longmans, Green and Co. pp. 101, 460

Winniczuk, L. 1983. Ludzie, zwyczaje i obyczaje starolytnej Grecji i Rzymu, tom. I. Warszawa: PWN.

Beyond Chitlins and Teepees:
The Limits of Multiculturalism
An Interview with William Reynolds

Robert Lake

Editor's Note: *Dr. William Reynolds is a major voice in the field of curriculum theory. He along with Dr. William Pinar, Dr. Patrick Slattery and Dr. Peter Taubman wrote* Understanding Curriculum[1], *which has become one of the most important works in curriculum theory. He has written a number of books, articles and chapters in books (see http:// coe.georgiasouthern.edu/foundations/ bill.html) for a complete list. There is one central philosophy in all of his writing: he believes that is far more important to change the way teachers think than it is to offer them a plethora of methods.*
He is also an avid runner. In the last year alone he has participated in a number of running events including the New York City marathon. He teaches at Georgia Southern University in Statesboro, Georgia.

Reynolds and Reconceptualization

LAKE: The first thing we'd like to do is talk a little bit about your background. Dr. Reynolds, I understand that when you were in school you came in at a very unique time, which has since been called the "reconceptualization." Can you tell us a little about that?

REYNOLDS: Yes, when I went to the University of Rochester for my doctoral work, I had the honor of having Dr. William Pinar, Dr. Philip Wexler and Dr. Madeline Grumet as my committee, and also people that I worked with pretty extensively while going to the University of Rochester. This all relates to the reconceptualization. Prior to that, I did a master's at the State University of New York at Brockport, in English Education. Most of those courses that I took in that particular program were very much oriented to curriculum development: "How to teach a novel," "How to teach an expository essay" and those sorts of things. Then, when I went to the University of Rochester, lo and behold they weren't talking about curriculum development at all. And, that's kind of what the reconceptualization did. It moved us as a field from a primary focus on curriculum development to the focus on understanding curriculum, and that did a number of things.

It's not that we ignore the developing of curriculum, but that's only one aspect of the total picture of curriculum or what we all now call "Curriculum Studies." But what understanding curriculum does is bring all kinds of different viewpoints to the study of what it means to be in school. What curriculum means—so you can look at it from a political standpoint, a racial standpoint, a gender standpoint etc. So that was going on when I was in graduate school. It really started probably in the mid-70s and Bill Pinar probably was the prime motivator for the reconceptualization. By the time I got into graduate school, in 1981, the field was really moving towards this reconceptualization, although it wasn't an easy transition. There were quite a few battles that happened over whether it should be developing curriculum or whether it should be understanding curriculum. I would say by '85, the curriculum field had been pretty much reconceptualized, but it wasn't another ten years before we published our findings in *Understanding Curriculum*.

Multiculturalism as a Buzzword

LAKE: Most of the readers of this journal are ESL teachers or people that are involved in Language Arts teaching. In these areas of study, we have what we call a multicultural curriculum now. I think it would be appropriate to talk about that. We have informally settled on a title for this interview adapted from a quote by James Banks: *Beyond Chitins and Teepees*[2].

REYNOLDS: I've always loved that quote. I think what Banks is referring to is what makes me feel most uncomfortable about contemporary approaches to multicultural education in public schools, although it's at universities and pre-service teacher education as well. I never liked the word multiculturalism anyway.

LAKE: Why not?

REYNOLDS: I just think it becomes like a buzzword and it becomes one of those words that if you use it over and over again and it means everything, then it means nothing. And so I'm a little concerned with that. But what I see happening is that multiculturalism becomes this way of homogenizing everything, homogenizing other ethnicities, and other races into a white norm. Because what I think you see in most schools and in most universities is this very conservative kind of multiculturalism. That is what Banks is talking about when he talks about *Chitlins and Teepees*. It's the notion—especially in public schools—that if we cook a Chinese dinner, then we understand the Chinese culture. Or we build a teepee we somehow understand Native American culture. So we need to get, sort of, away from that. When I consider multiculturalism, I always think it's more about a dialogue with the other. Levinas, a philosopher, said that the more we try to define and even understand the other, the more we are able to do violence to the other.[3]

Of course the extreme example of that would be the Holocaust, where Hitler defined the Jews and was able to do violence to them. I'm certainly not comparing multiculturalism to fascism or anything like that, but the notion that we can develop a packet on African Americans and then understand them or a packet on Asian Americans and a packet on Hispanics and that sort of notion is what Banks is talking about when he talks about going beyond chitins and teepees. Another negative aspect of multiculturalism seems to be this notion that we need to accommodate and assimilate people and not recognize the differences and see how important those are. So, I'm not in favor of packetizing anything, especially people or other groups. And then you have sort of the liberal approach to multiculturalism legislation. Then, there's this third one.

Whiteness

I think it's Peter McLaren that talks about this. He calls it *Revolutionary Multiculturalism*[4]. In this book, he talks about critical multiculturalism, which studies whiteness as another ethnicity.

LAKE: Is that related to why the dominant culture tends to like lighter more than darker skinned African Americans?

REYNOLDS: Possibly. That's one example of how we measure up to that white norm, and I mean it would explain why the great books of Western civilization are studied. Behavior, punctuality, all those kinds of things that are there which of course fit nicely into the industrial model.

Postcolonial Hope

REYNOLDS: So, I think we need to get beyond that. I see great hope in the stuff that's coming out on post colonialism. Which, I know within the field of multiculturalism and post colonialism and in those fields, although I'm not a big student of that. I know that there are all kinds of debates between them. Like which one has the better tact on understanding things, whether it's multiculturalism or post colonialism. But I think post colonialism opens up a lot of things that multiculturalism might not. And of course, post colonialism talks about the relationship between first world and third world. So, there is a lot that can be discussed about the African nations and India and those kinds of things, but you can also talk about slavery, because that's an example of colonialism. There's a big debate about whether the United States is a colonial nation or a post colonial nation. I have a feeling that given the current state of affairs that we do see some examples of colonialism in our present day.

LAKE: One of my major issues in this area has to do with the IQ test and the "Bell Curve Controversy" posited by Herrnstein and Murray[5], which states that some races have an inherently lower IQ than others. I think that would figure right in to a colonial attitude.

REYNOLDS: Yes, but then post colonialism allows you to do a lot of things, I suppose you could do it out of the rubric of multiculturalism, but I don't know. In Post colonialism, you can talk about things like music, art and how there's evidences of this in the artwork, in the music. In the book, *Reading and Teaching the Postcolonial* by Dimitriadis and McCarthy[6], they do a big chapter on artists and one of the artists they use is Basquiat. There's a great film about him called *Basquiat*[7], which talks about how he had to deal with the establishment in the art world and try to sort of carve out a place for himself in that. So there's colonialism and there's colonialism.

I think that opens up a lot of things with students, especially in public schools and with undergraduates and graduate students. You can begin to bring in some of this cultural stuff, such as art and music and begin to discuss ways in which we see evidences of colonialization in art and in music and in other things and attempts to break out of that.

Hip-Hop music is a great example because you can have all kinds of discussions about it. I remember I was teaching a graduate class where we did a book by Dimitriadis about Hip-Hop music[8]. And, that was one of the best discussions I've had in a graduate class in 20 years. But the talk about it was the relationship of race within this Hip-Hop music because there are white Hip-Hop artists.

LAKE: That's a very interesting question for students to consider.

REYNOLDS: And there's this whole notion about whether there's a solely African American cultural thing, or whether whites can participate in that, you know like Bubba Sparxxx, Eminem, and those people. And so you can hit that conversation although I don't know if you could play some of that music in public but you could certainly have that conversation with high-school students. And that begins to open that conversation in a very different way but yet, it's a dialogue, rather than "Okay here's the packet on African-Americans." So yeah, there's that alternative.

Tolerance and Beyond

LAKE: How do you like the word "Tolerance"?

REYNOLDS: Well, you know tolerance—I've never liked the word. I suspect we have to have tolerance before we can go any further but, tolerance always reminds me to tolerate something. To me, it's to kind of put up with something that's annoying.

LAKE: Yes, you acknowledge the existence of the "other" but try to keep them out of your way.

REYNOLDS: Yes, like a mosquito. I can tolerate the outdoors, I mean I can be outdoors and tolerate the mosquitoes, or the gnats or whatever the case may be. I think understanding might even be wrong. I think, dialogue might be the word we want to use with this, or a complicated conversation, or a critical caring conversation or something. But the notion is to keep the conversation going, not to stop.

Flight from Dualism

LAKE: In your book *Expanding Curriculum Theory*[9], you talk about discovering lines of flight. In the introduction there is a quote from Deleuze and Parnet:

> We do not escape dualism in this way since the elements of any set whatever can be related to a succession of choices which are, themselves binary. It is not the elements of sets which define the multiplicity. What defines, it is the and as something which has its place between the elements or between the sets

How would you apply that to dialogue with the other across the differences?

REYNOLDS: Well, that's it. So, with the packet idea, I'll go back to that. With the packet idea, what you're saying is, African-Americans, are this. Hispanics are this. And that drives me crazy. And we do that with almost everything. So we say, "White is this," "Black is this" and there you have the binary which is dangerous. So I think the interesting place is in the middle. And so there you can say "African-Americans are this and this and this and this and this and this and this and this and this." And it never stops. Like, what is curriculum theory? Well, it's cultural studies, it's post structuralism, and it is Deleuze. It's this and this and this and this and this. And, it's by doing that and that opens up those spaces where we can kind of challenge the modernesque notions of what things are.

LAKE: Instead of the binary either/or.

REYNOLDS: Right. So it's like this: What is multiculturalism? Well, it could be post colonialism, and it could be Hip-Hop music, and Bosquiat's paintings and on and on and on and on. It opens up so many more things than it shuts down things. Of course, you know, our 20th century thing is we want to know. We want to define. And I'm not saying definitions are bad, but if we just stop at those definitions then we're really missing a while lot.

LAKE: Yes, that reminds of a dream that a friend of mine had. In this dream he saw a rare and unusually beautiful butterfly which he captured and mounted in the pages of a book.

REYNOLDS: Yep, Michelle Seres says that, and I quote this in the introduction to *Expanding Curriculum Theory*—that for modern man, knowledge is always the hunt. You know, we want to hunt things down and tack them in a book, and then we know them.

LAKE: Yes, it's like "on page 10, we have information about the people of Cambodia and for more information, visit www.cambodia.com.

REYNOLDS: Now we have it. Now we know it, right.

Fishing from Within

LAKE: I wanted to have you talk a little bit about the metaphor that you use in your book, *Curriculum, A River Runs through It*[10]. And that is, fishing from within, and how this principle can take us beyond "Chitlins and teepees" or the packet multiculturalism approach.

REYNOLDS: Right, well, I took that notion from two things, from *A River Runs through It*, and from the movie, but mostly from the novella[11]. Where there's a family and the father—forgive me, I forget the character's names right now. The father is a minister and he has two sons. He wants to teach them to fly-fish and he says he wants to do it, he's a minister, and so he's going to do it Presbyterian style and marine style. And so he does this thing where he's showing the kids that you do it at 10 and 2 o'clock, when you cast you do it at 10 and 2 o'clock. And so one son, he's got it down; he's doing the Presbyterian marine style. But the other son doesn't do that at all.

There's a scene in the film where it shows him doing this casting and it's nothing like the staccato thing that the other two were doing and he calls it "shadow casting." And, you know, it's very creative, it's very imaginative and it's very open, and the other two people can't understand what he's doing. But the father says: "He's shadow casting." And I sort of interpret that like he's fishing from within, so he's not constrained by all this methodology that comes down and says this is what you should do—he figures it out for himself. And, I think that's really what I'm talking about. We don't really need—I know this really flies in the face of everything that's done right now in public schools—but we don't really need more methodology. We don't really need more how-tos; we don't really need more packets on curriculum development. What we need to do, is to have teachers who begin to think up their own stuff. And, of course, you know, I mean, I had an argument one time with fairly famous curriculum scholar about this very thing. And I said: "The only way to change the way teachers practice is to change the way teachers think." And that's what "Fishing from within" is about. It's changing your practice, because you think differently. And Bill Pinar wrote this article years and years ago, it might have even been in the seventies. It was called *Working from Within*[12] and that's exactly it. That we work from within, to work out. So you work on yourself and then you can change the world. So, I think that, I mean, I don't have any simple answers. But it seems like if teachers were a little less trained, and a little more educated, a little less given prescriptions for success and a little more given the, or allowed given the chance to think about things. You'd have a very different kind of thing going on in the public schools. You know, Dewey said that if you want someone to think, you've got to give them something to think about[13]. And, I don't think we give people much to think about these days.

126

LAKE: I'm reminded while you were talking about a phrase from Kliebard's book[14]. He talks about a period in the earlier part of the 20th century, that he called an era of the orgy of testing. This was at the height of the machine age, when efficiency and output were the order of the day. That seems so appropriate for what's happening now. The current climate of testing certainly has had an effect on language and ESL teaching. What would you have to say as a word of encouragement in this time of such an extreme standardized test atmosphere or environment?

REYNOLDS: Right, well, it can look pretty hopeless, even for progressive educators there comes a time when you say: "Oh my goodness, it's bad. I don't think we can get out of this." But, I can't do that. And there's a part of me that says: "No, we can't storm the testing barricades. But there are ways to try to find, pardon the phrase, these lines of flight within contemporary context. So that while we can't destroy the testing machine completely, although I think it may self-destruct, we can find ways to do things as teachers, despite all that horrendous stuff that's going on. And sort of, it's like when we talk about expanding curriculum theory it's like when we talk about the debates about the curriculum studies field. And, you know, sometimes debates are just very unproductive. And I think, if I have to engage in one more debate about testing, I just don't want to do that. So my idea is, okay, testing is terrible, most people know it, but it exists. So, how do we find ways to work within that context? You know, "Develop these lines of flight," and develop this fishing from within, whatever you want to call it. How do we do that? And that's what we need to do and you won't get that if you continue to train them in a skill and a drill kind of mentality which is what's going on.

LAKE: That's all the questions I have, but if you have any closing comments...

REYNOLDS: Okay, I know the name of this journal is *The Journal of the Imagination in Language Learning*. I'm reminded, of course, of Maxine Greene whenever I hear the word "Imagination." And, I think, I agree with a lot of what she had to say. And, one thing she does say is that we need to wake up to what's going on. In his new book, *What is Curriculum Theory*[15], Pinar says that we are in a nightmare. So we need to wake up to the fact that we're in this nightmare. But we shouldn't give up hope. And the only way to keep hope alive is to continue to struggle to find those openings—those "and" moments, if you will—to try and do something different. And Maxine Greene called that "releasing the imagination[16]."

End Notes

[1] Pinar, W.F., Reynolds, W.M., Slattery, P., & Taubman, P.M. (1995). *Understanding Curriculum: An Introduction to the Study of Historical and Contemporary Curriculum Discourses*. New York: Peter Lang.

[2] Banks, J. A. (1993). Multicultural education: Characteristics and goals. In J. A. Banks & C. M. Banks (Eds.), *Multicultural Education: Issues and Perspectives* (2nd ed., pp. 3–28). Boston: Allyn and Bacon

[3] Levinas, E (1998). *Entre Nous: On Thinking-of-the-other*. New York: Columbia University Press, p.9.

[4] McLaren P. (1996). *Revolutionary Multiculturalism*. Boulder CO. Westview Press.

[5] Herrnstein, R. & Murray, C. (1994). *The Bell Curve: Intelligence and Class Structure in American Life*. New York: Free Press.

[6] Dimitriadis, G. & McCarthy, C. (2001). *Reading and Teaching the Postcolonial: From Baldwin to Basquiat and Beyond*. New York: Teachers College Press.

[7] Allen, J., Brant, P. & Yoshizaki, M. (producers) Schnabel, (Director). (1996). *Basquiat* (Video recording) Miramax home entertainment.

[8] Dimitriadis, G. (2001). *Performing Identity/Performing Culture: Hip Hop as Text, Pedagogy, and Lived Experiences*. New York: Peter Lang.

[9] Reynolds, W. M. & Webber, J. A. (Eds.). (2004). *Expanding Curriculum Theory: Dis/positions and Lines of Flight*. NJ: Lawrence Erlbaum Associates Publishing.

[10] Reynolds, W.M. (2003). *Curriculum: A River Runs Through It*. New York: Peter Lang.

[11] McLean, N. (1989). *A River Runs Through It*. Chicago: University of Chicago Press.

[12] Pinar, W.F. (1972). Working from within. *Educational Leadership*. 29(4) p. 329-331.

[13] Dewey, J. (1910). *How We Think*. Lexington, Mass. D.C. Heath publishers.

[14] Kliebard, H. (1986). *The Struggle for the American Curriculum: 1893-1958*. Boston: Routledge and Kegan Paul.

[15] Pinar W. (2004). *What Is Curriculum Theory*. Mahwah, N.J. Lawrence Erlbaum Publishers.

[16] Greene, M (2000). *Releasing the Imagination: Essays on Education, the Arts, and Social Change*. New York: Jossey-Bass.

How to Read a Movie:
Using Multiple Intelligences to Interpret Film

Barbara Le Blanc and Hilary Thompson

This article describes a series of activities that were piloted with grade five, six and seven students in Nova Scotia, Canada. The lesson plans were created to accompany a video called *Rain* (Winner of Best Short Film, Atlantic Film Festival 2000). The plans reflected the curriculum outcomes of drama, language arts, social studies and visual arts programmes established by education departments in some Canadian Provinces. Using these outcomes, we developed imaginative and creative strategies to encourage the use of language skills for interpreting media other than print. During these activities, students used movement, music, still-life tableaux, and poetry within a drama structure to learn how to "read" a movie.

Background

In 1996 *Flashfire Productions* in Halifax, Nova Scotia, contacted Thompson during the casting process of the video *Rain*. Using drama in education methods, she facilitated the selection process of a cast that was made up of children aged eight to eleven. She then organised a workshop on character development for the cast. Shortly after this, the producers requested an educational guide to accompany the video that was to be distributed to school across Canada by *Moving Images* of Vancouver, British Columbia. Having successfully collaborated on the creation of the drama structure *Candlemas in the Classroom (124-138),* Thompson contacted Le Blanc at Universite Sainte-Anne to help create and pilot a drama structure for *Rain.* In November of 2000, they took the project to Kingston Elementary School in the Annapolis Valley of Nova Scotia. Before discussing the lesson plans, we will outline the scenario of the video that served as the basis for the activities that we developed.

Scenario of the Video Rain

A group of children are playing hide-and-seek in a field. Most of the children are hiding. One boy, Eliot, is playing at being a fighter pilot. One girl, Winifred, is curled up, dreaming in the grass. Another girl, Sal, is counting. Eliot confuses his game of war with the game of hide-and-seek. He pretends to save his sister, Winifred, from the enemy. She does not want to play war. She prefers to dream. Teddy offers to be "It." Boots shouts to Eliot to "Get her!" Rusty is building a fort in the grass. Eliot chases Winifred. Rusty and Eliot collide. They argue and fight. Then Eliot picks on Winifred. All the children, except Sal, join in the fight. Sal steals Eliot's pilot's hat. Winifred runs away. He goes looking for her. She rejoins the other children and then wonders what Eliot will do without his pilot's hat. She goes to look for him. He is hidden and alone in another part of the field. It begins to rain. Winifred wears the hat and dances in the rain. Eliot sees her. He is moved emotionally. The rain passes and the game of hide-and-seek begins again. Winifred lies in the grass facing the sky in the field of tall grasses.

Instructional Procedure

We prepared three specific lesson plans. The general outcomes were that students would listen, speak, read, write, view and represent to explore thoughts, ideas, feelings, and experiences. The activities had worksheets that students used to guide them through their responsibilities to desired outcomes. The drama structure began with a brainstorming session where the students became film reviewers for a magazine called *Movies Today*. The two facilitators (Thompson and Le Blanc) were in role as editors of the journal. In drama we try "to pick up signals from them and to get into their minds as much as possible" (Wagner, 35).

Lesson One: Mantle of the Expert

In the first lesson, the students agreed to participate in a drama structure based on Mantle of the Expert. They became engaged in brainstorming the nature of the magazine *Movies Today*, providing reviews for discriminating film fans. Each student filled in a questionnaire creating a new identity as film reviewer, thereby entering the drama and beginning to build belief in the chosen role (Wagner, 67). The reviewers/students reminded themselves of the guidelines for reading a film: to listen attentively to sounds, words and dialogue; to notice how people move; and to listen and notice how the music changes. They then watched the video. While doing this, they listed and correlated words, sounds (including musical instruments), and movements. The reviewers/students chose a series of words, sounds and movements that they considered most important for their review. They drew a moment in the film when sounds, music and words interested them. While doing this, the reviewers/students were working on the musical-rhythmic level of sensory perception. In workgroups the reviewers read the scenario of the video *Rain* and listed the most important events. They divided the scenario into a sequence of scenes in order to integrate their individual perceptions into an overall group view of the story.

Lesson Two: Still-life Tableaux

In the second lesson the reviewers/students worked in groups exploring the verbal and non-verbal communication of the characters in the video. As a result of the scenarios that they created, they were able to move towards a kinaesthetic and affective level of sensory perception. In teams of six, the reviewers/students created rules and signed a contract to ensure the effectiveness of their group work. The reviewers/students read the scene descriptions of the video. In co-operation, they chose adjectives to describe each character in the video. As a group, they chose a character and described his or her behavior and feelings. They created a group movement to express one of the following feelings: happiness, sadness, anger or confusion. Each reviewer/student chose or accepted the role of one of the characters in the video. They created a still-life tableau of one of the assigned pivotal scenes. In such a tableau, students assume the motionless bodily positions that are expressive of the highest moment of a particular scene. For instance, a male might get down on one knee and extend an engagement ring to his beloved who has one hand atop the other hand placed near her neck as her eyes are fixed on her suitor. That pose is held for about ten seconds or so and constitutes the tableau. Finding the most positions that capture pointed relationships between the characters in such scenes provides an excellent opportunity for substantial conversation. They followed guidelines to help each group of reviewers act out and experience the scenes in the video in order to write a better review. The reviewers/students created still-life tableaux of their scenes. The tableaux were presented in scene sequence. While one group was in a tableau, the other groups observed, and individuals photographed the tableaux from different angles with either a Polaroid or digital camera. The reviewers (students) observed and filled a review sheet.

Lesson Three: Signs and Symbols

In the third lesson the reviewers/students moved from sensory perception to awareness of the meanings of signs and symbols in the video *Rain*. In order to appreciate the significance of the tableaux, they created posters of the photographs and drawings for reviewers to scrutinize. In their same work groups, the reviewers examined the photographs and drawings and in which characters were communicating without words and sounds. They discussed which photographs, and drawings, the Art Department of the magazine could use to inspire the artwork that would illustrate the reviewer's text. They noted and discussed the feelings that the faces and bodies were expressing. They described and discussed the significance of the objects and natural images in the video and in the tableaux (namely military - uniform, goggles, hat, tree, field, grass, rain). In so doing so, the reviewer/students explored the continuity and the changes of the meaning of the symbols in the video.

As they explored these changes, the reviewers/students were asked to make connections between (1) fighting as an aggressive act that endangers life, and (2) the conflict experienced during the children's game of hide-and-seek in the video *Rain*. They discovered that rain cleanses, transforms and gives the characters an opportunity to change. They discussed examples of other movies where children have been in conflict and crisis situations and have taken the opportunity to grow. The reviewers/students were encouraged to present their discoveries in a poem that would conclude their reviews.

Pedagogy and Theory

Educational drama strategies challenge and extend our experiences (Johnson and O'Neill, 1984, 82). Mantle of the Expert provides the means and medium for emotional, physical, intellectual, imaginative, aesthetic and social development. The simplicity of this strategy rests on the students' involvement with task. Any information the students require is provided to them in their role as workers who are involved in an ongoing work situation, such as archaeologists, journalists, historians, travel agents, entrepreneurs, and television producers (Heathcote and Bolton, 1995, 38). It is the task (here of reviewing movies) that holds the students' attention. With attention to task, comes the need to be professional, responsible workers. The students do not need to be accomplished writers, but they do take the job of writing a review seriously. Since all children in Western society are familiar with television, videos and films, the engagement with the role and the completion of the tasks of film reviewers comes easily. In undertaking these tasks, students use their individual abilities to explore their own imaginative and creative potential. This they can do safely with no concern for "what they sound or look like" (Morgan and Saxton, 1987, 119).

Howard Gardner's theory in his groundbreaking work *Frames of Mind: The Theory of Multiple Intelligences* (1983) resonates with this learning and teaching. The activities in our drama structure integrated most of the multiple intelligences identified by Gardner. Students used verbal-linguistic intelligence when they read and discussed the scenario, and when they wrote poetry and their reviews. They drew on logical-mathematical intelligence in the sequencing exercises and the correlation of items in tables. Students utilised visual-spatial intelligence when creating their still-life tableaux, photographs and drawings. When they students made comparisons between sound and movement, they explored their musical-rhythmic intelligence. Group exploration of emotion through movement, creation of tableaux and dance provided the opportunity to practice bodily-kinaesthetic intelligence. In their group work and cooperative learning, students tapped into their interpersonal intelligence. When they explored and reflected on the image of rain as transformation and on the symbolic significance of the metaphor of the field as a place of play and change, students used intra-personal intelligence in their high-order thinking about signs and symbols. They put this intelligence into concrete form when they wrote their poetry.

Conclusion

Our work creating an educational guide for the video *Rain,* using a drama structure such as Mantle of the Expert, challenges thinking patterns and precipitates an examination of the potential of media to expand sensory perception, symbolic awareness and higher-order thinking. The process we endorsed entailed developing activities that brought together the drama strategies created by Dorothy Heathcote, Howard Gardner's Theory of Multiple Intelligences, and the learning outcomes of a variety of Education Departments of Canadian Provinces in Elementary Language Arts and Drama. Development of material based on the drama strategy of the Mantle of the Expert permits students to use their multiple intelligences, encouraging an active use of imagination to discover and experience language creatively.

References

Gardner, Howard. 1983. *Frames of Mind: The Theory of Multiple Intelligences.* New York: Harper and Row.

Heathcote, Dorothy and Gavin Bolton. 1995. *Drama for Learning: Dorothy Heathcote's Mantle of the Expert Approach to Education.* Portsmouth NH: Heinemann.

Johnson,Liz and Cecily O'Neill. 1984. *Dorothy Heathcote: Collected Writings on Education and Drama.* London: Hutchinson.

Le Blanc, Barbara and Hilary Thompson. 1995. "Candlemas in the Classroom: Relating Past Traditions to Present Realities." *Children's Voices in Atlantic Literature and Culture,* pp. 124-138.

Morgan, Nora and Juliana Saxton. 1989. *Teaching Drama: A Mind of Many Wonders.* Cheltenham, UK: Stanley Thornes Publishers Limited.

Verrall, Ann. *Rain.* 2000. Halifax, NS: Flashfire Productions. (video)

Wagner, Betty Jane. 1976. *Dorothy Heathcote: Drama as a Learning Medium.* Washington, DC: National Education Association.

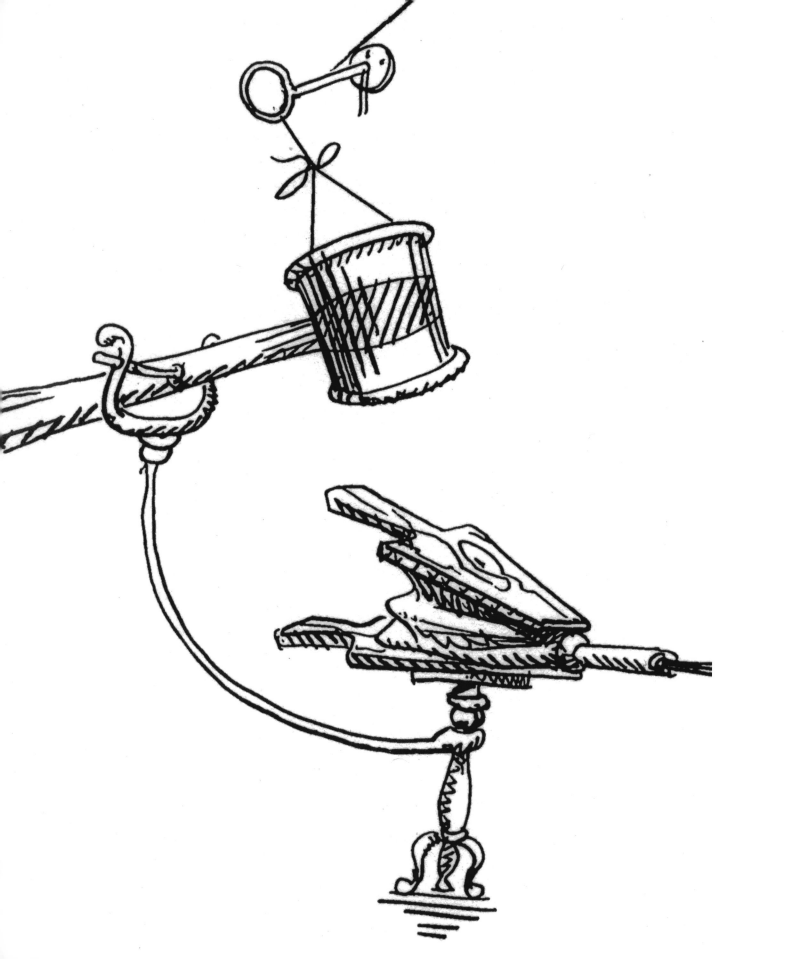

Three Controversial Feature Films for the ESL Classroom

Walter Petrovitz

The versatile nature of video technology has proven to be of great value in instruction English as a Second Language (ESL). It has enabled the development of a wide range of presentation strategies, as explored broadly in works such as Lonegran (1984) and Stempleski (1992). This flexibility is particularly helpful with feature films. While such films can provide interesting and extended contexts for a variety of activities, they have three major disadvantages. First, their length might cause certain teaching points to become obscured. Second, they often involve cultural presumptions; and third, they make formidable linguistic demands on ESL students. Dividing a film into segments, replaying certain scenes, turning off either the sound or the image, or showing closed captions allows the instructor to elucidate the content and use it for specific pedagogical goals. It is important to keep in mind, however, that the feature film is itself a universal artifact of modern culture and brings with it its own norms for appreciation. These films are usually regarded solely as an enjoyable, leisure-time activity and viewed from beginning to end, interrupted only by commercial breaks in the case of television transmission. Other forms of presentation must struggle against these expectations and habits. Students from very traditional educational backgrounds might regard watching feature films in the classroom as a waste of time. Others may welcome it, but grumble at having their attention diverted from an appealing scene or interesting plot line. For these reasons, it is helpful for the instructor to provide some rationale for the viewing strategies being employed and the activities involved. While all of the techniques described above could conceivably be used to some benefit with any film, there are certain films that are more naturally suited to particular forms of presentation, providing in themselves the rationale. This is a great help in lessening the sense of artificiality students might otherwise feel. In this article, I will discuss three award-winning films that can be used in this way.

Sensory Perception in Films

A number of techniques for the classroom use of video involve changing the channel of reception from visual to auditory or both. For this reason, they are a natural choice for films that have difficulties in sense perception as their central theme. Two of the films recommended below are of this category. Such materials can of course serve purposes beyond the introduction of classroom video techniques. Attitudes toward disabilities vary significantly across cultures, and the greater awareness in the United States of the needs and distinct perspectives of persons who are physically challenged is relatively recent. Films dealing with these issues can therefore be used as consciousness-raising tools and vehicles for teaching an important aspect of contemporary American culture.

Pre-viewing activities should include a discussion of attitudes towards people who have physical disabilities. Ask your students how such persons are treated in their own cultures, what special accessibility provisions, if any, are made, and whether they had contact with these people in everyday life. An important part of the preparation, especially in the current atmosphere of heightened sensitivity, is the vocabulary used to discuss these issues. As in other areas, language learners must be made aware of which terms are acceptable and which are offensive, and instructors themselves may need to review the generally accepted usages. Your school's office which handles accessibility compliance should have appropriate materials. If not, excellent resources have been prepared by various governmental and private agencies. (I have found the pamphlet "Choosing Words with Dignity," put out by the State of Oregon's Department of Human Resources, to be a succinct and helpful guide.) As a follow-up activity, you may ask your students to notice whether the characters in the films you are presenting follow the suggested norms. The usage varies quite a bit, as might be imagined.

Soundtrack Listening

A technique which is often used with video is to turn off the picture and allow students to listen to the soundtrack while they speculate about the visual aspects of a particular scene. This is obviously of little use if most of the students have already seen the film, which is very often the case with popular recent releases. Few students, however, are likely to be familiar with the undeservedly neglected 1965 film *A Patch of Blue*, which was a box-office hit and features critically acclaimed performances by Shelley Winters, as an abusive prostitute; Elizabeth Hartman, as her unfortunate teenage daughter; and Sidney Poitier, as the African-American stranger who befriends the young woman. It will enhance students' appreciation of the acting to know that Hartman, whose character is unable to see, wore completely opaque contact lenses during the filming.

The film is a natural subject for soundtrack listening. Selina, who as a child was accidentally blinded by her mother, has never been to school and spends her days doing household chores and making necklaces, home employment for which she receives a small salary. She begins to visit a nearby park each day to string her beads. After a brief opening sequence which introduces Selina's highly dysfunctional family, the scene shifts to Selina in the park, where for the first time she meets a passerby named Gordon (Poitier). Students can at this point be asked to put themselves in Selina's place, meeting a stranger whom they can judge only on the basis of what they hear. A sample of their encounter illustrates Selina's attempts to size up this person who so intrigues her (this is, incidentally, the only instance I know of in film of a lesson on subject-verb agreement):

Selina:	I'm sorry, I don't usually talk so much. I gotta get movin'. I promised I'd get two day's work done by tonight. Oh cripes! The damn things is all mixed up.
Gordon:	"The damn things are all mixed up," you should say.
Selina:	What?
Gordon:	"...are all mixed up."
Selina:	You sound like the radio.
Gordon:	I do? How's that?
Selina:	Different. Kinda sure. Lotsa things is different on the radio.
Gordon:	"...are different on the radio."
Selina:	I'm sorry. Are different.

In this and subsequent meetings, Gordon does not reveal his racial identity, an element which becomes an important undercurrent in the film. After the students have listened to the dialogue (I have them listen twice, the second time with a script in order to clarify Selina's use of contractions and quaint exclamations), they are asked to describe their impressions of Gordon in terms of background and personality as well as what they imagine his physical appearance to be. Students recognize Gordon's refined diction as an indicator of the class distinction between the two and are invariably startled when the scene is replayed for them with the picture turned on. This scene can serve as an introduction to a discussion of racial stereotyping, which can be broadened to a consideration of stereotypes in general, including those involving disabilities. The grammatical features of informal speech and the use of different kinds of expletives can also be worked into a discussion of the scene.

Selina's encounters with Gordon are discrete episodes in the film. Thus, if the entire film is to be viewed over several class periods, the teacher may wish to switch to only the soundtrack for each of their meetings until Gordon's race is finally revealed to Selina. With each encounter, the students can be asked to develop their mental image of Gordon and then later to speculate as to whether the racial difference will matter. Some of the vocabulary referring to race is either pejorative or dated, but an explication of such terms and alternative expressions should also be part of an ESL student's cultural education. The film ends ambiguously with regard to the future relationship between Gordon and Selina. Although some students feel cheated by this, it makes a good topic of discussion.

Silent Viewing

Another technique often used with videotape is to switch off the soundtrack, so-called **silent viewing**. A film which would naturally lend itself to this sort of treatment is *Children of a Lesser God*, the story of a romance severely tested by opposing views on how to deal with the inability to hear. Jim (William Hurt), a new teacher at a school for teenagers who are deaf, falls in love with Sarah (Marlee Matlin), an angry and reclusive young woman who is a former student of the school and now works as a janitor there. Sarah's refusal to speak or read lips becomes an ongoing source of discord between the two. An excellent selection of background material (including both positive and negative newspaper reviews) and a variety of comprehension and vocabulary-development exercises based on the film are available in Mejia, Xiao, and Pasternak (1992). Lane, Hoffmeister, and Bahan (1996) will provide a good resource on sign language and the culture of the hearing impaired. Students will be interested to learn that Matlin, who won an Oscar for this performance, is herself hearing impaired.

Just as with *A Patch of Blue*, students can be asked to put themselves in the place of a person dealing with a sensory limitation. One ample source of material for silent viewing and description is the sign language used in the film. Signs vary of course in their degree of obvious iconicity, and much of the signing is done very quickly. There are, however, a number of scenes in which, for one reason or another, more literal signs are delivered in isolation. One such scene is the encounter after many years of separation between Sarah and her mother (Piper Laurie). Up until that point, the mother has displayed indifference and even hostility when speaking about Sarah. Knowing a few signs, but never having become fluent, Sarah's mother uses slow and deliberate gestures to communicate with her daughter. If you have not seen the film, view the scene first silently yourself and try to imagine the content of the discussion. Ask your students to note the signs being used. List these by brief descriptions ("spread fingers," "stroke across the palm") on the board and see if the class can agree on their meanings. The conversation is short enough (less than three minutes) to review a few times with your class in a single session. The meanings of less easily interpretable signs can then be provided, such as the one for "father," and the conversation progressively deciphered on repeated viewings.

Other scenes can also be used in this way. In one of the early encounters between Sarah and James, she mocks his poor comprehension of quick signing by slowly gesturing in an exaggerated fashion. The emotional intensity of their reunion in the final scene is also marked by more demonstrative movement. Again, as in the case of *A Patch of Blue*, the ending leaves many unanswered questions about the future relationship of the two, which students can be asked to predict.

Closed Captioning

The use of closed-captioned video for language instruction has been explored in a number of studies: Goldman and Goldman (1988), Vanderplank (1988), and Neuman and Koskinen (1990), among others. This strategy accords well with current constructivist approaches to language teaching since through captioning, students receive input from a variety of channels. Much of the work on the use of closed captioning has focused on educational videos or television programs, rather than on feature films. In fact, the claim has been made (Vanderplank, 1993, 13), with some justice, that closed captioning is ill suited for use with feature films:

> *Perhaps surprisingly, closed-captioned feature films have also failed [along with TV dramas and natural-history programs] to be useful as language learning resources. There is no shortage of students who want to watch them in self-access, but on the whole, they learn little language from them. The associations with the cinema are too strong and they become absorbed into film watching as a distinctly different experience from language learning.*

While this judgment is perhaps a bit too negative, it does reflect the aforementioned difficulties that most presentation strategies encounter with feature films. Here again, the use of material which seems to call for closed captioning can help to introduce students to this device as a language-learning tool.

The film *Dead Man Walking* can be an excellent component of preparatory activities for a discussion or essay on capital punishment. Based on the true story of Sr. Helen Prejean's struggle against the death penalty, it is the most comprehensive and unbiased treatment of the subject I know of in any medium. I had used this film a few times with advanced students, but nearly decided to abandon it because of the comprehension difficulties it presented. Regional and social dialect variation, the use of voice-over in a number of scenes, and the large amount of germane but unfamiliar vocabulary make parts of the film nearly incomprehensible to most ESL students. It was quite by accident that fiddling with the controls on the monitor, I turned on the closed captioning, much to the relief of my students, who persuaded me to leave it running. The difference in the students' response to the film was dramatic. Nearly all began to jot down words which they later asked about in the general class discussion, and the increased use of vocabulary specific to the topic was noticeable in their essays.

The film incorporates details from a number of stories found in Sr. Helen's own account of her work (Prejean, 1993) into a single fictionalized case. Matthew Poncelet (Sean Penn), a young tough, is convicted of rape and murder and condemned to die by lethal injection, while an accomplice turns evidence against him and is spared. Sr. Helen (Susan Sarandon) and the lawyer she finds to represent Poncelet make eloquent and thorough arguments against capital punishment, which are countered by the victims' families, the prison chaplain, and other characters in the film. While the gruesome portrayal of the death penalty evokes pity for its victims, Poncelet himself is a rather unsympathetic character: a violent white supremacist as well as a brutal criminal, who does not take responsibility for his actions until (literally) the eleventh hour. The families of the victims are portrayed as complex individuals, whose cries for what they see as justice and whose anger against Sr. Helen, as well as Poncelet, although discomfortingly vindictive at times, are quite understandable. Thus, the viewer is forced to decide the question of capital punishment on its merits, rather than relying on easy sympathy with oversimplified characters.

Activities using closed captioning with feature films will benefit from Vanderplank's (1993) suggestion (with regard to television programs) to allow the rhetorical structure of the material to determine its pedagogical use. While the instructor may be presented with questions involving violent crime in the United States, grammatical and lexical features of the dialects used, or certain norms of the Roman Catholic Church (some of these issues can be relegated to a pre-viewing discussion), the focus of the activities should be the extended and well-handled expositions of the differing views presented, which serve as the focal points of the film. These include a great deal of the necessary vocabulary for discussing the topic, as shown in the following excerpt from the ironic history of capital punishment which Poncelet's lawyer gives to the parole board:

> *In this century, we kept searching for more and more humane ways of killing people we didn't like. We shot them with firing squads, suffocated them in a gas chamber. But now, now we have developed a device which is the most humane of all: lethal injection.*

The use of closed captioning can also help in reinforcing the correct use of collocations ("spare a life," "try a case," "carry out an execution"), which are difficult for even advanced learners. Existing proficiency with these can be evaluated by a cloze exercise before viewing, and the results reviewed with the students, preferably with self correction, after they have seen the film. These usages can be highlighted again in associated activities. For example, ask the students to summarize point-by-point the argument which Poncelet's lawyer makes before the parole board. Have them compare the differing reactions of the parents of the victims in their often uncomfortable encounters with Sr. Helen. Allow them to speculate as to whether Poncelet would have ever admitted his culpability had he not been facing certain death. In each case, note any errors, replay the relevant scene, and ask questions to elicit the target vocabulary. Here are some examples:

> What does the parole board decide?
> They decide to *deny clemency* to Poncelet.

> Why did Poncelet's accomplice escape the death penalty?
> Because his lawyer created a *reasonable doubt* in the mind of the jury.

> What does Sr. Helen want Poncelet to do?
> She wants him to *take responsibility* for his actions.

Conclusion

Feature films are one of the most important aspects of contemporary American culture. While their use in the classroom presents various difficulties in terms of students' expectations concerning the medium, not utilizing this resource would rob ESL instruction of a means of presenting material in a contextualized and interesting way. An essential component of any educational strategy is for the participants to understand and accept its use. Choosing films with subject matter that lends itself to a particular form of presentation allows for the introduction of tested and proven techniques for the utilization of video in the ESL classroom in ways that will seem natural to students.

References

Berman, P. (Producer), & Green G. (Director). (1965). *A Patch of Blue* [Videotape]. (Santa Monica, CA: MGM/UA Home Video).
Choosing Words with Dignity. (n.d.). Salem, OR: State of Oregon Department of Human Resources.
Goldman, M., & Goldman, S. (1988). "Reading with Closed-Captioned TV." *Journal of Reading,* **31,** 458-461.
Klik, J., Robbins, T., Simmons, R. (Producers), & Robbins, T. (Director). (1996). *Dead Man Walking* [Videotape]. (New York: PolyGram).
Lane, H., Hoffmeister, R., & Bahan, B. (1996). *A Journey into the Deaf-World.* San Diego, CA: Dawn Sign Press.
Lonegran, J. (1984). *Video in Language Teaching.* Cambridge: Cambridge University Press.
Neuman, S., & Koskinen P. (1990). Captioned Television as "Comprehensible Input": Effects of Incidental Word Learning from Context for Language Minority Students. Falls Church, VA: National Captioning Institute.
Prejean, H. (1993). *Dead Man Walking.* New York: Vintage.
Stempleski, S. (1992). "Teaching Communication Skills with Authentic Video." In S. Stempleski and P. Arcario (Eds.), *Video in Second-Language Teaching* (7-24). Alexandria, VA: TESOL.
Sugarman, B., Palmer, P. (Producers), & Haines, R. (Director). (1986). *Children of a Lesser God* [Videotape]. (Hollywood: Paramount).
Vanderplank, R. (1988). "The Value of Teletext Sub-titles in Language Learning." *ELT Journal,* **42,** 272-281.
—. (1993). "A Very Verbal Medium: Language Learning through Closed Captions." *TESOL Journal,* **3** (1), 10-14.

Les Miserables: Combining Music and Story in College EFL

Chih-hsin Tsai

Background

In my second year of high school, our new music teacher led us to an audio-visual classroom where she showed us the concert version of a Broadway musical *Les Miserables*. Without a piano, without any musical textbook, I experienced the most unforgettable music class ever. The music teacher introduced us only to the story while showing the video. English lyrics, not included in her pedagogy, were scarcely comprehensible to me. Yet with great enthusiasm for *Les Miserables*, I bought the complete CD recording containing a lyric sheet. The beautiful melodies and intriguing plot propelled me to comprehend all the lyrics. Such passion for a musical helped to build up my English ability in a non-pressured way.

Planning a new syllabus last year, I seriously considered integrating *Les Miserables* into my college freshman English course. The goal of this idea, which originated from my past experience, was to arouse students' interest in English through a musical comprising beautiful music, touching stories, and most of all, abundant English learning materials. My 247 college freshman students were from four different departments: Healthcare Administration, Childcare and Education, Applied Cosmetology, and Food Science and Nutrition. The students' gender and dispositions varied; their English levels ranged from low to intermediate. A questionnaire was conducted in our first meeting to detect students' viewpoints about language learning. Around 61% of my students admitted that they didn't like English. Nevertheless, 58% of them enjoyed English songs, and up to 88% thought they would feel less pressured when songs were incorporated in English lessons. Despite the differences in their backgrounds and levels of English proficiency, these teenagers generally thought they would get more pleasure in learning English through songs.

Language through Songs

A considerable amount of literature has discussed how music helps in language learning. Ample websites that provide tips on teaching English through songs are easy to access. In spite of the fact that the majority of these sources aim at children, benefits of incorporating music into English courses are also highly recognizable in teenage and adult EFL classrooms. Murphy in his book *Music & Song* (1996) states that music and song have motivational appeal to many age groups and different types of learners. Lems (2001) also recognizes English proficiency as well as cultural knowledge to be the advantages of using music in the adult ESL classrooms. As to the psychological aspect of learning, Adkins (1997) and Eken (1996) both found that music aids in raising students' responsiveness to language input. Smith (2003), from the students' comments on his "English Through Songs" courses at the University of Hong Kong, found that improvement in English could result from a pleasurable way of learning. And when the enjoyment in a language classroom is evoked, more learning is likely to occur outside the classroom.

Story-Based Songs

The power of music is universal; the application of songs to language learning is widely suggested. Adkins (1997) highlights the use of music "as a memory aid because a major goal of second language teaching is to enable students to remember what they have learned, and to call upon that material when needed as they begin to produce language." Yet simply playing songs and explaining lyrics may not be effective enough to motivate students. The fact is that students tend to be bored with lyric translation and soon lose interest in the songs. If we aim at making the melodies as well as phrases from a song "stick" in students' heads (Murphy, 1990), so as to fortify a natural process of using English vocabulary, grammar, and even conversational patterns, we should not neglect the necessity of building students' background knowledge of the targeted song and its related information. People of all ages like stories, especially those related to their personal experiences and viewpoints of their living environment. When asked about acquiring background information of a song, 69% of my freshman students appeared to be more curious about "the story implied in the song" than "the singer" or "the production of the song." They agreed that getting a picture of the related story, if there is any, before a song is played would enable them to be more engaged in lyric-reading and listening. My students' positive attitude toward learning English through narrations and music fortified my plan to introduce them a musical, one that is composed mostly of story-based songs.

Musicals

Musicals thrive in the United States. Their broad appeal to people is primarily due to the dramatic stage effects, diverse subjects, and the use of everyday language in the form of attractive songs. Since musicals were almost all written and are sung in English, they serve as ready-made English learning materials. Milano is one of the first professionals who brought musicals into a language classroom. She shared in her "Teaching English Through Broadway Musicals" (1994) the beneficial experience of using musicals as a stimulating alternative for ESL classes:

> Bringing musicals to the classroom provides wonderful opportunities to expand vocabulary and gain familiarity with colloquial expressions and certain grammatical structures. Exploring musical videos can also create an awareness of American speech patterns and nonverbal expression. Furthermore, students benefit from exposure to the variety of socio-cultural issues that are addressed in many musicals.

Following are several characteristics of musicals worth attention when introduced in class:

CHARACTERISTICS OF MUSICALS

1) **Rhyming**: Rhyming creates a magical touch and adds a poetic tone to a song. Creative and entertaining use of rhymes has been a hallmark of musical theater. For ESL/EFL students, rhymes facilitate the memorization of lyrics and provide phonetic practice.

2) **Wording**: Repetitions, which are an element of a pop song, are not commonly seen in a musical. All the songs in a musical are connected from beginning to end; they have to be exact in wordings to help tell a comprehensible story. The lyrics of a musical are usually long and less recitable or memorable than pop songs; on the other hand, they provide inviting reading materials, because students are tempted to find out what happens next by following through all the songs.

3) **Plot**: Time and place are usually precise in a musical. Characters, which are usually implicit in pop songs, are a lively component with clear identities in a musical. These features combine to make the lyrics of a musical help tell a clear story similar to a shorter, simpler version of a novel.

4) **Expressions**: Scenes in a musical cannot be dramatically changed. Instead, performers' facial as well as vocal expressions attract the audience's most attention. Students who listen to CD recordings are encouraged to focus their attention on the characters' tone of voice so as to sense the subtle and strong emotions each song conveys.

5) **Theme**: Themes in musicals are universal. They are about human and cultural issues such as history, relations, power, life, and death. Students, whatever backgrounds they have, will easily relate their experiences to the themes. With discussion sections provided, students can voice their feelings about such themes and identify with some of the musical's controversial subjects and characters.

Why *Les Miserables*

Having little chance of going to musical theaters, people in Taiwan generally acquire their basic knowledge of musicals from the media (CD/movies/news). Very few of my freshman students (3%) understood the definite contents of the Broadway musicals. Around 16% had heard recordings of musicals but had not paid attention to the lyrics. 39% said they only knew *Phantom of the Opera* or *Les Miserables* because these two musicals were once made into films and there were books on them.

Other than the fact that *Les Miserables* is one of the most popular and successful musicals of all time, several reasons prompted me to choose it as my teaching material:

1. **Adaptation**: *Les Miserables* is one of a few musicals adapted from a classic novel.

The epic novel Les Miserables by Victor Hugo has its great influence and reputation in the history of literature. For students who may be interested in more in-depth reading, there are abridged, unabridged, and bilingual copies available in bookstores and libraries.

2. **Availability/Attractiveness**: The concert recordings of the musical *Les Miserables* can be obtained in the form of CD, VCD, or DVD. Among them, DVD serves my need because of its music/lyrics/image combination, and particularly the selectivity of bilingual

(English/Chinese) lyrics subtitles. *The Les Miserables 10th Anniversary* concert features a special audio and visual effect with an orchestra, chorus, and singers who wear costumes. The singers stand at their microphone stands, but they also participate in some movement. At certain points, the video switches to action from a stage production. Although the DVD does not show the genuine stage performance, it offers enough attraction to the viewers.

3. Universal Themes: As in Hugo's own word, "I don't know if it [*Les Miserables*] will be read by everyone, but it is meant for everyone…Social problems go beyond frontiers." Based on Hugo's novel, the musical conveys no fewer messages: despair, salvation, evil, goodness, progress, love, hope, etc.. The characters are ordinary people with flaws, not figures from some imaginary world. Students from any background can easily relate themselves to the themes and characters involved. Discussions of the themes can provide them a good chance to verbalize their opinions and personal experiences. Abundant lesson materials are obtainable from several *Les Miserables* websites. The official site (http://www.lesmis.com) alone provides a plenty of information. The on-line synopsis can be downloaded and abridged into one that suits students' English levels. The complete libretto is only available with *Les Miserables'* CD recordings.

Schedule and Methods

The college freshman English course met two hours a week, spanning two semesters. It aimed at developing students' all four skills of reading, writing, listening, and speaking. I arranged the course into several main topics. *Les Miserables* was joined as an extended material with the topic of Music and Movies. Ten hours of class were scheduled to present this musical.

First Week: The introductory session began with net browsing and brainstorming in the computer lab. The objects were to prepare students for a basic understanding of *Les Miserables*, and to arouse their interest in it. Tasks assigned were: (1) What makes you feel miserable? Discuss and share your answers with the class. (2) Locate the official website of the Broadway musical *Les Miserables*. (3) Talk about the logo (the portrait of young Cosette) you've found and how it may be related to the word "miserable;" what may the story be about?"The tasks being done, I passed out the abridged synopsis of *Les Miserables*, asked the students to underline all the capitalized words, most of which were names, and then directed them to a webpage demonstrating genuine French pronunciation of all the names in this musical. Meanwhile, students were showing obvious curiosity and eagerness to know the whole story. They were dismissed with the synopsis as a take-home reading assignment.

Second and Third Week: Students were directed to the multimedia language lab where they could watch *Les Miserable* concert DVD on individual monitors. The following are my steps of presenting ten selected songs that go with the synopsis:

1) Quickly go through/interpret one paragraph in the synopsis.
2) Play the song related to the paragraph in caption-off mode. Encourage students to practice guessing and inferring meanings from visual clues.
3) Ask students to recognize each singer's identity, emotions, the surroundings, and characters involved. Explain new words.
4) Play the same songs with English subtitles. Some fast songs give a good practice of speed-reading.
5) Pass out full lyrics of the song. Identify rhyme, idioms, grammar, and impressing sentences.
6) Play the song again with both English and Chinese subtitles. Have students speak or, if they can, sing with the singers.

Here is an example showing the typical strategies I used to present each song:

(1) Synopsis: Vajean repays the saintly Bishop by stealing some silver.

        Hurrying with the silver upon him, Valjean is caught and brought back by the police.

        The Bishop lies to the police to save him, also giving him two precious candlesticks.

(2) Show students "Valjean Forgiven" without lyrics subtitles:

But my friend, you left so early
Surely something slipped your mind
You forgot I have these also
Would you leave the best behind?
So, Messieurs, you may release him
For this man has spoken true
I commend you for your duty
And God's blessing go with you
But remember this, my brother
See in this some higher plan
You must use this precious silver to become an honest man
By the witness of the martyrs
By the passion and the blood
God has raised you out of darkness
I have bought your soul for God!

(3) Having read the related paragraph in the synopsis, students should be able to recognize the singer to be the Bishop, who is singing to Jean Vajean in the church. The Bishop's voice sounds gentle at first but it later turns into a serious low tone. Valjean seems astonished at the Bishop's words.

(4) Direct students attention to the English subtitles when listening to "Valjean Forgiven" again.

(5) Rhymes are in pairs: "mind" with "behind," "true" with "you," "plan" with "man," and "blood" with "God." Grammar, idioms, and impressive sentences may vary.

(6) Finally, students have the chance for oral practice: speak/sing to the music.

Fourth Week: In the past four periods of class, students had read the whole synopsis and heard all of the ten songs. In this session, students were asked to join a group discussion about themes in Les Miserables. Their ideas and examples were later reported to the class. Toward the end, students had to write a short essay on one of the following topics:

(1) The most impressing character(s) in *Les Miserables*

(2) The scene or song that relates to your personal experiences.

Fifth Week: Group role play. Students had been informed of this final task in the second week. Each group was assigned a selected scene from *Les Miserables* which they had to transform into a short play. Their group role plays were recorded.

Conclusion

Domoney and Harris (1993) found that music is often the major source of English outside the classroom for EFL students. However, with the prevalence of pop music, students tend to neglect the possibility of contacting English through other forms of music. Although musicals were a novel genre to most of my students, after five weeks of the *Les Miserables* experience, they expressed a very positive attitude toward this unusual way of learning English. The percentage of students who disliked English dropped significantly from 61% to 14%. Students' attendance and participation during this period of time was improved. Many of them inquired about abridged bilingual copies of Hugo's novel *Les Miserables*. Some were enthusiastic in adapting the song "Do You Hear the People Sing" into one that aims at fighting SARS, an infectious disease causing drastic panic in Taiwan. One student made a comment on this experience and it is what I meant to achieve with a musical—to make English "stick" in students' head: "English has given me a headache, but after these five weeks' of English class, the characters often come back in my mind, and they are singing to me—in English!—This is incredible."

References

Adkins, Sandra. (1997). Connecting the powers of music to the learning of languages. *The Journal of the Imagination in Language Learning*, 4. Retrieved June 18, 2003 from http://www.njcu.edu/CILL/journal-index.html.

Beliavsky, N. (2001). English through opera. *The Journal of the Imagination in Language Learning*, 6. Retrieved June 18, 2003 from http://www.njcu.edu/CILL/journal-index.html.

Brown, H. D. (2000). *Principles of Language Learning and Teaching*. White Plains, NY : Addison Wesley Longman.

Domoney L. & Harris, S. (1993). Justified and ancient: Pop music in EFL classrooms." *EFL Journal*, 47, 234-241.

Eken, D. K. (1996). Ideas for using pop songs in the English language classroom. *English Teaching Forum*, 34, 46-47.

Lems, K. (2001). Using music in the adult ESL classroom. Eric Digest, ED459634. Retrieved June 19, 2003 from http://www.ericdigests.org/2002-3/music.htm.

Milano, G. (1994). Teaching English through broadway musicals. *The Journal of the Imagination in Language Learning*, 2. Retrieved June 18, 2003 from http://www.njcu.edu/CILL/journal-index.html.

Murphey, T. (1996). *Music & Song*. Oxford: Oxford University Press.

Murphey, T. (1990). The song stuck in my head phenomenon: A melodic din in the LAD? *System*, 18(1), 53-64.

Schoepp, K. (2001). Reasons for using songs in the ESL/EFL classrooms.

The Internet TESL Journal, 7(2). Retrieved June 20, 2003 from http://iteslj.org.

Smith. G. P. (2003). Music and mondegreens: Extracting meaning from noise. *ELT Journal*, 57(2), 113-121.

http://www.lesmis.com/

http://www.lesmis.de/en/index_e.html

http://www.geocities.com/Broadway/2403/lesmis1.html

Student-Made Video in a Language Class

Ekaterina Nemtchinova

How many students can say that their oral final exam was an extremely enjoyable experience? This is what my second year students think about the course requirement to make a video in the Russian language. Several years ago, I offered the video as an alternative to a traditional oral exam format during students' final quarter in the program. At first they looked puzzled and even terrified, but gradually they found the idea appealing and became very involved. They created a story line, wrote the script, cast roles, had several rehearsals, and finally videotaped the skit that demonstrated what they had learned during the year in a very creative way. The success of the project and obvious benefits of using video for evaluation purposes made me introduce it as a requirement worth twenty percent of the final grade. Drawing on the successful use of student-made video in assessing of the linguistic progress, I will point out its advantages, explain the process, and provide tips for using the technique in a language class. (Many of these steps can be used in other parts of the course.)

Dramatization in Language Learning

Because video requires performance, it can be regarded as a creative drama technique similar to role-playing, simulation, improvisation, skits, pantomime—all of which are known to immensely assist language learners in development of reading, writing and listening (Maley and Duff, 1993; Verriour, 1985). Dramatizing a story enriches the language classroom by increasing communicative and authentic language use in verbal and non-verbal form. Incorporating both the cognitive principle that information is processed more effectively through more than one sensory channel and the behavioral notion that repeated action imprints knowledge upon the mind, scripts produced by students allow them to actively acquire and practice vocabulary, grammar and syntax of the target language. They offer students a dynamic encounter with language that comes closest to traditional communication (Berlinger, 2000).

Creative drama techniques have a strong potential for developing creativity and self-esteem. But perhaps the most important reason for using dramatization techniques is that they make the learning of the language an enjoyable experience (Ernst-Slavit and Wenger, 1998). In the dynamics of a group interaction process, numerous opportunities to apply one's imagination and personality make them appealing to students. And, as noted by Ladousse (1987), "although there does not appear to be any scientific evidence that enjoyment automatically leads to better learning, most language teachers would probably agree that in most case this is surely so" (5).

Student-made Video in a Language Classroom

Video has many practical applications in a foreign language classroom. Students are exposed to the dynamic of interaction while watching a video in the target language. They can also benefit from contextual clues (setting), linguistic variations (accent, register), and paralinguistic cues (postures, gestures) (Secules, Herron, & Tomasello, 1992). Another use of video technology is the possibility of filming language learners to develop aural/oral proficiency and to examine and improve their individual language production and communicative styles (Forrest, 1992). Brooke (2003) argues that videotaping can be helpful in practicing

140

presentation skills in front of the audience because it lowers apprehension as students engage in a situational group role-play. He stresses the affective impact of the media on students and describes possible formats (e.g. mini-documentaries, interviews, advertisements) for students to film. Dubriel (2004) points out that the medium transfers the focus of the task to the student who becomes more engaged in the learning process. Interestingly, these and other authors indicate that it is a daunting task, but at the same time encourage teachers to undertake such a project.

Video can be an invaluable tool in monitoring and assessing students' language abilities. As Lonegran (1992) notes, "Feedback and evaluation sessions with students can be the most fruitful aspect of working with a video camera" (p. 93). As the video replays students' actions, they can study, analyze and discuss the fine points of their verbal and non-verbal behavior. By examining their performance in context, students can gain insight into their communication styles thus improving their learning (Forrest, 1992). Feedback sessions provide students an opportunity to see themselves functioning in a foreign language; this in turn can motivate them to take more risks and improvise with the language.

Lonegran (1992) points out that first, the video should be played back to students as soon as practical. "Filing the tape away can arouse…suspicions and even hostility among learners" as they speculate "what will happen to the tape, who will see their efforts, why they cannot see themselves" (p. 116). Second, students' performances should be evaluated in an atmosphere of understanding. It might be necessary to instruct the class to provide constructive and diplomatic feedback to each other. Finally, giving students observation tasks during feedback sessions will focus them on specific language points and increase their awareness of the language learning process.

Using the Student-made Video Exam

The benefits of student-made video as an assessment tool are manifold. I treat this assignment as another activity to practice specific communicative skills.

1. **The project ensures the maximum student involvement while the teacher assumes the role of an observer.** As students write, act out, direct and edit the video, they create a student-centered environment.
2. **Producing the video increases students' motivation.** They are empowered by authentic experiences with a professional looking product they can view and demonstrate to others with pride.
3. **The task allows students to contextualize the previously learned vocabulary, structures, and intonation.**
4. **Both accuracy and fluency skills are practiced.**
5. **An open-ended assignment motivates creativity and imagination in the target language expression.**
6. **The collaborative nature of the project combined with a non-threatening format alleviates test anxiety.**
7. **Video technology affords detailed study essential for evaluation.** The instructor can replay the video as many times as necessary while assessing individual students' performance, reviewing actions and speech, and paying attention to intonation and non-verbal communicative responses. In a traditional exam, the elusive nature of oral communication presents problems for evaluators.
8. **After the test a student-made video can serve as a teaching and self-evaluation tool.** Students can comment on their own and their classmates' performance of various language skills and reflect on ways of improving them. Students in other classes can do listening, grammar and vocabulary activities based on the same video.
9. **An additional benefit for a small program is popularizing the Russian courses.** The video is usually filmed on campus. Russian students invite "passers-by" for episodic appearances. They might even teach them some Russian words. These people become interested in a "cool class" and sign up for Russian the following year.
10. **In a multilingual class, all communication surrounding the production of the video will be in the target language.**

Procedure

At the beginning of the quarter, students receive the course syllabus including the description of the video project as the oral component of the final exam. The only formal requirements are that the video should be at least five minutes long, that it should include the linguistic material covered during that quarter, and that it should grant equal amount of involvement to each class member. One video can accommodate up to six students. For more, get two projects going. Evaluation is based on development and sequencing of the plot, on delivery, on language structures, pronunciation, intonation and vocabulary. This method of testing also provides a review of specific topics and presents students with an incentive to perform.

To facilitate the preparation process, provide structure to the assignment and keep students on the task. Hand out guidelines which break the project into manageable steps and specify the deadline for each step (see Appendix 1). Students plan, invent and negotiate among themselves with no interference on my part. Several times during the quarter, I ask students about their progress with the video and remind them to seek help from me if needed, but other than that they work independently. They use their knowledge of the language and consult dictionaries, outside texts, and native speakers to charge their wonderful ideas with content. Sometimes I am asked to check the grammatical accuracy and/or the choice of vocabulary of individual parts of the script; however, students prefer to keep it secret to create a feeling of surprise.

Actual Filming

The actual filming is done outside of class after several rehearsals. The plot usually revolves around the adventures of the class members on campus. Since students realize that using notes in front of the camera may look unprofessional, they choose to memorize their lines, which benefits them by helping to internalize language patterns (Ernst-Slavit and Wegner, 1998). On the other hand, the creative nature of the task invariably leads to improvisation on the spot. Student actors have to think on their feet and to find a way to respond appropriately as the situation unfolds. Thus they are forced to activate their speaking and listening skills and generate new language as required by the plot (Berlinger, 2000).

After the film is shot, students edit it. This part of the project is optional; nevertheless, students invariably prefer to edit the video to produce a quality final product. They use video editing software such as iMovie, Windows MovieMaker or Adobe Premiere to import the footage into the computer and enhance visual and auditory impact with black and white versus color slides, slow motion, background music, voice-overs, and still images. Once a group of students even included "extras" for additional humorous effect. Although only one person is usually involved into the actual editing process, the whole group participates by providing comments and advice. The end product is saved on a tape or a CD-ROM.

Time for Tea and Russian Sweets

Finally, at the end of the quarter we all gather to watch the video. Students proudly display their creation, comment on episodes and tell how this or that scene was shot (all in the target language!) while we drink tea and eat Russian sweets. During this time, students also informally evaluate their own and their classmates' linguistic performance by praising others and critiquing themselves. After the class, viewing, I watch the video several times for grading purposes, each time focusing on an individual student's performance. Presentations are evaluated using a scoring rubric adapted from Alaska Department of Education & Early Development web site. Every rubric has a set of statements describing what the learners are expected to do at each level (see Appendix 2). In addition to a numeric score, students receive written narrative feedback on their exam presentation that offers encouragement as well as suggestions for improvement.

Suggestions For Avoiding Pitfalls

The following suggestions may be helpful for teachers interested in implementing a video project in their classrooms.

- Consider the level of language proficiency of the students. The project can be successfully carried out by language learners at the low-intermediate level and above. Beginners or first-year students might not have yet acquired sufficient linguistic means to achieve flexibility and creativity of expression.
- Explain the benefits of the project to the class since the unfamiliar format of the assignment may be intimidating. Remind camera-shy students that they will appear in front of the camera as part of a group, they have several weeks to prepare, and their classmates and you as their teacher will provide all kinds of assistance.
- Find a way to regularly check students' progress on the project to ensure that they have plenty of time to develop it into a quality product. Providing a set of guidelines, asking students to write about the project in a journal, including an appropriate question into a quiz, or simply asking in class will prevent students from putting the video off until the last minute.
- Make certain that students are aware early in the course of the criteria by to which their presentation will be evaluated early. This encourages self-monitoring and improves their performance at the test. Remember that the aim of the project is to evaluate the learners' linguistic performance; grading should not be affected by their acting or technical abilities.
- Split larger classes into smaller groups: four to six people seem to be the optimal number of participants. A larger group would face more coordinating problems as well as need to produce a longer video.
- Discuss technological support and equipment with your class. While many students have experience with shooting and editing video, teachers cannot safely rely on that. Master the essentials of video production yourself or, better yet, invite a colleague or a tech support person with more expertise to help with the project.
- A plausible script with a beginning, middle and end is necessary. For that function, ask for one or two volunteers.

Student Reaction

Course evaluations continuously reveal that students are very enthusiastic about the project. They embrace the opportunity to display their creativity and show what they have learned. One student remarked that she "really enjoyed making our Russian video because we got to take control of the whole project by creating the plot, writing the script and then filming it. It was fun to work with the other Russian students and to see how much of the language we could actually use, especially funny expressions that we could ad-lib into the video." Another wrote, "It was fun using language in a creative way, and I think it was especially helpful to have the chance to speak nothing but Russian for the video." Other students noted that they "liked making the video because it was a good chance to review past vocabulary, and to force yourself to remember a variety of different words" and that "the process of inventing the script and deciding what to do for the exam was very engaging." Many comments concern the evaluative aspect of the task: "It was also a good experience to be able to see and hear myself using a foreign language after the taping. I was able to identify the things I need to work on and pat myself on the back for the things I have learned" or "I liked hearing myself speak on TV. It gave me a better idea of what I sound like when speaking Russian." In general, students believe that "making a video for the final was both hilarious and extremely enjoyable" and "it really pushed us to figure out how to say new things with our still-limited vocabulary, making us aware of our limitations but also of ways to work around them."

Conclusion

Using student-made video for evaluation of oral communicative skills can be very beneficial for students as well as teachers. Students enjoy the opportunity to use meaningful language for communicative purposes in a creative way and to evaluate themselves. Recording a rehearsed presentation on video diminishes test anxiety allowing students to perform to their best ability and turns an intimidating oral examination into a rewarding group project and a confidence-booster. At the same time, the medium of video permits the instructor to bring a creative element into language testing, to assess students' linguistic progress in a dynamic situation that mimics a real-life language encounter, and to consider various aspects of students' oral performance in a careful way that is not provided by traditional testing media.

Appendix 1.

VIDEO PROJECT GUIDELINES

Your video is due on the last day of class, but it is wise to start early. This is a group project, so you will have to accommodate everybody's schedule as well as to provide equal opportunity to participate for all class members. You are welcome to choose any subject for the video; it is important, however, that all the material that we study during this quarter is included (see syllabus). The following guidelines will help you to stay on task.

A. Planning your video   Due_____

- o Agree on a general plot line.
- o Decide on every person's role: who will say what?
- o Write each one's individual lines.
- o Find an interesting way to present your script. Would you like to use music, props, costumes etc.?

B. Rehearsing your video   Due_____

- o You have to have several rehearsals to ensure the smooth presentation of the script. It is your responsibility to schedule these before the date of filming.

C. Filming your video   Due_____

- o When you are satisfied with your rehearsals, record your video. You may do it yourself, recruit your friends to film you, or ask me to enlist help from the technical service department (ITS). If the latter is the case, I should be told at least a week in advance to make the necessary arrangements.

D. Editing the video (optional)   Due_____

- o This is the most time consuming part of the project; however, in the past students have chosen to edit the video to create a high-quality product. ITS web site provides instructions on how to use Apple iMovie (see http://www.spu.edu/depts/ its/multimedia/imovie.htm). If you have no experience with video editing software, ask your friends for help; ITS can be of assistance too. And don't forget to save the final version of the video and bring it to class!

This project is worth 20 percent of your final grade. The project will be presented in class on June 3. It will be graded based on the following criteria:

Development and sequencing	20%
Delivery	20%
Language structure	20%
Pronunciation/intonation	20%
Vocabulary	20%

Please let me know if there are any problems or concerns at any stage of the project. I will be more than happy to help!

Appendix 2.

VIDEO SCORING GUIDE					
	Developing and Sequencing	Delivery	Language Structure	Pronunciation/ Intonation	Vocabulary
5	creatively developed; many details; holds audience's interest; entertaining;	effortless and smooth, no unnatural pauses; sounds like natural speech	consistent and accurate use of structures; may contain a few minor errors that don't interfere with the communication	mostly correct with only minor flaws	is used accurately with creative variety; reveals breadth of knowledge
4	adequately developed; includes all required story elements; has beginning, middle, and end	fairly smooth with few unnatural pauses; slight choppiness and/or occasional error in stress	generally uses correct structures with some errors	is influenced by first language	is appropriate
3	partially developed; missing a few required story elements; beginning, middle, and end may be unclear	occasionally halting and fragmentary with some unnatural pauses, choppiness, or inappropriate stress	demonstrates an inconsistent use of correct structure	shows strong influence from first language	is simple with some inappropriate use
2	minimal development; missing many required story elements; hard to follow	halting and fragmentary with many unnatural pauses; speech sounds mechanical	shows many errors in use of structure	is dominated by first language	is limited or incorrect
1	unsatisfactory development; inadequate amount of material; no sequencing	very halting and fragmentary with excessive unnatural pauses	has no apparent understanding of structures	interferes with comprehension	is very poor or inaccurate for topic; first language word may be used; speaker may create a target language from the first language

References

Alaska Department of Education & Early Development Curriculum Frameworks Project. 12 Feb. 2004 <http://www.eed.state.ak.us/tls/ frameworks/wrldlang/wlinstr3.html#Skit>

Berlinger, Manette. "Encouraging English Expression through Script-based Improvisations." *The Internet TESOL Journal* 6 .4 (2000). 6 Feb. 2004 <http://iteslj.org/Techniques/Berlinger-ScriptImprov.html>

Brooke, Sebastian. "Video Production in the Foreign Language Classroom: Some Practical Ideas." *The Internet TESOL Journal* 9. 10 (2003). 6 Feb. 2004 <http://iteslj.org/Techniques/Brooke-Video.html>

Dubreil, Sebastien. "When students become directors: Redefining the role of the learner in the foreign language classroom." Eds. Lomicka, L. and Cooke-Plagwitz, J. *Teaching with technology.* Heinle and Heinle, 2004.129-138.

Ernst-Slavit, Gisela, and Wenger, Kerri. "Using creative drama in the elementary ESL classroom." *TESOL Journal* 7. 4 (1998): 30-33.

Forrest, Tracey. "Shooting your class: The videodrama approach to language acquisition." Stempleski and Arcario 79-92.

Heining, Ruth Beall. *Creative Drama for the Classroom Teacher.* Prentice Hall, 1993.

Ladousse, Gillian Porter. *Role Play.* Oxford: Oxford University Press, 1987.

Lonegran, Jack. "Using a video camera to evaluate learners' classroom performance." Stempleski and Arcario, 93-108.

Maley, A. and Duff, A. *Drama Techniques in Language Learning.* Cambridge: Cambridge University Press, 1993.

Secules, T.,Herron, C., and Tomasello, M. "The effect of video-context on foreign language learning." *Modern Language Journal* 76 (1992): 480-490.

Stempleski, S. and Arcario, P., eds. *Video in Second Language Teaching: Using, Selecting, and Producing Video for the Classroom.* Alexandria, VA: Teachers of English to Speakers of Other Languages, 1992.

Stempleski, S. and Tomalin, B. *Video in Action.* New York: Prentice Hall, 1990.

Verriour, P. "Face to face: Negotiating meaning through drama." *Theory into Practice,* 24 (1985): 181-186.

Wessels, Charlyn. *Drama.* Oxford: Oxford University Press, 1987.

Haiku Poetry
in the Language Classroom

Kristin Lems

I have to go now
I am meeting my good friend
It has been too long
EVA RAISON

The *haiku* poem has its origins in Japan, but can now be found in many countries. Its strict three-line format—split into consecutive lines of five syllables, seven syllables, and five syllables—is a challenge to poets and provides a rich writing opportunity for the language arts or ESL classroom. The haiku is a form of poetic expression that evolved out of the mystical awareness of the Zen Buddhists in Japan in the 17th century. The greatest traditional poet of Japan is Basho (1644-1694), who combined spiritual depth with seemingly simple observations of nature. Buson (1715-1783) followed, along with Issa (1763-1827), and the more modernist Shiki (1866-1902). All these masters and many others have been widely translated into English in versions which sometimes retain the same classical format, and other times render freer translations. Haiku themes revolve around nature and the changing of the seasons, but also paint human nature and relationships, often highlighting a humorous irony. Each haiku, like a shining pearl, can provoke a great deal of reflection, despite its seemingly simple exterior. The following are a few classical Japanese haikus in English translation:

Staring delighted
Even at walking horses
in new morning snow
Basho

Under my tree-roof
slanting lines of April rain
separate to drops
Buson

You hear that fat frog
in the seat of honor, singing
bass? that's the boss
Issa

Nightlong in the cold
monkey sits conjecturing
how to catch the moon
Shiki

Haikus in Culture, Internet

Recently, haikus have assumed a new life, aided by the technology of email and the Internet. A set of "Computer Haiku," which circulated widely through email inboxes, can be traced back to a contest sponsored by the online journal *salon.com*, which solicited "haiku error messages" from computer users. The outpouring of witty, Zen-flavored haikus entered in

146

the competition may have captured better than any prose form the nuanced interaction of computer and user. The first-place haiku, created by David Dixon, appears in the contest's archive at the *salon.com* site:

Three things are certain:
Death, taxes, and lost data.
Guess which has occurred.
David Dixon

Haikus are also making an appearance in newspapers and listservs. For example, a weekend features section of the *Chicago Tribune* recently solicited haikus from readers on current events themes and got a huge response. Here are two of them; the first refers to the unfortunate mauling of a circus animal trainer by the tiger he had worked with for years; and the second references the famous nonexistent "weapons of mass destruction" which were the pretext for Bush's invasion of Iraq:

Beware white tigers
Lurking behind sequined sets
Instinct betrays glitz.
Julia Buckley

Searching everywhere
They must be hidden well, like
Double you em dee.
Ed Nemmers

Listservs also feature haikus. Shortly after Thanksgiving weekend, the following one, reprinted by permission, was written by a folksinger and posted on a listserv to which we both belong. Like the Nemmers haiku, it illustrates the plastic nature of the haiku—it can be both classical and very colloquial. (Tryptophan is a chemical naturally occurring in turkey, which has a soporific effect. It is still used as a treatment to help insomniacs).

Thanksgiving Haiku

load the dishwasher
quick, before the tryptophan
nails us to the couch
Sebastian Mendler

A Haiku Journal and Conference

At Millikin University, the haiku is celebrated with an ongoing yearly festival, the Global Haiku Festival, and a credit-bearing English class entitled Global Haiku Traditions. The same group publishes a haiku magazine, *World Haiku Review*. It contains photo essays and other graphics along with essays on haiku traditions and contemporary haiku poets writing in many languages. Millikin University has become a gathering place in North America for the study of this deceptively simple form and its many variations.

Clearly, the haiku form is immensely versatile. In addition to its malleability, the structure allows those who believe themselves to be non-poets a task-based activity at which they cannot fail as long as they can count syllables, while at the same time giving the more poetically-inclined a chance to flex their creativity within challenging limits. This ability to create a workmanlike project for some and at the same time a sublime activity for others is the remarkable zen of the haiku. An extra bonus is that haikus, both in Japanese and in translation, seem to lend themselves easily to illustration, from calligraphy pen to collage, or to musical accompaniment.

Haiku in the Classroom

I discovered these features inadvertently while teaching English to Korean undergraduate students in an intensive exchange program in Chicago last summer. The subject of haiku came up, and I quickly showed the haiku form on the blackboard. Several heads nodded in recognition. On the spot, we created a rather unexceptional but tidy haiku about our classroom. Everyone smiled with satisfaction to see a finished poem created by group process. It inspired me to ask all the students to write a haiku for the next day's class. Fortuitously, they were taking a field trip to the Botanic Garden, so I suggested that they use the field trip as a possible haiku topic. The assignment was greeted with a mixture of groans, head scratching, and mystified smiles. I really didn't know what to expect. Sure enough, every single student had a haiku ready the following day—a mixed bag, to be sure, but there was something from everyone. I asked everyone to write their haiku on the board (they don't take up much room!), and we counted syllables together for each one. Half of the haikus did not match the syllable count—because of a mispronunciation of one or more of the English words. What a teachable moment! It was a revelation for them to see that certain words had reductions which resulted in collapsed syllables in American English, such as the one-syllable word "orange." It was a productive, authentic language practice activity. After that class period, I asked them to revise their haikus, hand letter them onto blank white paper which I provided, and illustrate them. They were given until the end of the week.

When I began to receive them back one by one, and beheld the quality of the work, I realized that I had stumbled upon something very special. The haikus were captivating, each one in its own way, and each revealed some special wit or sensitivity on the part of its writer. Everyone hovered over each others' papers, and there was a murmur of excitement. I decided the poems deserved a larger audience than just the class. I suggested we gather all the haikus into an anthology, and it was greeted with smiles. After receiving the students' written consent to reproduce their work, I brought the colorful pages to my mother, who owns a slow but trustworthy color printer. She faithfully duplicated a color copy of each page during the long weekend, setting up a large paper bag for each slow copy to fall into, and laboriously loading each original. (For this monumental effort, she deserves the High Order of Haiku.) I then found a binder into which each set of pages could be inserted, with a clear plastic cover. By the last day of class they were ready to be given out as souvenirs, one to each student. The anthologies were enthusiastically received and created quite a stir at the final party. Here are a few of my favorites from the anthology. This feisty haiku has humor and "spunk," which matched so well with its author.

Here are rose gardens
Many colorful roses
I want to snap them!
Sunnyeo Joo

Another student wrote this haiku about the Chicago Botanic Garden, which she illustrated with crying trees. Together, the image and words showed her revulsion toward the idea of taking trees out of their natural setting and putting them into a landscaped exhibit:

They cry bitterly
We want to go back dwelling
not exhibition!
In Hee Kim

And my favorite, a haiku which shows both a sense of place and deep changes the author is undergoing, is this one, based on downtown Chicago's famous Loop, where the trains turn around overhead and then return from the way they came:

Life....differs from Loop
Can see the right track or not
It is not easy.
Young Ji Hong

Although each of these has a slightly different syntax or grammar from that found in the writing of a native speaker, each writer has been able to show nuanced emotions and thoughts at a level that may exceed the writers' ability to communicate in accurate English sentences.

Haiku in the Chicago Public Schools

The next frontier for my expanding haiku unit was a fourth grade classroom in one of the Chicago Public Schools, where I serve as a reading consultant. The fourth grade class was composed of largely Hispanic students fluent in conversational English but using Spanish in the home. These students work hard and want to succeed, but often experience delays in consolidating the academic skills needed to master content area topics. They also tend to show weak performance on the extended writing sample sections of the high-stakes standardized tests. The teacher had been working on making text-to-self connections, in preparation for the state tests they would soon be taking. Following up on my demonstration on the overhead projector, the students tried to write their own haiku. They read them to each other, and the teacher was able to use these sketches as powerful examples that the students were able to make personal connections to nature. This illustrated text-to-self very organically; a rich discussion ensued. The syllable-counting was also useful in this classroom, and the teacher supplemented it by having students look up the syllable breaks of some words in the dictionary. We discovered that some dictionaries consider "interesting" a four-syllable word, and others consider it to be three syllables. The class had a chance to talk about the varied pronunciations of the "ed" ending.

Illustrations

When the kids wrote and illustrated their own haikus, a great deal of excitement occurred. There was much syllable counting on fingers, and frantic hand-raising to see if they'd gotten it right. When everybody had a usable haiku, they took out their art supplies, illustrated the poems, and then shared the result with the rest of the class, one-by-one in front of the room. As it was 11:20 a.m., a striking number referred to the delights of lunch, which was coming a few minutes later.

When I looked later at the haikus and illustrations of these young learners, I realized they served as a sort of Rorschach test in their ability to show what was on the minds of the children. One boy whom the teacher had identified to me as "seeing a psychiatrist" wrote and illustrated a haiku which showed a single stark flower sticking stiffly up out of the earth under a cold sun, and the haiku stated that he like the flower preferred warmth to cold. Others talked about the joys of candy, hamburgers, and snow. One boy wrote an angry haiku about having the windows of the family's new car broken by vandals. All in all, the simple activity was rewarding, revealing, and affirming of the students' lives. Each child left the room that day a published poet.

Haiku with Teachers

For my next haiku exploration, I brought haiku writing to a group of ESL teachers at a workshop I offered at the 2004 Illinois TESOL/BE convention. Teachers had no trouble getting in the zen-zone. By now, I knew that I wanted to write up a haiku unit, and when I asked the teachers to create haikus on the spot, they were happy to oblige. They wrote them, read them aloud to each other, and, at the close of the workshop, handed them in to me along with a signed permission to allow me to include their gems in a future article. Here are some of those choice gems.

Twenty five people
or is it twenty seven?
lovers late to class

Julie Steinhaus

Where my two worlds meet
is a place of great beauty.
You must come and see

Tanya Thomas

My children are big
why must it happen so fast?
fish swimming away

Laura Kristek

The lowly haiku is a miniature "trojan horse" for bringing magic and imagination into the classroom for many kinds of language learners. How good it feels to tumble and play one's way into self-expression by juggling seventeen golden syllables, lighting sparks of truth in a few short strokes.

References

"Challenge No. 65: The world according to haiku." *Chicago Tribune*, Jan. 16, 2004, The Q Section, 2.

The Four Seasons: Japanese Haiku written by Basho, Buson, Issa, Shiki, and Many Others. New York: The Peter Pauper Press, 1958.

"The 21st Challenge." (1998). *The culture of technology; the technology of culture.* salon.com Archive. Retrieved January 26, 2004 from http://archive.salon.com/21st/chal/1998/02/10chal2.html

Mendler, S. (2003). *Thanksgiving Haiku.* Retrieved January 26, 2004 from http://www.well.com/~smendler/creative/poetry/thnxhaiku.html

World Haiku Review: the Magazine of the World Haiku Club. Retrieved May 10, 2004 from http://www.worldhaikureview.org/

The Sublime

A Phenomenon of Imagination—*From Heraclitus to Trotsky*

Hyun Höchsmann

If beauty is a promise of happiness, the sublime is a fulfillment of the promise—

The Sublime as a Phenomenon of Imagination and not of Cognition

With beauty, the sublime is at the summit of aesthetic encounters. The sublime—from the Neo-Platonist Longinus, Burke, and Kant to Schiller—has been conceived as a phenomenon invoking astonishment in contrast to the beautiful as eliciting delight.[1] In the classical conception, beauty flourishes as harmony, balance, and ordered arrangement. The sublime embodies grandeur, power, awe, and soars aloft in the boundless realm of nature. The sublime does not pertain to nature alone. The aesthetic sublime is linked to the moral sublime. Human actions are deemed sublime when they transcend the expectation of what is right or good.

While delight in the beautiful results, in Kant's view, from the "harmonious interplay of faculties of imagination and understanding" freed from the rules of reason and the imposition of categories, the encounter with the sublime extends the bounds of sense beyond reason. The aesthetic sublime is not an object of rational cognition but an occasion of wonder and imagination. Imagination presents in the realm of action that which cannot be known rationally. Imagination extends beyond rational understanding. The sublime cannot be known by a rational analysis as it borders on the incommensurable and does not fall under the categories of understanding. Recognizing that it is the enigmatic which is enticing, in *A Philosophical Inquiry into the Origins of Our ideas of the Sublime and Beautiful*, Burke declared that "It is our ignorance of things that causes all our admiration and chiefly excites our passions."

Is the sublime known in intuition? Bergson emphasized the intuitive aspect of learning and the communication of the subject with the object.[2] In intuition we "know" an object by "entering into it." Science and reason yield only a relative, partial and fragmented knowledge; intuition, an "absolute" knowledge. The sublime is not a consequence of an *a priori* deduction but like the universe, a process in which the contrary dynamic forces are continuously changing and intertwine ceaselessly. The philosopher of the flux, Heraclitus, illuminates the metaphysical sublime:

All things come into being through opposition and all things are in flux, like a river (DK 22 A 1).[3]

The Sublime as the Flux in Heraclitus

Heraclitus turned to nature in wonder and sought to study the ultimate structure of reality. The world-order is likened to fire.

This world-order (kosmos), the same for all, no god or man has made but it always was and is and will be an ever-lasting fire, kindling by measure and going out by measure (DK 22 B30).

Heraclitus visualized the world not as a sum total of all things, but as the totality of events, or changes, or facts.[4] There are no changing things but only changes. To know the truth is to have grasped the essential being of nature as implicitly infinite, as a process in itself.[5] Man is part of the *kosmos* and as such he is subject to the laws (*nomos*) of *kosmos* in the same way as all its other parts.[6] But since, by virtue of his intellect, he harbours within himself the eternal law of the life of the universe, he can share the highest wisdom, from whose counsel springs the divine law. Heraclitus elevates the moral character of the *kosmos* to "divine *nomos*" and" "bases the moral code of the philosophical man upon the moral law of the entire universe."[7]

> Of this *logos*, although it is true for ever, men have no understanding before they hear it and after they first hear it. Although everything happens according to this *logos*, they seem quite inexperienced when they make trial of such words and works as I tell of by explaining each thing according to its own nature and stating how it is (DK 22 B1).

In the process of reality, which is in constant flux, there is an ever-present rational pattern (*logos*).[8] Justice (*dike*) is a balance of forces in nature. Morality is conceived as a mean between opposites, a balance and a proper attunement or a harmony of the soul. Heraclitus refers to the world-order simultaneously as "justice" and "harmony." The adverse is concordant: from discord the fairest harmony (DK 22 B8).

There is measure in accordance with which the contraries are to be balanced. The process of the world-order is a harmony achieved from strife and conflicting natural elements and forces. The organizing constitutive principle of the physical world creates order from conflict and strife.

> For those who are awake the *kosmos* is one and common, but those who are asleep turn aside each into a private *kosmos* (DK 22 B89).

We should not act and speak like men asleep (DK 22 B73).

The somnambulists conjure up private worlds of their own making. Heraclitus' remarks might startle the subjectivists who are enmeshed in private world of dogmatic slumber. Equipped with nothing other than the principle of pre-established harmony, we could set the metaphysical sublime aloft in the *kosmos*, the ordered harmony of the world of nature and the moral sublime aloft in the realm of unmitigated good will, for perception of evil in but a partial glimpse of the harmonious whole. But that was in another country, and besides—Heraclitus is long dead.[9] Humanity no longer openly gazes at the *kosmos*.[10] Now nothing short of "destructive creation, creative destruction"[11] will suffice to produce an axe to break the frozen sea in each of us.[12]

The moral sublime is not beyond good and evil. The sublime as the construct of imagination does not only soar in the region of light. The moral sublime must be prepared to meet the onslaught of all magnitude—even that of the "race of devils."[13] Conscious and deliberate pursuit of destruction for the sake of destruction, as in Goethe's Mephistopheles who utters, "All that exists should perish," and Milton's Lucifer in *Paradise Lost*, who declares, "Evil be thou may good." The vigorous self-assertion of Lucifer as an act of daring against the authority of an absolute deity merits admiration but the act of revolt is one of rage and not of strength.[14] The paradox of the Romantic rebellion afflicts Lucifer. The validity of the rebellion against the established authority is inseparable from the recognition of the established authority as an antagonist. Lucifer's defiance is not autonomous but dependent on the existence of the adversary whose extinction propels his momentary striving. Were he to attain his goal, the sole ground of his being would evaporate since that which fuels the rebellion would no longer exist.

The Sublime and Individual Terror

Can the voice of the sublime be individual? Trotsky asks "Is individual terror, for example, permissible or impermissible from the point of view of pure morals?"

> If we shall say, a revolutionist bombed General Franco and his staff into the air, it would hardly evoke moral indignation even from the democratic eunuchs.[15]

Trotsky makes the distinction between intentions which are deserving of sympathy and those that are not:

> Our relation to the assassin remains neutral only because we know not what motives guided him.[16]
> The oppressed condition of those who adopt terrorism as a means elicits sympathy.
> Our sympathies are fully on the side of Irish, Russian, Polish or Hindu terrorists in their struggle against national and political oppression.[17]

Here is the voice of a compassionate revolutionary. But a course of political action cannot be derived from the basis of sympathy.

> However, not the question of subjective motives but that of objective efficacy has for us the decisive significance.[18]

Here a consequentialist strategist speaks.

> Thus even in the sharpest question—murder of man by man—moral absolutes prove futile. Moral evaluations, along with political ones, flow from the inner needs of struggle.[19]

This leads Trotsky to renounce "the meridian of the categorical imperative" and "moral absolutes" insofar as "morality serves politics," and moral principles are appropriated for pragmatic ends of legitimizing power: "Conservative bourgeois now even render official praise to the terrorist William Tell."[20] Is political action, then, severed from all morality? In his reply to the terrorist Trotsky invokes moral universals regarding the ends and means: Act only in accordance with that which is conducive to liberating humanity. The only justifiable means are those which involve the participation of the people. To the question, "Are we to understand that in achieving the end anything is permissible?" Trotsky replies, "That is permissible, we answer, which really leads to the liberation of humanity. The ends and the means are so closely interwoven with one another as path and goal that a change in one means a change in the other. And a different path gives rise to a different goal."[21] There is a "dialectical interdependence of end and means:" "A means can be justified only by its end. But the end in its turn needs to be justified."[22]

> From the Marxist point of view, which expresses the historical interests of the proletariat, the end is justified if it leads to increasing the power of humanity over nature and to the abolition of the power of one person over another. [23]

Trotsky's reply to the further question, "Just the same, does it mean that in class struggle against capitalists all means are permissible: lying, frame-up, betrayal, murders and so on?" illuminates the ongoing debate between consequentialists and deontological moral theorists.

> Permissible and obligatory are those and only those means, we answer, which unite the revolutionary proletariat, fill their hearts with irreconcilable hostility to oppression, teach them contempt for official morality…imbue them with consciousness of their own historic mission, raise their courage and spirit of self-sacrifice in the struggle. Precisely from this it flows that *not* all means are permissible.[24]

The only justifiable choice of means is that which involves the participation of the people.

> When we say that the end justifies the means, then for us the conclusion follows that the great revolutionary end spurns those base means and ways which set one part of the working class against other parts, or attempt to make the masses happy without their participation; or lower the faith of the masses themselves and their organization, replacing it by worship for the 'leaders'.[25]

Trotsky's investigation of individual terror probes into a turbulent topic in current international relations.

> [T]o the terrorist we say: it is impossible to replace the masses; only in the mass movement can you find effective expression for your heroism.[26] Only within the context of civil engagement, can an individual action have a political significance.

It is the inseparability of the means and goals which leads Trotsky to conclude that "individual terror" cannot achieve the "liberation of the workers": "the liberation of the workers can only come through the workers themselves."[27] In sharp contrast to political realists or legal positivists who sever the connection between morality and politics in calling for a simultaneous justification of ends and means, Trotsky avows the necessity of moral evaluation of all political activity. Trotsky's conviction that human beings can work towards "liberation of humanity" revitalizes the Heraclitus' conception of the oneness of *kosmos*.

> One should follow the common. But while the *logos* is common, the many live as though they had a private understanding (DK 22 B82).

L'invitation au Voyage

The meeting ground of the metaphysical, the aesthetic, and the moral sublime is not the Elysian fields but a region which from time immemorial has been regarded as the true field of philosophy: the teaching of the good life. The moral sublime carries the metaphysical sublime into the field of concrete action in global justice, human rights, economic production and distribution, and environmental ethics. The moral sublime is a synthesis of values of friendship, equality, and freedom into a harmonious whole.

A grand unification theory of the sublime would take the path of drawing upon the philosophical, poetic, and historical legacies of world civilizations. Aristotle's distinction between philosophy, poetry, and history can be reformulated as not one of hierarchy or grades of truth conveyed by each but one of successive understanding. Philosophy explores the spheres of the real and the true, poetry, the possible, and history, the actual. Philosophy is a comprehensive endeavour which aspires to incorporate and enhance the insights of poetry and history. The scope and the range of philosophical approach to the sublime would correlate the ideas within each discipline with its specific methodology. Philosophical comprehension of the sublime would build upon the empirical investigations of history and the imaginative endeavour of poetry.

Kant's thesis of the beautiful as the symbol of the good is amplified by Shelley in "Defense of Poetry." Shelley explains that if we are less than wholly good it is not for the lack of worthwhile principles. In order to be good, man must imagine intensely and vividly. It is not reason but imagination which leads to the moral good. In Lev Vygotsky's words,

> The possibilities for the future for art as well as for life are inscrutable and unpredictable. As Spinoza said,
> 'That for which the body is capable has not yet been determined'.[28]

On the horizon of anticipation we glimpse the sublime, new and immense—

> Là, tout n'est qu'ordre et beauté,
> Luxe, calme et volupté. [29]

Bibliography

Barnes, J. *The Presocratic Philosophers*. London: Routledge, 2000.

Bourke, V. *History of Ethics*, vol. I. New York: Doubleday, 1968.

Burke, E. *A Philosophical Inquiry into the Origins of Our ideas of the Sublime and Beautiful*. London: Penguin, 1998.

Diels, H. and W. Kranz. *Die Fragmente der Vorsokratiker*. Berlin: Weidman, 1956.

Jaeger, W. *Paideia, The Ideals of Greek Culture,* **vol. 1**. Oxford: Oxford University Press, 1986.

Kant, I. *Critique of Judgment*, J. H. Bernard, trans. London: Hafner, 1951.

Kirk, G. S. and J. E. Raven, eds. *The Pre-Socratic Philosophers*. Cambridge: Cambridge University Press, 1962.

Longinus, *On the Sublime*. New York: AMS Press, 1935.

Popper, K. *Conjectures and Refutations: The Growth of Scientific Knowledge*. New York: Harper and Row, 1965.

Schiller, F. *NaÔve and Sentimental Poetry* and *On the Sublime*. New York: Frederick Ungar Publishing,1980.

Trotsky, Leon. *Their Morals and Ours*. New York: Pathfinder Press, 1973.

—*Literature and Revolution*. Ann Arbor: University of Michigan Press, 1960.

Vygotsky, Lev. *Psychology of Art*. Cambridge, MA: MIT Press, 1971.

End Notes

[1] Burke, *A Philosophical Inquiry into the Origins of Our ideas of the Sublime and Beautiful*. Kant, *Critique of Judgment*, J. H. Bernard trans. (London: Hafner, 1951).

[2] *The Two Sources of Morality and Religion* (Notre Dame, IN: University of Notre Dame Press), p. 177.

[3] [DK] refers to H. Diels and W. Kranz, *Die Fragmente der Vorsocratiker* (Berlin: Weidman, 1956).

[4] *Ibid*. Popper, *Conjectures and Refutations and Popper,* "Kirk on Heraclitus and on Fire as the Cause of Balance," *Mind* 72, 1963, pp. 386-92.

[5] Quoted in Barnes, J. *The Presocratic Philosophers* (London: Routledge, 2000), p. 68.

[6] Jaeger, W., Paideia, *The Ideals of Greek Culture*, vol. 1. (Oxford: Oxford University Press, 1986), p. 183.

[7] Ibid., p. 184.

[8] V. Bourke, History of Ethics, vol. I (New York: Doubleday, 1968), p. 17. Heraclitus, Fragments, 1:2. 45, 50, 72 and 115 in Kathleen Freedman, *Ancilla to the Pre-Socratic Philosophers*.

[9] Echoing Marlowe, "But that was in another country. And besides, the wench is dead," *The Jew of Malta*.

[10] Longinus, *On the Sublime* (New York: AMS Press, 1935), chap. 44.

[11] Dylan Thomas's words to Vernon Watkins about what a poem should be.

[12] Kafka's phrase.

[13] In Kant's phrase.

[14] Or "resentment"—Nietzsche's characterization of an action stemming from rage and weakness and not strength.

[15] Leon Trotsky, *Their Morals and Ours* (New York: Pathfinder Press, 1973), p. 51. If Trotsky were writing at present, he would find in the empires of the four corners of the world those who would be well-qualified to join the ranks of Franco.

[16] *Ibid.*, p. 50.

[17] *Ibid.*, p. 50.

[18] *Ibid.*

[19] *Ibid.*, p. 51.

[20] *Ibid.*, p. 50.

[21] *Ibid.*

[22] *Ibid.*, p. 48. See also Trotsky, *Literature and Revolution* (Ann Arbor: University of Michigan Press, 1960), Ch. 5.

[23] *Ibid.*, p. 48.

[24] *Ibid.*, p. 49

[25] *Ibid.*

[26] *Ibid.*

[27] *Ibid.*

[28] Lev Vygotsky, *Psychology of Art* (Cambridge, MA: MIT Press, 1971), p. 259.

[29] Baudelaire, "L'invitation au Voyage," *Les Fleurs du Mal.*

American vs. British English: Bridging the Gap

Mónica Tosi and Gustavo González

American English and British English are the two most important varieties of English students in many parts of the world are exposed at present. There comes a time when they do want to know where the differences lie. It is our role as teachers to help them become aware of these differences and try to find a way to "bridge the gap," not just by telling them the way things are but by having them explore these two varieties (and eventually others) and savor the process of discovery on their own. English—the language of business, tourism, entertainment and professional growth—enables us to understand others and be understood anywhere in the world. With the influence of the media, our students are constantly exposed to different kinds of English, especially through movies and songs—American and British being the predominant ones. We do not want to teach them either one or the other. We do want to help our students become aware of the differences they might encounter when dealing with these varieties so that they are prepared to handle them when they have to make a choice of their own.

After all, variations also take place in their native tongue. More often than not, Argentineans have difficulty understanding Spanish-speaking people from other countries. There is no reason why this should not apply to English as well, with all its different varieties, accents and dialects. It would be somewhat difficult for us to deal with dialectical differences in this short article, but in a world where globalization seems to be "the star of the show," we do know that American and British English are the varieties our students are most exposed to. We strongly believe that we, teachers of English as the language of international communication, must be aware of the most important differences between these two varieties of English so as to be prepared to clear out any queries our students may have.

Lorry or Truck

We have always been interested in the differences between these two varieties. However, our concern became even more acute over the years, as our students kept asking questions like "What's the difference between a lorry and a truck?" or "Which one is correct: *write me* or *write to me*?" One day, at the computer lab, a group of students wanted to know why certain words in their documents appeared underlined in red, if their spelling was correct. And the answer was simple: because the set language in their word processing software was English, but the variety corresponded to the US, among many other options, and students were using UK spelling. Our main objective is to help ourselves, teachers whose L1 is not English, and therefore our students, be consistent in the use of English. What we mean by this is that we should make our students aware of the fact that, whichever variety they choose to use, they should conform to it as much as possible. If they wrote the word *traveler*—with only one "l"—somewhere in a piece of writing, then it would not be right for them to spell *colour* or *theatre* in the same document. The same happens with the choice of words: purses and pants are not the same thing in the US and the UK. Needless to say, we must warn our students that many words may be offensive in either of these varieties, so they must be extremely careful when using words that may result in embarrassment.

One of the first things we had to admit was that we were overcorrecting our students. How many times have we found spelling mistakes in words such as *neighbor* or *enroll*? How many times have we emphasized the stress on the first syllable in *in*teresting or *de*tail? Yes. We are to blame because most teachers in Argentina have blindly chosen the British variety as if it was the only acceptable one. Of course, this has to do with the fact that British schools have enormous impact and prestige in this part of the world. The European origin of most families may also have played an important part when choosing this variety. But this is not all. Most of the course books available are published in Britain. The second problem we came across was the following: how can we teachers deal with the differences between British and American English when we have never lived in either of those countries? How can we, River Plate Spanish speakers, handle such subtle differences in the use and occurrence of certain words and expressions considering we are talking about the United States, with its 50 states, and the United Kingdom—with its different dialects all over the north, south, east and west?

So, we decided to take a much narrower approach and to focus on some of the most visible and obvious variations that occur in standard English and group them into five areas of difference: spelling, grammar, vocabulary, pronunciation and culture. Spelling was the easiest one, for there are standard rules available, as well as high occurrence of both spellings in the same country. As regards grammar, we didn't encounter great trouble. Some differences do occur, but they definitely do not impede communication. The toughest area was vocabulary, since there are many words that have different meanings on each side of the Atlantic. In order to develop awareness-raising activities, we knew that we had to work with something equally appealing to student and teacher, for the only way to motivate our students is to be self-motivated as teachers. The American sitcom "Friends" was the answer. It is very popular in Argentina and our students just love it! We focused on the episode called "The One with Ross's Wedding" because, in it, these friends travel from New York to London for Ross's wedding. His getting married to a British woman provided us with lots of elements to cover the areas we were concerned about and it could be great fun as well.

The Activities

We wanted our students to explore and find their own way with language, so the activities were meant to be engaging and challenging. We started by analyzing a picture taken from the opening scene of the episode. Eliciting information was our number-one task so that, when shown the scene, students would be ready to check whether their predictions had been right or not. By discussing the kinds of problems one may encounter when going to England or the States, they began to become familiar with some communication difficulties that even Americans going to Britain or British people going to the USA may face.

After watching and discussing the scene, we asked our students to get together in groups, read the script of the scene they had just watched and underline all the words that they thought might be different in British English. To their surprise, they found that the variations were numerous. Once they were able to spot some of them, they wanted more. They felt like going deeper into it. After this warm-up activity, they were ready to start working. By showing the second scene selected, we invited students to analyze an area not covered in the first activity: culture. Gestures are not international, and a perfectly "innocent" gesture in one country may be highly offensive in another one. So, we chose a particular scene in which Ross gestures the American "time-out" sign and his British fiancé is deeply offended.

Trying hard to be extremely tactful, we had a lot of fun dealing with situations that may result in embarrassment, not only by using gestures, but also using words and expressions with different meanings according to the language variety used. The following activity was also about cultural differences, but this time leaving "unintentional obscenities" aside. We showed the third scene, a telephone conversation between a young American and an elderly British woman, with the sound off. The students had to guess the tone of the conversation taking into account the paralinguistic features. After checking their predictions with a second sound-on watching, we discussed many of the conventions used when making a telephone call. As a follow-up activity, the students role-played different kinds of conversations, bearing in mind that they had to be extremely polite, especially when talking to a British person.

Having dealt thoroughly with cultural differences, we asked our students to focus on spelling differences. We gave them a chart with words they were familiar with, spelled either in American or British English, for them to try to recognize them. They found it rather difficult, and they realized that, up till then, they had used the two varieties indiscriminately, without considering the distinction. After this, we moved on to lexical differences. Following patterns such as *same word - different meaning* and *different word - same meaning*, we explored in a fruitful way the many possibilities these varieties provide us with. Pronunciation was the last item discussed. After dealing with the most common variations, we listened to the song "Let's Call the Whole Thing Off" (see Appendix), where these differences are clearly shown.

International Examinations

Students should be as consistent as possible when communicating in English, especially when dealing with international examinations. If they choose to sit for an international exam like TOEFL, it would be advisable for them to stick to the American variety. The University of Cambridge ESOL Examinations board will respect American spelling, grammar and lexicon if they find that students have been consistent in their use.

Conclusion

As language educators, we want to show our students that there are different varieties of English. We know that the acquisition of such differences requires constant exposure and it is at this point that we, teachers, play an important role. However, raising awareness does not mean that we have to spoon feed our students by providing relevant materials and activities all the time. It is a process that needs research and reflection on their part, and the ultimate goal is to trigger curiosity, let them draw their own conclusions and choose which variety they would like to use in order to be consistent when communication takes place. Needless to say, the process is long and it involves hard work. We are more than satisfied with the results we have obtained so far: our students now realize that spelling and grammar differences will rarely lead to misunderstanding, whereas pronunciation may sometimes do so, and vocabulary, in turn, is bound to cause misunderstanding and even embarrassment. Being aware of this, they have started paying more attention to the sources they encounter (books, movies, etc.) and to their own use of English. We hope that other teachers around the world will profit from our experience.

Appendix:

SONG: From *Let's Call The Whole Thing Off* Ella Fitzgerald, Louis Armstrong (words by Ira Gershwin; music by George Gershwin). Introduced by Fred Astaire and Ginger Rogers in the film *Shall We Dance?*

You say <u>eether</u> and I say <u>eyether</u>,
You say <u>neether</u> and I say <u>nyther</u>;
<u>Eether</u>, <u>eyether</u>, <u>neether</u>, <u>nyther</u>,
Let's call the whole thing off!

You like <u>potato</u> and I like <u>potahto</u>,
You like <u>tomato</u> and I like <u>tomahto</u>;
<u>Potato</u>, <u>potahto</u>, <u>tomato</u>, <u>tomahto</u>!
Let's call the whole thing off!

But oh! If we call the whole thing off,
Then we must part.
And oh! If we ever part,
Then that might break my heart!

So, if you like <u>pajamas</u> and I like <u>pajahmas</u>,
I'll wear <u>pajamas</u> and give up <u>pajahmas</u>.
For we know we need each other,
So we better call the calling off.
Let's call the whole thing off!

You say <u>laughter</u> and I say <u>lawfter</u>,
You say <u>after</u> and I say <u>awfter</u>;
<u>Laughter</u>, <u>lawfter</u>, <u>after</u>, <u>awfter</u>,
Let's call the whole thing off!

You like <u>vanilla</u> and I like <u>vanella</u>,
You, <u>sa's'parilla</u> and I <u>sa's'parella</u>;
<u>Vanilla</u>, <u>vanella</u>, <u>Choc'late</u>, <u>strawb'ry</u>!
Let's call the whole thing off!

References

Burke, D. 1993. *Bleep! A Guide to Popular American Obscenities!!!* Beverly Hills: Optima Books.

Gershwin, I. & Gershwin, G. "Let's Call The Whole Thing Off," originally sung by Fred Astaire and Ginger Rogers, in *Shall We Dance?*, 1937 directed by Mark Sandrich. This version by Ella Fitzgerald and Louis Armstrong, Polydor, 1998.

Longman, B. 2000. *A guide on the differences between American and English culture.* Available at: http://us2uk.tripod.com/

RJH Productions. 2003. *Friends' Scripts.* Available at: http://www.friendscafe.org/scripts/s4.shtml

Stallings, P. 1998. *Making FRIENDS in the U.K.* London and Basingstoke: Macmillan Publishers Ltd.

Harnessing the Imagination to a Neglected Ear

Clyde Coreil

NOTE: *These remarks were delivered as a featured presentation at the 2003 Conference of the Imaginative Education Research Group at Simon Fraser University near Vancouver, Canada.*

When I was a kid, one of the most popular comic strips around was L'il Abner. Boy did it have imagination! One of the creatures was named the "Schmoo." Schmoos loved human beings. They laid eggs, gave milk and died of sheer ecstasy when someone looked at them with hunger. The Schmoo loved to be consumed and tasted like any food desired. Anything that delighted people delighted a Schmoo. One brooding character in the comic strip however, warned that the Schmoo was the greatest threat to humanity that the world had ever known. Why? Not because they were bad but because they were so darn good! Among other things, the character was afraid that we would become too dependent on them. To shorten a long story, the Schmoos were reportedly hunted down and exterminated by the U.S.Government.

The Imagination as Schmoo

I want you to think of the imagination as a Schmoo, that is, as a very willing workhorse, one that is certainly not limited to singing, dancing and the other arts. Those are indeed suitable for the imagination but so are problems dealing with physics, biology and the marvelous rings of Saturn. One of my main points today is that the imagination is excellent at two activities: (1) fantasizing, that is experimenting with rich variations of human consciousness, and (2) hypothesizing—which it can do until the cows come home. For us, there is quite a difference between a fantasy and a hypothesis. When one hears the word "fantasy," one thinks of something wild and visionary, of cows flying on gossamer wings. On the other hand, when the word "hypothesis" comes up, one thinks of scientific formulations and strong evidence possibly yielding a thesis and a new idea that would replace an older idea. For the imagination, however, fantasizing and hypothesizing are essentially minor variations of the same thing. For them, a stable, unchanging world would seem to be a falsified reality. It is probably from that profound capacity for variation and change that the concept of a "hypothesis" derives the right to exist and has meaning for us. Without fantasy and the imagination, we would know only frustration when things don't go as expected. And we would have no Tarzan, no Peanuts, no Superman. Without the imagination, we would have no thoughts of "What if?"

Solid Balls Sink

But, you say, a solid lead ball will sink in the ocean. And that's a fact. If you are operating within certain parameters, it will. If you are not operating there—if you are plumb loco, completely out of your mind—you might even believe me when I rant and rave with a wild look in my eyes about a metal object that rides a rising plume of flame, travels for months, and then settles on a distant planet and sends back snapshots, marvelous pictures of itself as it examines rocks, rolls around, gets stuck and waits for Mama to send up a message that will free it. "Lock him up! God knows what that man has been smoking." So every day, science in fact depends on fantasy for broad ideas that it can begin to move to. Lately, with the ubiquitous computer, fantasy seems to have been given a run for its money. We are conditioned to think of science as rigorous, based largely on experiment and careful observation,

158

and having nothing to say about angels. And indeed science is exactly the way we define it: essentially, as fantasy with strongly guarded perimeter. I would like to take up other aspects of the neglected imagination, but that would use up my scant forty-five minutes. Kieran Egan said that the backstage crew had a very effective long-handled hook designed for people who talk too much. So I will get to the neglected ear with only a little further ado.

The Silent Kindergarten Student

The following is a true story. A couple of years ago, there was a shy kindergarten student in the USA who refused to speak in the classroom—ever. For weeks, it went on. Then the teacher got an idea. He began talking to the child through a hand puppet named Hilda. You know, one of those things where you sew a couple of buttons for eyes on a sock. It worked wonders. The child began, timid at first, to ask questions—not about the school or teacher or her fellow students, but about the puppet's life. Soon the great difficulty of silence faded away. So, a little imagination solved a problem that might have resulted in an ominous diagnosis by the school psychologist.

Such positive reports on the "Scooter that made it to Mars" and on the kindergarten student make one wonder. Why hasn't the imagination been given the respect, stature and resources of an academic discipline? That would focus research and at least help us to define the phenomena that are now like the invisible man who had to wrap his body in strips of gauze so that people would know he was there. How sad. But what can we do? Well, what would you think creating a couple of courses and calling them "Imagination 101" and "Imagination 102?" How about a "Department of Imagination?" If that isn't enough, what about creating a "Bachelor of Arts in Imagination," or indeed a "Bachelor of Science in the Imagination?" I have one more suggestion that will make your minister of education swoon—and that is "The Canadian University of the Imagination." The surprising thing is that if a dean or a minister were to support the establishment of a "B.A. in Imagination," you can be sure that there would be bloody fights in each academic department about who would get to teach the courses. I would also wager that such a curriculum would attract incoming students like bees to honey, like eds to coeds. Enough of that! I must get to the ears.

The Ears

One of the loveliest things about having tenure and being 63, which I am, is that you don't have to worry too much about the latest pedagogical buzzwords. You can waste your time not on Critical Thinking, Multiple-Choice Tests, Portfolios, Outcomes, Assessments, World Languages and whatever else is on the list of Best Buzzers this year. If you don't like them, go back inside and come out next year—they will have changed. No, we old guys are free to work on ideas that begin with, "What if…?" About a year ago, one possibility, one "what if", occurred to me. I will share it with you today as an example of the close relationship of the imagination to the kind of language-learning research that is based on hard evidence. It seems that compared to generations past, we have tons of things to stimulate our visual sense, things that we can use in teaching language. The internet explodes with thousands of ways to explore new printed texts and gives us things to see and think about.

What's missing from this really marvelous picture? Possibly nothing. But then there's the possibility that the ears are being overlooked-not completely but enough to be a problem. "What? Rubbish. There are more CD's, audiocassettes and videos with sound than you can shake a stick at. Too many if you ask me." I agree. You're probably right. But let's try to imagine that I am just a little less wrong than you think. The first piece of evidence I would present is that there seems to be a close link between the ears and the part of the brain that constructs an enormously complicated language from limited evidence. Linguists tell us that babies come all wired up for language. It has even been suggested that infants yet unborn begin to perceive the patterns of intonation spoken by the mother during the third trimester of her pregnancy. As time goes, information continues to be processed, stored, accessed and articulated—information that comes mainly through the ears of a child. Visual experience provides valuable motivation and helps the child to integrate stimuli. But almost always, it is the perception of sound that seems extraordinarily important to the acquisition of a particular language.

To repeat—the ears and the eyes are apparently connected to different terminals in the brain. Are these different terminals equally adept at figuring out language? In other words, do both ears and eyes contribute equally to language learning? These questions are of enormous importance to the acquisition of both a first and a second language. However, judging from the second language materials now available, it seems to be assumed that ears and eyes are only slightly differentiated parts of a single perceiving whole. There is little point, it seems to have been assumed, in differentiating between the two. And this might be correct. Language may well be more basic than speech, hearing or gesturing. What might rescue my hypothesis is the fact that in hearing children, sign language is not developed but rather a strong dependence on the production and interpretation or sounds coming through the mouth. If I am right, then we have been neglecting the ears, the auditory channel and it's most influential connections in the brain. It seems that we have allowed the circus barkers of the visual to upstage the proponents of the auditory.

Differences between Written and Heard Text

I also think there might be an enormous difference between written text and heard text. Another way to get at this is by suggesting that the emotional quotients of writing and of hearing are very, very different. I am not underestimating the marvels of the written word or of the enormous benefits of reading or indeed of signing. I consider myself a writer and an editor, and struggle every day to conceive of and express ideas in a straightforward, easy-to-understand manner. I will, however make four suggestions this morning about non-signed language. First, that heard language has access to emotions that are infinitely more varied and rich than their written counterparts. Second, that the human voice with its expressive textures and thousands of intonation patterns is truly a wonder and has no parallel in the paltry commas and exclamation points of written language. Third, that the word "voice" can be used as a metaphor for one or more imagined persons with a complex set of reaction patterns. Fourth, we use "voice" to express something from deep within our inner conscience. We can spend some very valuable class time explaining these different meanings of voice. We can help students to practice creating one or more voices related to the characters and situations in the stories we read. (If you're interested in this, check out "readers theater" in a book or on the internet.) Together, these four less-technical and more humanistic considerations are as important as they are neglected.

No Record Button

For a number of years, I was pleased to see that virtually every audiocassette player had a record button and came with a microphone. But now, it is indeed difficult to find a cassette player with a function for recording. That button is now hooked to the CD player. I think that this somehow reflects the present underestimation of the human voice. The Greeks, who would put pebbles in their mouths to practice clear articulation, would indeed be sad. Curiously enough, this parallels the current crisis in cursive handwriting which is absent from the curriculum of many elementary schools. It is not uncommon to find a native English-speaking graduate student who can't really connect letters. Eloquence, elocution, articulation, rhetoric, storytelling, the spoken poem, stories that are read aloud, dramatized stories, and many other aspects of the human voice having to do with the imagination seem to be somehow neglected along with the ear. This neglect affects education in broad terms and needs to be examined.

In the USA, for example, this situation seems pronounced in graduate programs in the Teaching of English as a Second Language. In their curriculum, a strong emphasis on technical linguistics has eclipsed more humanistic elements like literature, legends, music and the visual arts. Once those students become professors in the graduate programs, it is understandably quite difficult to get them to consider this argument because it is so far from their training. For them, it is icing on a cake that needs no icing. I think that the pendulum will be in large part moved by individual classroom teachers as they reintroduce the humanities in their second language classes. I don't think change will come from above in the near future. If the theme of this wonderful conference is taken up in other venues, the pendulum will begin its backswing sooner. Let's consider a couple of examples of what awaits us.

The Power of the Voice

An excellent example of the power of the voice lies in the almost forgotten mode of radio-drama. I remember when I was about ten—before my family had bought a TV—there was a radio story on a program called "The Inner Sanctum" which started with the sound of medieval door creaking open. In one particular story, a couple ran out of gas on a lonely road, near where a cunning but strong and extremely violent woman had escaped from a mental hospital. Suddenly, a woman was tapping on the window of the car, her face distorted, begging refuge from the madwoman who was stalking her with a huge hunting knife. Should the husband open the door and take her in, or was this the madwoman herself, hungry to feed her bloodlust. I was terrified and literally trembling deep beneath the covers of the bed. But I listened to every word, every breath, and every tone of voice.

Lost in Saudi Arabia

Another time, I was a young, new English teacher in a rather remote area of Saudi Arabia. I was a Yank and had been given, at my request, the worst class possible by my British supervisors. Why? Deep down, I was unsure of myself and wanted students I could blame possible failure on. "These guys cannot learn English," the Brit said. "We have suggested dismissal, but the headmaster says no. Good luck and don't send any of them to my office. None! No matter what!" So I went into the classroom, clicked my heels and said, "Hi! I'm Clyde." I drew not a smile. Forgetting what I had prepared, I proceeded to read them a simple story. They seemed to quieten down. So I read it again. And again. Each time, I asked simple questions about the story, and a couple of students blurted out very short and barely understandable but generally correct answers. Their ears had been working far better than their tongues. Anyway, later that afternoon, I recorded a couple of stories and copied the tapes one-by-one on my recorder. Then I wrote ten true-false questions about the story. At the end of class next day, I handed out the tapes and exercises and gave them three days to finish. I did not include the printed version of the tape scripts.

After the three days, they had completed the assignment but were grumpy and implied that it was far too difficult but asked where was the next one. They were even more upset when I said there was no next one, but that I would make another that afternoon and have it ready in a couple of days. If I hadn't, I fear that my motorcycle tires would have been sliced by a curved dagger. They weren't lazy. But many of them had grown up on the desert. They were fiercely independent and hated normal English class because it involved for them humiliation, embarrassment and frustration. On the other hand, the listening work was difficult, but they could do it, and they needed something they could be proud of. It was incredible to me how well they mimicked my tape-recorded voice: "Oh, no," Ali said, "I can't go back there!" I could hear traces of my Cajun accent in their voices. That class learned a lot of intonation, pronunciation and even grammar with me hardly ever mentioning it.

With my raspy voice, I am in no way a professional reader. I made up for this deficiency by hamming it up unashamedly and doing some slightly questionable things myself. For instance, I would pause occasionally and—breaking the narration—sternly say something like: "Abdul, wake up! This is not a tent!" Subsequently, in middle of class, one or another of them would repeat one those admonitions in exactly the tone of voice I had used. So it wasn't only targeted speech production that they learned, it was a number of aspects of speech patterns that I wasn't even aware that I had, much less had put on tape. I became more aware than ever of the great, extremely subtle interpretive powers of the human ear. If I had given them the printed tape script instead of the tapes, I don't think I would even remember the class now. Again, there's something very special about the human voice, the human ear, and the human imagination, and I am afraid that we are neglecting all three in many of our classrooms.

New Jersey and Arabia

I recently made some tapes for ESL students in New Jersey. I treated these much as the tapes I had made many years before with the Arab students but in considerably more sophisticated presentation. Again, students were not playing and re-playing the tape because I asked them to. Rather, they wanted to find the answers to the true-false items to demonstrate that they could do it or so that they would make a better grade. This does provide practice in comprehension, but essentially I was tricking them. What I really was interested in was their intense exposure to a limited number of English words and phrases. This might be called "Induced Unconscious Memorization." Among the many advantages of this approach is that it provides practice in different stress and intonation patterns for a single sentence like, "James said John doesn't know," which would result in very different interpretations by a native speaker: "**James** said John doesn't know. James said John doesn't **know**."

They had all successfully accomplished this in their native languages and very likely would have intuitively divided a sentence in that language into some approximation of noun, verb and object. They would have also said that the words of a particular phrase belong together. Virtually all linguists agree that everyone shares this intuition, part of which results from wiring. My purpose in exposing the students to English sentences was not in hopes that they would memorize every sentence they encountered, but that their brains would take the sentences apart and use the phrases and other elements to interpret and produce new combinations of the structures. In other words, the auditory channels that had performed this structural analysis in their first language were being asked to perform the same type of analysis in a far more limited group English words.

Memorization and Language

Let us turn our attention to the generation of hypotheses, which can be preceded by a question such as the following: Does memorization in early childhood make the brain more able to integrate other pieces of information and patterns? That is, does more advanced processing occur in brains that have a lot of data already memorized? The advantage of such a question is that it helps us to focus our hypothesis precisely on our new idea. This leads us to ask another, more specific question: Does memorization result in brains that learn a first and/or a second language more quickly? These questions are important. They must be answered if our store of relevant information is to keep growing.

However, also of utmost importance is the matter of how we come up with such questions, such hypotheses. I think that there are two parts to this answer. The first is a fundamental assumption of science: that the ultimate can never be attained. Science is a path, never a final answer. That sounds like some sort of mysticism, but virtually any scientist would agree, after some grumbling about context.

The second is more fundamental. It is central to the artist and to the humanist as well as to the scientist. It is this extremely simple question: Since the imagination is pivotal, how do we develop it to the maximum? I once interviewed Carolyn Graham, who is known for her "Jazz Chants" method of teaching ESL, and asked if she had a suggestion on how to cultivate the imagination. She paused, and said slowly in a measured fashion: "The child already has lots and lots of it. The question is how to avoid whatever it is that stifles the imagination in children as they grow up." That was a simple but profound answer. It should be a fairly simple process— learning to avoid destroying something as vital and as vibrant as the imagination. Yet that process of self-destruction is still very much with us. A great many educators treat the imagination like an unwelcome mosquito.

Responsibilities

It is our responsibility as teachers to help students learn to trust, value and use their fragile imagination, despite the fearsome, seemingly metaphysical opposition from some dark realm. I don't think I am overstating the case when I say that the struggle of the imagination to survive and prosper is darkly Faustian and universal in scope. The challenge is formidable. But again, what can we do? We can begin by forgetting for a moment about the danger of taking risks. And make no mistake: finger painting and such is dangerous business. I believe that it is outlawed in some schools, having been replaced by that smelly Abominable Snowman, the Multiple Choice Test. Generally, those tests measure how much snow has prevented real learning from taking place. Equally important is sheer courage, for when we open ourselves to the methods of the imagination, it is we who are really vulnerable. Oh we can search for safety by hiding behind academic titles, high professional and powerful positions, and subject matter and formality and propriety and current buzzwords and committees that cut the arts. But that isn't safety—it's shame. If we open ourselves to the Lady of the Imagination, what will come after the initial nervousness is excitement, trust and deep appreciation.

Conclusion

Recently, I decided to pursue the line of inquiry I had begun in Arabia. It was my good fortune to have as colleagues Dr. Ninah Beliavsky, Junko Takahashi, Gilda Reyes, and Sarah Dugger. My hypothesis was that texts encountered through the auditory channel are more efficiently memorized than texts encountered through the visual channel. Accordingly, materials for homework assignments had nothing printed. They consisted of a recording with a narrative of about 200 words, and 10 to 20 true-false items. These items were dictated on the tape itself and had to be written out and answered. The questions were based on information assembled from several parts of the narrative. The students had to listen repeatedly to the text—which of course was my real purpose—in order to find the answer. They did surprisingly well on the central task, which was scored and figured in the final grade. All of the students—admittedly for different reasons—wanted more of this type of listening and writing exercise to use after the course had ended.

Several interesting points emerged. Prof. Takahashi suggested that when students are very familiar with a given text they are better able to manipulate the ideas as well as the verbs and nouns in that text. She added that they seemed more confident about using their imagination to extend the text. Dr. Beliavsky suggested several ways to make the inquiry more valuable as a legitimate research project. She suggested that one of her classes be exposed only to the written text and that another be exposed only to the aural in order to form a control.

For me, the most encouraging thing about this small project is the chance that it just might result in the re-evaluation of listening in learning. The second most encouraging thing has to do with two Schmoos that were recently sighted off the coast of Nova Scotia. I do believe that they will find Canada more to their liking than they did the USA. If that sighting report is accurate and the Schmoos are rescued, I think that Simon Fraser University would be their residence of choice. I know that if I were a Schmoo, it would be mine.

About the Authors

Dr. Ninah Beliavsky

Dr. Ninah Beliavsky is an Associate Professor of Eenglish as a Second Language (ESL) in the Department of Languages and Literatures of St. John's University in Queens, New York. She holds an M.A. and a Ph.D. in Applied Linguistics from Northwestern University and a B.A. in Linguistics and Psychology from the University of Wisconsin in Milwaukee and Madison. Her interests include child language acquisition, bringing music and art into the classroom, and applying Lev Vygotsky's and Howard Gardner's theories to ESL teaching. Her e-mail address is beliavsn@stjohns.edu

Chih-hsin Tsai

Chih-hsin Tsai holds an M.Ed. Degree from Harvard University and has been teaching college English Foreign Language (ESL) courses in Taiwan for nine years. Her research interests include students' out-of-class English learning and discovering ways to help low-motivated students learn English.

Andrzej Cirocki

Andrzej Cirocki teaches English at H. Derdowski Secondary School at Kartuzy and Pomeranian School of Higher Education in Gdynia, Poland. His teaching experience also includes short-term contracts at Eliot College (UK) and Studio Cambridge Language School (UK). Mr. Cirocki holds an M.A. degree in Teaching English as a Foreign Language (TEFL) from Adam Mickiewicz University (Poland). He also received a Certificate in English Language Teaching to Adults (St. Giles' College, London Highgate) in 2003. His particular interests are in teaching English to adults, second language acquisition, and Elizabethan literature (Shakespeare). His research interests include Communicative Language Teaching (CLT) and English language teaching through literature.

Dr. Clyde Coreil

Dr. Clyde Coreil, professor of English as a Second Language at New Jersey City University, has edited *The Journal of the Imagination in Language Learning and Teaching* and *Multiple Intelligences, Howard Gardner, and New Methods of College Teaching* as well as this anthology. Coreil holds a M.F.A. in playwriting from Carnegie Mellon University, and a Ph.D. in linguistics from the Graduate Center at the City University of New York. www.clydecoreil.com

John Courtney

John Courtney teaches English as a Second Language (ESL) at the Islamic Saudi Academy in Alexandria, Virginia. He taught English for twelve years in Thailand and was the Managing Editor of *The English Teacher: An International Journal.* He has an M.A. in Teaching English as a Second Language (TESL) from Saint Michael's College, and an M.A. in English Literature from the University of Massachusetts at Boston. His research interests include creative methodology, L2 writing, and reflective and cross-cultural learning. e-mail: jjc_tesl@yahoo.com.

Dr. Elliot W. Eisner

Dr. Elliot W. Eisner is professor of education and art at Stanford University, where he works in arts education, curriculum studies, and educational evaluation. His research focuses on the development of aesthetic intelligence. Dr. Eisner has published more than 15 books and is the recipient of numerous awards, including a John Simon Guggenheim Fellowship, and a Fulbright Fellowship. He has served as president of the National Art Education Association, the International Society for Education through Art, the American Educational Research Association, and is currently president-elect of the John Dewey Society.

Dr. George Gadanidis

Dr. George Gadanidis is Chair of Continuing Teacher Education at the Faculty of Education, The University of Western Ontario. His most recent research is on students' and teachers' mathematical thinking, and the nature and aesthetics of their mathematical attention. He also designs, develops and researches online interactive mathematical stories. His research website is at http://publish.edu.uwo.ca/george.gadanidis.

Kevin Gaudette

Kevin Gaudette began his EFL teaching in 1968 as a Peace Corps Volunteer in Sierra Leone, West Africa. Over the years, he has taught at universities, schools, and corporations in Mexico, Hong Kong, Macau, Taiwan and in Mainland China for the past five years. In addition to teaching English to foreign students at California State University at Los Angeles, he engaged in long-term part-time graduate study at CSLA, with a focus upon Global Education.

Katherine Granelli

Katherine Granelli is an Assistant Professor in the Child Study Department at St. Joseph's College on Long Island, New York. Having taught children with special needs for many years, she now teaches pre-service teachers special education curriculum, methods and materials. Her academic interests include teacher education, special education, literacy development, and imagination and how these seemingly diverse areas all relate to each other.

Dr. Maxine Greene

Dr. Maxine Greene is well known across the United States and internationally and is regarded by many educators as The First Lady of the Imagination. Her most recent book is *Releasing the Imagination: Essays on Education, the Arts and Social Change* published by Jossey-Bass.

Dr. Hyun Höchsmann

Dr. Hyun Höchsmann teaches at New Jersey City University. Having studied philosophy, art history, and literature at Ludwig Maximilian University in Munich and at the University of Sorbonne in Paris, she received a Ph.D. in philosophy from the University of London. Höchsmann was a visiting professor at Deree College in Athens and at the American University in Cairo. She was also a visiting scholar at the East China Normal University in Shanghai. Her publications include *On Chuang Tzu, On Peter Singer, On Philosophy in China*, and *Zhuangzi*.

Dr. Cornelia Hoogland

Dr. Cornelia Hoogland is a poet, play-wright and scholar at the University of Western Ontario, Canada. She recently launched her fourth book Cuba Journal: Writing and Language. Hoogland has performed and lectured internationally (Cuba, Brazil, Philippines, U.S. and England) in the areas of poetry and drama. Her website is http://publish. edu.uwo.ca/cornelia.hoogland/

Jane King

Jane King, holds a M.A. in Education and is a Texas certified teacher of English as a Second Language (ESL). She is currently teaching at Soochow University where she is conducting elementary/secondary teacher training. Her research interests include communication strategies for cross-cultural interaction and computer-assisted English learning.

Dr. Stephen Krashen

Dr. Stephen Krashen is currently Emeritus Professor of Education at the University of Southern California. Krashen is best known for his work in establishing a general theory of second language acquisition, as the co-founder of the Natural Approach, and as the inventor of sheltered subject matter teaching. His recent books include *Explorations in Language Acquisition and Use, Condemned Without a Trial: Bogus Arguments Against Bilingual Education, Three Arguments Against Whole Language and Why They are Wrong,* and *The Power of Reading* (second edition). He also holds a black belt in Tae Kwon Do and was the 1978 Incline Bench Press Champion of Venice Beach California.

Dr. Elena Kravtsova

Dr. Elena Kravtsova is the grand-daughter of Lev Semenovich Vygotsky. Dr. Kravtsova was born in Moscow in 1950. In 1972, she graduated from the Department of Psychology at the M.V. Lomonosov Moscow State University. She has worked at the Institute of Pre-school Teaching, the Institute of Psychology, and the laboratory of psychology and education of the Moscow regional administration. Presently, Kravtsova is director of the L.S. Vygotsky Institute of Psychology of the Russian State Humanities University. She studies various aspects of psychological readiness for school, develops the principles of the building of play activity, elaborates the periodization of psychological development, and realizes the principles of Vygotsky's cultural-historical theory in educational psychology. Elena Kravtsova is one of the authors of developing educational programs for children and adults built on Vygotsky's ideas.

Robert Lake

Robert Lake is Assistant Editor of this anthology and a doctoral student at Georgia Southern University.

Dr. Barbara Le Blanc

Dr. Barbara Le Blanc teaches for the Department of Education at Université Sainte-Anne in Nova Scotia, Canada. She holds a B.A. in Theatre and a B.Ed. in Teaching French as a Second Language from Dalhousie University, Halifax, Nova Scotia as well as a M.A. in Les Arts et traditions populaires and a Ph.D. in L'Ethnologie des francophones en Amérique du Nord, from Université Laval, Quebec, Canada. She has published a number of articles on Acadian culture.

Kristin Lems

Kristin Lems writes and perform songs, in addition to being an Associate Professor at National-Louis University in Chicago. She loves the arts, and enjoys the company of children. Her email is kristinsong@yahoo.com and her website is www.kristinlems.com.

Dr. Geoff Madoc-Jones

Dr. Geoff Madoc-Jones grew up in Wales, came to Canada in 1968, and taught both elementary and secondary Language Arts from 1969 to 1985, mainly in small rural communities. Since 1985 he worked in the Faculty of Education as a teacher educator as well as a program developer in Graduate Programs. During this time he also completed his M.A. and Ph.D. in the area of philosophy, hermeneutics and language arts education. He is currently an Assistant Professor in the Faculty of Education and his research interests include hermeneutics, teaching poetry and the history of literacy.

Ms. Ferradas Moi

Ms. Ferradas Moi teaches Literary Theory and Contemporary Literature at the Universidad Nacional del Litoral, Argentina. Founder and former co-director of the T.S. Eliot Bilingual Studies Centre in Buenos Aires, she is also a teacher-educator for the Norwich Institute for Language Education, UK, a well-known presenter at international conferences and an English Language Teaching (ELT) author. Consultant, web editor and materials designer for the British Council, she has co-chaired the Oxford Conference on the Teaching of Literature, Corpus Christi College, UK, on four occasions.

Sylvain Nagler

Sylvain Nagler has been on the faculty of New York's Empire State College since 1972 where students are encouraged to develop individualized and original programs of study tailored to address their unique personal needs and interests and the academic standards of the institution. This educational process provides an opportunity for the design of creative and imaginative studies, an example of which is described in this case study authored jointly by mentor and student.

Ekaterina Nemtchinova

Ekaterina Nemtchinova is an Assistant Professor of TESOL and Russian at Seattle Pacific University. Her research interests involve technology in foreign language teaching and teacher education, particularly the issues of nonnative English speaking professionals.

Dr. Nel Noddings

Dr. Nel Noddings is the Lee L. Jacks Professor of Education, Emerita, at Stanford University. She has written thirteen books—among them, *Caring: A Feminine Approach to Ethics and Moral Education, Philosophy of Education*, and, in 2003, *Happiness and Education*. Noddings is also author of some 200 articles and chapters on various topics, ranging from the ethics of care to mathematical problem solving. Professor Noddings is a former teacher, administrator and curriculum developer in public schools, and is the recipient of numerous teaching and excellence in education awards. She is currently the President of the National Academy of Education.

Walter Petrovitz

Walter Petrovitz teaches at St. John's University in New York City. His research has focused on the application of linguistic analysis to a number of diverse areas, including second-language instruction, philosophical argumentation, and literary analysis. In teaching both ESL and linguistics, he has explored the applicability of various media to the presentation of instructional materials.

Dr. William Reynolds

Dr. William Reynolds teaches at Georgia Southern University in Statesboro, Georgia. He is also an avid runner, including the New York City marathon.

Claudia Gellert Schulte

Claudia Gellert Schulte teaches English as a Second Language (ESL) at John Bartram, a public high school in Philadelphia. A published poet and aspiring singer/songwriter, she especially loves art that dips deep into the well of unruly emotion and transmutes it into the gold of the awakened heart. She can be reached at Naila786@verizon.net.

Dr. Rupert Sheldrake

Dr. Rupert Sheldrake has been active in this area of the human psyche and has given us the term "Morphic Resonance" which has proven to be of considerable interest to persons and various fields.

Sarah Springer

Sarah Springer graduated from Empire State College in September of 2003 with a B.S. in Human Services. For fifteen years she ran her own Day Care business utilizing her Associates in Early Childhood Education. Using music and imagination has always been in her repetoire of teaching tools not only for her clients, but for her own children. She is currently working in the field of Special Education and is married with three children.

Dr. Hilary Thompson

Dr. Hilary Thompson taught children's literature and children's theatre at Acadia University in Nova Scotia from 1976 to 1999. She has recently retired to work as a drama consultant on projects such as the educational activities to accompany the video Rain. She has published articles on children's literature, as well as on image and text. Her M.Ed. work in drama education informs her article published in *Canadian Tertiary Drama Educators: Perspectives on Practice*. She edited *Children's Voices* in *Atlantic Literature and Culture: Essays on Childhood* and she is currently a contributing editor for *Canadian Children's Literature*.

Mónica Tosi and Gustavo González

Mónica Tosi and Gustavo González are ELT practitioners from Argentina. Both teach teenagers and adults and train students for international examinations. They also teach in-company courses in Buenos Aires, for IdiomaNet and ABS International respectively. They have been in charge of teacher development sessions in Argentina and abroad, most recently at The Fifth Southern Cone TESOL Convention in Montevideo, Uruguay.